Radical Religion
in the
English Revolution

Radical Religion
in the
English Revolution

edited by
J. F. McGregor and B. Reay

OXFORD UNIVERSITY PRESS
1984

Oxford University Press, Walton Street, Oxford OX2 6DP
London New York Toronto
Delhi Bombay Calcutta Madras Karachi
Kuala Lumpur Singapore Hong Kong Tokyo
Nairobi Dar es Salaam Cape Town
Melbourne Auckland
and associated companies in
Beirut Berlin Ibadan Mexico City Nicosia

Oxford is a trade mark of Oxford University Press

Published in the United States
by Oxford University Press, New York

British Library Cataloguing in Publication Data
Radical religion in the English Revolution.
1. England—Church history—17th century
2. Great Britain—History—Puritan
Revolution, 1642–1660
I. McGregor, J.F. II. Reay, B.
291'.0942 BR756
ISBN 0–19–873044–6

Set by Hope Services, Abingdon
Printed in Great Britain
at the University Press, Oxford
by David Stanford
Printer to the University

Preface

The subject of this book is radical religion during the English Revolution, religious movements and ideas which were fundamentally in conflict with official, institutionalized, established religion and theology. But as well as being radical, the religious expressions dealt with in this volume were popular, popular in the sense of articulating the hopes and grievances of those outside the ruling groups in English society. Let it be emphasized that this book does not represent an attempt at a *histoire totale* of the religion of the people in seventeenth-century England. It is concerned with religion that was either taken up or produced by the people, but religion which in numerical terms represented only a small proportion of them — though a number, Christopher Hill has recently pointed out, greater than that of the nation's 'natural rulers'.[1] In short, this collection of essays deals with 'oppositional forms' during the English Revolution.

Nor is it our intention to minimize the importance of popular conservatism in English religious history. From the early stages of the English Reformation there had been divisions at the popular level:[2] on the one side those attached to the old ways; on the other, the zealous reformers, the supporters of reformation; and in the middle, probably the vast mass of the population about whom we still know tantalizingly little. The radical–conservative division was there a century later in the early 1640s after a parliamentary ordinance for the removal of idolatrous images from parish churches: popular iconoclasm versus popular defence of the crucifix and church images — by 'poor journeymen and servants' in Richard Baxter's Kidderminster.[3] When, in Cornwall in the 1640s, a local office holder of radical Protestant persuasion attempted to use a stone cross as rubble

[1] C. Hill, B. Reay, and W. Lamont, *The World of the Muggletonians* (1983), 9.
[2] S. Brigden, 'Popular Disturbance and the fall of Thomas Cromwell and the Reformers, 1539–1540', *Historical Journal*, xxiv (1981), 259, 261.
[3] *The Autobiography of Richard Baxter*, ed. N.H. Keeble (1974 edn.), 38–9.

for highway repairs he encountered staunch opposition from fellow parishioners. Some said that the stones were too heavy for the oxen. One said 'in Cornish that it was a holy cross and if it were good before it is good now'.[4] So we need to be aware of both sides of the coin, popular traditionalism as well as popular radicalism. The Revolution had its popular radicalism in the form of radical sectarianism. It had its popular conservatives in the form of the Clubmen who opposed rapid religious and social change and who rose in direct reaction to the 'glorious flux' of the 1640s. As John Morrill has recently demonstrated, stubborn adherence to the rituals of traditional Anglicanism is an important, and neglected, factor in the history of the civil wars and Interregnum.[5]

However, this volume concentrates on popular *radicalism* during the English Revolution. Recent research has shown the importance of these groups and ideas: as expressions of popular religious experience; as outlets for class or social protest; as important contributions or contributors to the history of political and economic theory (the ideology of liberty, toleration, the labour theory of value, and so on); and most recently, as a neglected chapter in the history of English literature.[6] During the Revolution ordinary people attempted to come to grips with the problems of their age and, in Christopher Hill's words, 'impose their own solutions'. They campaigned for notions that have yet to be realized; there is much that we can learn from them.

Hill's *The World Turned Upside Down* has demonstrated an interest in the radicals of the Revolution — an interest not confined to institutions of learning. *The World Turned Upside Down* (together with the work of Bernard Capp, A.L. Morton, Keith Thomas, and some of the other contributors to this volume) has stimulated research and debate.[7]

---

[4] Cornwall RO, DD SF 285/68-9.   [5] See p. 9 below.

[6] See C. Hill, 'Radical Prose in Seventeenth Century England', *Essays in Criticism*, xxxii (1982); N. Smith (ed.), *A Collection of Ranter Writings* (1983), esp. the Foreword by J. Carey.

[7] A.L. Morton, *The World of the Ranters* (1970); K. Thomas, *Religion and the Decline of Magic* (1971); C. Hill, *The World Turned Upside Down* (1972); B. Capp, *The Fifth Monarchy Men* (1972); Hill, Reay, and Lamont, *World of the Muggletonians*.

There is now a considerable literature on this subject, in the form of scholarly articles and monographs; we even have a three-volume *Biographical Dictionary of British Radicals in the Seventeenth Century*.[8] This volume is intended as a synthesis of recent work in the area, a survey of those religious alternatives which have captured the interest of historians over the last century and generated debate about their historical significance and modern relevance.

Chapter I is an introductory chapter; it sets the historical context; and it teases out the main themes of the volume, arguing that 'the religious factor' is central to any understanding of mid-seventeenth-century English radicalism. Contributors then go on to look at some of the radical groups and movements in more depth. Chapter 2 by J.F. McGregor looks at the Baptists, a group curiously neglected by historians. There was always an inner tension in the Baptist movement between the desire for involvement in the turmoil of the period and the Baptist obsession with the minutiae of organization. In the end obsession won, but not before the Baptists had provided recruits for the Levellers and Quakers. A Baptist apprenticeship was often an important stage in the making of a radical. Chapters 3 and 4 are devoted to those who are probably the best known of the Revolution radicals: the Levellers, and Gerrard Winstanley and the Diggers. Brian Manning discusses the role of religion in the formation of Leveller ideology, an important issue which has tended to suffer at the hands of historians who are usually concerned with the more secular aspects of the movement. The reverse is true of Winstanley and the Diggers. There has been vigorous debate about the exact role of religion in the formulation of Gerrard Winstanley's ideas, and Winstanley studies have reached something of an impasse. G.E. Alymer provides an overview of the problem in chapter 4. The next two chapters cover other popular sectarian products of the Revolution: Seekers, Ranters, and Quakers. In his chapter on Seekers and Ranters J.F. McGregor re-examines the evidence for them, cutting beneath the hostile comment, misinformation, and exaggeration to arrive at what he

[8] Edited by R.L. Greaves and R. Zaller (Brighton, 1982–4).

considers to be a more accurate picture of the heresies than that normally provided. He argues that the Ranters and Seekers provide a valuable illustration of the difficulties faced by the spokesmen of orthodoxy when they had to comprehend and describe the often confusing tenets of popular religion. Modern critical studies of early Quakerism have gradually eroded the image of the sect as fairly mild and moderate seventeenth-century pacifists. Chapter 6 establishes the revolutionary nature of the early Quaker movement and examines its impact on seventeenth-century politics and society. The remaining chapters seek to escape from a strictly denominational approach to radicalism by concentrating on some general themes rather than specific manifestations, and indeed by demonstrating that much of the radical ferment during the Revolution sought to rework the familiar themes of popular religious culture. Bernard Capp's essay (chapter 7) deals with popular conceptions of the millennium, notions which were often vastly different from the academic speculations of the élite; and he argues that at this lower level astrology and millenarianism often meshed, producing vague expectations of a shortly expected life of ease and security. Finally, Christopher Hill's chapter (the only previously published piece in the volume) develops one of the main themes of his book *The World Turned Upside Down*: popular religion articulating opposition to the received wisdom and conventions of the ruling classes. In this chapter he deals with irreligion during the Revolution; the way in which the common people rejected 'the religious orthodoxies of their betters'.

The editors would like to thank a number of people — other than those whose names appear between the covers — who have contributed to the making of this volume. John Morrill and Wilfrid Prest read sections of the typescript, while Colin Davis ploughed valiantly through the whole book; their comments, criticisms, and suggestions were most valuable. Christopher Hill's chapter, which in its original form was the Barnett Shine Foundation Lecture for 1974, appears by permission of Queen Mary College, London. We would also like to record our gratitude to Freda Christie, Barbara Batt, Sisilia Tonga, Bev Arnold, Sonia Zabalocki, Marilyn Connor, Marion Pearce, and Jill Stevens for transforming illegible manuscript into legible typescript. Finally the editors are more than aware of their obligation to the patient consideration of Sally McGregor and Athina Reay during the excessively lengthy gestation of this volume.

B. Reay
J.F. McGregor
June 1983

Contents

Abbreviations

The place of publication in all footnotes is London unless otherwise stated.

AR	*Association Records of the Particular Baptists of England, Wales and Ireland to 1660*, ed. B.R. White (1971-4)
BIHR	*Bulletin of the Institute of Historical Research*
BL	British Library
BQ	*Baptist Quarterly*
CSPD	*Calendar of State Papers, Domestic Series*
DNB	*Dictionary of National Biography*
FHL	Friends House Library, London
FPT	*The First Publishers of Truth*, ed. N. Penney (1907)
Gangraena	Thomas Edwards, *Gangraena* (1646; reprinted by The Rota, Exeter, 1977)
GBS	MS 'Great Book of Sufferings', Friends House Library, London
Haller	W. Haller (ed.), *Tracts on Liberty in the Puritan Revolution, 1639-1647* (3 vols., New York, 1933-4).
Haller and Davies	W. Haller and G. Davies (eds.), *The Leveller Tracts, 1647-1653* (New York, 1944)
JFHS	*Journal of the Friends' Historical Society*
NY	New York
P. and P.	*Past and Present*
PRO	Public Record Office
QS	Quarter Sessions
*RDM	K. Thomas, *Religion and the Decline of Magic* (1971, and 1973 Penguin edn.)
RO	Record Office
Thurloe	*A Collection of the State Papers of John Thurloe*, ed. T. Birch (7 vols., 1742)
TBHS	*Transactions of the Baptist Historical Society*
Winstanley, *Works*	G.H. Sabine (ed.), *The Works of Gerrard Winstanley* (Ithaca, 1941)
Wolfe	D.M. Wolfe (ed.), *Leveller Manifestoes of the Puritan Revolution* (1944)
*WTUD	C. Hill, *The World Turned Upside Down* (1972, and 1975 Penguin edn.)

* Contributors refer to different editions of *RDM* and *WTUD*. The relevant edition is cited in the first reference to the work in the notes to each chapter.

1 Radicalism and Religion in the English Revolution: an Introduction

B. Reay

I

There were many factors at work in England's slide into civil war during those bewildering months from the meeting of the Long Parliament in November 1640 to the raising of the royal standard at Nottingham in August 1642. The intrusion of events in Scotland and Ireland, fear of popery, economic crisis, social unrest, class conflict, the continual tension between Court, Parliament, City, and Country, individual personality, indeed sheer blunder and chance, all played a role in the emerging conflict. But it was the religious factor — what Sir Benjamin Rudyerd described as 'our *primum quaerite*' — that was perhaps uppermost in those months.[1]

For it was religion which in a real sense stimulated and fired revolution. Discontent with the counter-reforming policies of Archbishop Laud during the 1630s was among the precipitants which (in the schema of Lawrence Stone) 'brought the collapse of governmental institutions from the realm of possibility to that of probability'.[2] Fear and hatred of popery, a widespread conviction that there was 'some great design in hand by the papists to subvert and overthrow this kingdom',[3] mobilized the nation in 1642: 'For many contemporary writers', Robin Clifton has observed, 'the essence of the conflict' between Parliament and King 'was

---

[1] See Anthony Fletcher's excellent synthesis: *The Outbreak of the English Civil War* (1981). The Rudyerd quotation comes from G. Yule, *Puritans in Politics* (Appleford, 1981), 304.

[2] L. Stone, *The causes of the English Revolution 1529-1642* (1972), 118.

[3] John Pym, 3 May 1641, quoted in Fletcher, *Outbreak*, 26.

in fact a collision between true religion and popery.'[4] And it was the issue of church reform, the question of whether government by bishops was to be reformed or abolished root and branch, which helped to polarize the country in the early 1640s and which played no small role in changing England from a nation in which initially (as several historians have pointed out) everyone was a royalist to a nation of which it is perfectly accurate to talk in terms of royalist and parliamentarian.

A succession of preachers primed Parliament with apocalyptic sermons which proclaimed the fall of Babylon and the establishment of Zion. 'Oh, let us set God on work this day, to destroy the implacable enemies of his church; arise oh Lord, and scatter the Irish rebels! Arise oh Lord, and confound antichrist, and build the walls of Jerusalem!' 'The lamb's followers and servants are often the poor and off-scouring of the world, when kings and captains, merchants and wisemen, being drunk with the wine of the whore's fornications, proceed to make war with the lamb, and to give all their strength unto the beast till the words of God shall be fulfilled.'[5] It was religion in the form of militant Protestantism or Puritanism — hostility to the Church of Rome, attachment to Calvinist doctrine, an obsession with preaching and the message of the Scriptures, a penchant for godly discipline, and a vision of the New Jerusalem — which in the words of William Hunt 'gave rebellion its cultural validation'.[6] We can agree with the author of the best history of the early 1640s that there is indeed 'a real sense in which the English civil war was a war of religion'.[7] 'Kings and Armies and Parliaments might have been quiet at this day', observed a speaker at the Whitehall debates in December 1648, 'if they would have let Israel alone.'[8]

[4] R. Clifton, 'Fear of Popery', in C. Russell (ed.), *The Origins of the English Civil War* (1975), 162.

[5] See P. Christianson, *Reformers and Babylon* (Toronto, 1978), ch. 5, and pp. 225, 227 for the quotations. See also J.F. Wilson, *Pulpit in Parliament* (Princeton, 1969), esp. p. 195: 'In certain respects emphasis upon the anticipated new "age" — explicitly millenarian or not — was the most striking and fundamental characteristic of the formal preaching before the Long Parliament.'

[6] W.A. Hunt, *The Puritan Moment* (Cambridge, Mass., 1983), 312. Dr Hunt very kindly provided me with a pre-publication copy of his typescript.

[7] Fletcher, *Outbreak*, 417-18.

[8] A.S.P. Woodhouse (ed.), *Puritanism and Liberty* (1974 edn.), 147.

This should not surprise us. It was an age in which everyone thought in religious terms. Oliver Cromwell, it is well known, was eager to detect the hand of God in contemporary events: 'I am one of those whose heart God hath drawn out to wait for some extraordinary dispensations, according to those promises that he hath held forth of things to be accomplished in the later times, and I cannot but think that God is beginning of them.'[9] The memoirs of the radical republican Edmund Ludlow are steeped in biblical imagery.[10] For such men religion and politics were inseparable.

We should not think of religion in any narrow sense. Our own neat division between religion, politics, and society would have made little sense to the majority of the women and men of the seventeenth century and it is better to think in terms of overlap and interaction. It could hardly have been otherwise in an age of *à la mode* absolutism and Protestant–Catholic conflict, when religion was the touchstone of political freedom and patriotism. The economic, the cultural, the moral, the theological: they all meshed in antipathy towards the regime of Charles I.[11]

Religion was both the legitimizing ideology of the rulers and, as we shall see in due course, the revolutionary idiom of the ruled. For the élite, religion was 'the glew and soder that cements a Kingdom or church together'. The Anglican work *The Whole Duty of Man* told its poorer readers to be content with their lot, for 'whatever our Estate and Condition in any respect be, it is that which is allotted us by God, and therefore is certainly the best for us, He being much better able to judge for us, than we for ourselves'. Charles I believed that people were 'governed by the pulpit more than the sword in time of peace'.[12] Episcopacy was the 'counterscarp or outwork' of the whole political system. Hence the bitterness of the conflict of the early 1640s. As Edmund Waller explained

---

[9] Woodhouse (ed.), *Puritanism and Liberty*, 103–4. See also C. Hill, *God's Englishman* (1972), ch. 9.

[10] E. Ludlow, *A Voyce from the Watch Tower*, ed. A.B. Worden (Camden 4th series, xxi, 1978), esp. Worden's introduction.

[11] See R. Ashton, *The English Civil War* (1978), esp. ch. 2.

[12] S. Clarke, *Golden Apples* (1659), 38; [R. Allestree], *The Whole Duty of Man* (1719), 166; C. Hill, *Century of Revolution* (1972 edn.), 74.

in May 1641 (he was referring to plebeian agitation), 'if by multiplying hands and petitions they prevail for an equality in things ecclesiastical, the next demand perhaps may be *lex agraria*, the like equality in things temporal'.[13] This idea of the thin end of the wedge was to recur in conservative and moderate polemic.

II

As Christopher Hill has eloquently demonstrated in *The World Turned Upside Down*, the decade of the 1640s was a time of immense overturning. Well-established, if not always well-respected, institutions collapsed like the proverbial house of cards. The Star Chamber, Court of High Commission, the Councils of Wales and the North, had all been abolished before the end of 1641. Episcopacy and church courts followed in 1646, the House of Lords three years later. The Earl of Strafford (1641) and the Archbishop of Canterbury (1645) were executed; and then, in 1649, the King was tried and suffered the same fate. Censorship collapsed — in fact if not officially. New bodies, the county committees, had the power to haul errant ministers and politically suspect land-lords before them and to deprive them respectively of their parishes and lands. Ordinary parishioners — husbandmen, artisans, even labourers and women — could testify before such committees to the competence and political reliability of those who had hitherto been their social superiors, men who had, in their own eyes at least, been beyond reproach.[14] It was through the committees that leadership changed in the provinces. By 1646 power in many, probably most, counties had shifted to men from outside the normal governing circle, usually gentlemen, it is true, but 'new men from lower down the social scale, lesser gentry and townsmen, often of radical Puritan inclinations'.[15]

It is difficult to recapture the atmosphere of those years.

---

[13] Quoted in Fletcher, *Outbreak*, 123-4.

[14] I.M. Green, 'The persecution of "scandalous" and "malignant" parish clergy during the English Civil War', *English Hist. Rev.* xciv (1979), 518.

[15] D. Underdown, *Pride's Purge* (1971), 29-36 (the quotation is from p. 34).

People's experiences varied. John Morrill cites a Midlands rector's entry in a parish register: 'when an uncivil war was being waged most fiercely between King and Parliament throughout the greater part of England, I lived well because I lay low.'[16] He was fortunate. For others the impact of civil conflict was more spectacular; and could be symbolized quite dramatically in the iconoclastic intrusions of the parliamentary armies with their destruction of stained-glass windows, holy pictures, and statuary, their burning of altar rails and service-books, their defecation and urination in church aisles and fonts, their mock baptisms of horses and cows.[17] The old reference points were crumbling — sometimes quite literally. In a celebrated incident in Canterbury in 1642 troopers took pot-shots at a statue of Christ.[18] In a less well-known episode, the future Quaker John Ellis, responsible for the upkeep of highways in his Cornish parish, proceeded to pull down a stone market cross to use as filler.[19]

The lower and middle sort of people entered the political arena to an extent which no one could possibly have antici-pated. At times it must have seemed as though anything was possible. And prompted by something approaching *la grande espérance*, or at the very least a feeling that while the nation's rulers were at each other's throats established laws were no longer inviolable, people seized the opportunity to settle grievances. An Essex woman told her minister 'she would pay him Tith when the King & Parliamt were agreed'. Throughout the country people quite simply stopped paying the hated tax.[20] Tithe-barns and manorial records were burned.[21] According to the researches of John Morrill at least twenty-six English counties experienced enclosure rioting during the years 1640-4.[22] The West of England witnessed attacks on enclosures off and on from 1642-8 in what has been called 'a

---

[16] J.S. Morrill, *The Revolt of the Provinces* (1976), 89-90.
[17] Hunt, *Puritan Moment*, ch. 11; B. Manning, *The English People and the English Revolution 1640-1649* (1976), 249-50; R. Clark, 'Anglicanism, Re-cusancy and Dissent in Derbyshire 1603-1730' (Univ. of Oxford D.Phil. thesis, 1979), 143-4.
[18] Ashton, *English Civil War*, 193.   [19] Cornwall RO, DD SF 285/68-9.
[20] B. Reay, 'Quaker Opposition to Tithes 1652-1660', *P. and P.* 86 (1980), 98-9.
[21] Morrill, *Revolt of the Provinces,* 34.   [22] Ibid.

second Western Rising' after its more famous predecessor of 1626-32.[23] The Fens experienced widespread rioting against enclosures and drainage works as fenlanders attempted to drive out developers and regain lost common lands.[24] Ordinary people petitioned and agitated. There were popular demonstrations in London and Southwark for the execution of Strafford, for the removal of bishops from the House of Lords, and over decay in trade. When in January 1642 the King attempted to arrest the 'Five Members', there was 'what amounted to a general strike: all the shops were shut and the citizens stood in the streets with their arms'.[25]

Brian Manning has argued compellingly that popular agitation forced the pace of the English Revolution (much in the manner of the French Revolution) and that this pressure from below, combined with the emergence of radical forms of religion, terrified many of the nobility and gentry, welding together a royalist party — 'the party of order', a party which stood for stability and the preservation of hierarchy in both church and state.[26] Naturally a great deal depended on local circumstances. In East Anglia the gentry was to plump for Parliament as the best guarantee of order, the force most likely to possess the power to smash plebeian unrest.[27] Elsewhere the men of property pressed for an early accommodation between King and Parliament, lest, as Sir John Hotham put it in 1642, 'the necessitous people of the whole kingdome . . . sett up for themselves to the utter ruine of all the Nobility and Gentry of the kingdome'.[28] However, the essential point is that popular agitation had an impact.

Then there were the Clubmen, popular conservatives, or rather traditionalists, who in the mid-1640s banded together in their thousands in Shropshire, Worcestershire, Herefordshire, Wiltshire, Dorset, Somerset, Berkshire, Sussex, Hampshire, and South Wales to protect their communities against

[23] B. Sharp, *In Contempt of All Authority. Rural Artisans and Riot in the West of England, 1586–1660* (Berkeley, 1980), ch. 9.
[24] K. Lindley, *Fenland Riots and the English Revolution* (1982), chs. 3–4.
[25] Manning, *English People*, chs. 1–5 (p. 96 for the quote).
[26] Manning, *English People*, 111.
[27] C. Holmes, *The Eastern Association in the English Civil War* (Cambridge, 1974), ch. 3.
[28] J.T. Cliffe, *The Yorkshire Gentry* (1969), 341.

marauding armies and to defend 'traditional values and rights' and 'the pure religion of Queen Elizabeth and King James'.[29] Sometimes they sided with Parliament, sometimes with the King, and sometimes they remained genuinely neutral — historians have still not agreed on the reasons for this.[30] The Clubmen are a reminder that religious traditionalism was a force to be reckoned with.[31] They are also a reminder that for vast numbers of the common people local interests were uppermost. But the Clubmen were not always *social* conservatives. The Mere and Gillingham Clubmen (on the Wiltshire-Dorset border) condemned 'all supperiors whatsoever' and attempted to keep the soldiers out so that they could have 'a free hand against the enclosures'.[32] The Dalesmen of the North Riding of Yorkshire refused to 'submit to anie power, either Civill or Militarie but stood upon their guard, and for most of them refused to pay tythes. And their was noe cours to be taken to compell them'.[33] Whether it was as militant defence of the community, riot, resistance to tithes, agitation in *favour* of episcopacy, or as political and religious radicalism, the mid-seventeenth century, to quote Keith Wrightson, witnessed 'the emergence of "the people" '.[34]

This situation was not entirely novel. Derek Hirst has demonstrated that popular participation in the political process pre-dated the Revolution. Perhaps 40 per cent of the adult population had the vote by the mid-seventeenth century. 'Those involved in the popular outbreaks of the 1640s had clearly had some form of political education beforehand.'[35] Anti-enclosure rioters in the Dorset–Wiltshire

[29] Morrill, *Revolt of the Provinces*, 98, 110.

[30] Two recent contributions to the growing literature on the Clubmen, which refer to previous work on the subject, are: D. Underdown, 'The Chalk and the Cheese: Contrasts among the English Clubmen', *P. and P.* 85 (1979); R. Hutton, 'The Worcestershire Clubmen in the English Civil War', *Midland History*, 5 (1979–80). See also the comments of Buchanan Sharp, *In Contempt of All Authority*, 247-8.

[31] In this context it is worth stressing that there was popular petitioning in *defence* of the church in 1641-2; in *favour* of episcopacy: Fletcher, *Outbreak*, 283-91.

[32] Sharp, *In Contempt of All Authority*, 248.

[33] North Yorkshire County RO, R/Q/R9/9.

[34] K. Wrightson, *English Society 1580-1680* (1982), 225.

[35] D. Hirst, *The Representative of the People?* (Cambridge, 1975), 105.

border area during the 1640s, it has been argued recently, were continuing a well-established tradition; they were largely indifferent to the issues of the Civil War.[36] The same was true of the Fenland rioters.[37] Nor should we exaggerate the spontaneity. Petitions were often gentry-organized. Accusations against 'scandalous' and 'malignant' clergy during the 1640s frequently had similar phraseology, suggesting that witnesses 'had been well primed'.[38]

III

'The years 1640-60 witnessed the most complete and drastic revolution which the Church of England has ever undergone. Its whole structure was ruthlessly demolished . . . .' So wrote William Shaw in his two-volume *History of the English Church During the Civil Wars and Under the Commonwealth* (1900).[39] A glance through *Acts and Ordinances of the Interregnum* would appear to confirm Shaw's impression. The assault on Anglicanism is clear enough. Ordinances of 1643 and 1644 ordered the removal of altar rails and the destruction of crosses, crucifixes, and images of the Trinity, the Virgin Mary, the angels, and the saints ('monuments of superstition and idolatry'). The use of surplices, roods, organs, and fonts was prohibited.[40] Those who attended a wake, feast, or church ale on the sabbath were to be punished with a fine.[41] An ordinance of June 1647 abolished the festivals of Christmas, Easter, and Whitsuntide.[42] As we have seen, episcopacy and the ecclesiastical courts went, as did the *Book of Common Prayer* and the Thirty-Nine Articles.[43] In place of Anglican government and liturgy divided reformers provided what has been called 'a shadowy form of Presbyterianism'[44] and the *Directory for Public Worship*.

[36] Sharp, *In Contempt of All Authority*, 220, 247.
[37] Lindley, *Fenland Riots*, 139, 160, 257-8.
[38] Green, 'Persecution of . . . parish clergy', 510-12.   [39] Vol. 1, p. vii.
[40] *Acts and Ordinances of the Interregnum 1642-1660*, ed. C.H. Firth and R.S. Rait (1911), i. 265-6, 425-6.
[41] *Acts and Ordinances,* i. 420-2.   [42] Ibid. i. 954.
[43] Ibid. i. 582-607.
[44] C. Cross, *Church and People 1450-1660* (Glasgow, 1976), 205.

Yet as John Morrill has pointed out in what is in many respects a path-breaking piece of work, there was a gap between legislative intent and reality.[45] Presbyterianism never succeeded in England. In some areas the experiment was never tried. In others a Presbyterian system was set up but because of the lack of co-operation of the local authorities discipline was unenforceable. About seventy classes (the Presbyterian units of organization) were established, but few were still operative by the 1650s. Historians are familiar with this; but there is more to the story. By means of some astute work with churchwardens' accounts Morrill has shown that the attempt on Anglicanism was less than successful. Of the parishes which he examined 'more churches possessed the Prayer Book than possessed the Directory', and there is little evidence (in quarter sessions and county committee records) of prosecutions for the use of the *Book of Common Prayer*, an offence punishable by fine and imprisonment according to an ordinance of 1645. Recorded purchases of bread and wine for communion suggest a stubborn survival of the celebration of the banned festivals of Easter and Christmas: 43 per cent of Morrill's parishes held communion at Easter in 1650.[46]

The aim of Morrill's piece 'The Church in England, 1642-9' is to demonstrate the importance of popular Anglicanism. The 'greatest challenge to the respectable Puritanism of the Parliamentarian majority', he writes, 'came from the passive strength of Anglican survivalism.' Despite some caveats, the import of his argument is the removal of the sects from the centre of accounts of religion during the English Revolution.[47] Of course he has a point. During the 1640s and 1650s less than a third of English parishes lost their ministers through sequestration: continuity constituted the norm.[48] All this is salient; historians need to be aware of the vitality of popular Anglicanism amidst the turmoil of the civil wars and Interregnum. Yet the single most important aspect of the

---

[45] J. Morrill, 'The Church in England, 1642-9', in Morrill (ed.), *Reactions to the English Civil War 1642-1649* (1982), ch. 4.
[46] Morrill, 'Church in England', 104, 105-6, 107.
[47] Ibid. 90.
[48] Cross, *Church and People*, 203; Green, 'Persecution of . . . parish clergy', 522-4, 530; Morrill, 'Church in England', 100.

religious history of the period is the emergence of hundreds of independent and semi-independent congregations, the disintegration of Puritanism as well as the Church of England. After all, the strength of Independency and more radical sectarian forms was an essential ingredient in the failure of Presbyterianism in England. And it was radical sectarianism which both terrified and tormented conservative and moderate during the events of 1640-60. *Organized* dissent was a minority movement but its impact (political, social, ideological) far outweighed its numerical importance.

The picture, then, for the 1640s is of a broadly based church, one which — by default rather than intent — permitted a wide range of opinions. In the 1650s, under Cromwell, the 'broad tolerance'[49] was rather more intentional. As always, certain qualifications have to be made. The teeming freedom of these years — I refer now to the whole period 1640-60 — was to a large extent *de facto* rather than *de jure*. One has only to think of Parliament's summary action against radicals and heretics, and of the fates of John Lilburne and James Nayler, to question clear-cut notions of toleration.

Tithes, a *sine qua non* of religious freedom as far as radicals were concerned, were never abolished. Acts of 1647, 1649, and 1653 provided cumulatively for the punishment of the authors, printers, sellers, and buyers of unlicensed pamphlets.[50] Ordinances of 1648 and 1650 carried penalties of death and imprisonment and banishment respectively for a wide range of 'blasphemous and execrable' opinions.[51] The picture is complex. We have to be aware of chronological change. Compulsory church attendance was abolished in 1650, but came back again (in diluted form) in 1657.[52] The Instrument of Government, the charter of the Protectorate, declared toleration for all who 'profess Faith in God by Jesus Christ', a clear attempt to encompass anti-Trinitarians who had previously been considered beyond the pale. This changed in 1657 with the Petition and Advice which contained clauses

---

[49] Cross, *Church and People*, 214.
[50] *Acts and Ordinances*, i. 1021-3, ii. 245-54, 696-9.
[51] Ibid. i. 1133-6, ii. 409-12.
[52] Ibid. ii. 423-5, 1162-70.

that excluded many of the radicals.[53] As we saw earlier, there was a gap between statute and practice, a subtle interplay between centre and locality which sometimes worked in favour of toleration, sometimes not. The history of early Quakerism, I suggest in chapter 6 of this volume, demonstrates that central policy often counted for nought when set beside the predilections of the rulers of the local communities. The indications are that the Blasphemy Acts were employed somewhat sparingly: Quakers and Ranters were prosecuted, though not in large numbers, and I am not aware of any case of an offender suffering the ultimate penalty. Similarly with the various ordinances for 'the better observance of the Lord's-Day' (1644, 1650, 1657).[54] Justices could (and did) use them to harass Quakers.[55] However, it is extremely unlikely that justices would have bothered enforcing the acts' intricate provisions too systematically. Such questions await their historian; at the moment we can only make educated guesses.

IV

England had a tradition of heresy and nonconformity. The Lollard movement lasted from the fourteenth century until the sixteenth when it merged imperceptibly with the milieu of the Henrician Reformation.[56] A small branch of the spiritual movement called the Family of Love had established roots in England by the 1570s, only to disappear in the sixteenth century amidst the ideological flux of the Revolution.[57] There were Anabaptists in England from the 1530s, although they are sometimes difficult to distinguish from the Lollards. The General (that is non-Calvinist) Baptists had come into being by 1612; by 1625 there were at least five

[53] Compare the texts of the Instrument and the Petition, reprinted in J.P. Kenyon (ed.), *The Stuart Constitution* (Cambridge, 1966), docs. 94 and 96.
[54] *Acts and Ordinances*, i. 420-2, ii. 383-7, 1162-70.
[55] See p. 160 below.
[56] Cross, *Church and People*, chs. 1-2; J.F. Davis, 'Lollardy and the Reformation in England', *Archiv für Reformationsgeschichte*, lxxiii (1982).
[57] A. Hamilton, *The Family of Love* (Cambridge, 1981), ch. 6; J.W. Martin, 'Elizabethan Familists and English Separatism', *Journal of British Studies*, xx (1980).

congregations in various parts of the nation.[58] But for the most part it is wrong to think in terms of coherent movements (let alone self-conscious gathered churches) when we discuss the 'sectarianism' of the sixteenth century; it is better to think in terms of a range of ideas and 'individual eccentricities'.[59]

Out-and-out separatism was a comparative rarity in the period before 1640. The policies of Archbishop Laud during the 1630s had the effect of alienating those who had until then been reconciled to working within the church, of nudging Puritans (often reluctantly) in the direction of separatism. But it was only with the start of the civil war that separatism became a substantial movement. London provides an interesting case-study. With only a handful of separatist churches in the 1630s and perhaps a population of 1,000 separatists in 1641, London could by 1646 boast thirty-six gathered churches; while by the 1670s London Quakers alone probably numbered between 8,000 and 10,000.[60] Before the Revolution, quasi- or semi-separatism was the most common form of dissent. The zealous would attend church, leaving perhaps when the Prayer Book appeared, or only turning up for sermons, but would also hold their own meetings where they would discuss various issues and read from Scripture.[61]

It is difficult to say to what degree the radical ideology of the Revolution was a product of the revolutionary milieu, to what degree it was a continuation of pre-existing ideas and attitudes. As we shall see, Christopher Hill has charted continuities: the ideas were there all the time, the breakdown after 1640 allowed them to come into the open. 'If the peasants kept these radical ideas to themselves when rebellion was out of the question, they put them forth fervently when revolt became a political possibility as well as a social necessity.'[62] This is someone talking about peasant revolt in

[58] M.R. Watts, *The Dissenters* (Oxford, 1978), 8–9; M. Tolmie, *The Triumph of the Saints* (Cambridge, 1977), 69–72.

[59] D. Loades, 'Anabaptism and English Sectarianism in the Mid-Sixteenth Century', *Studies in Church History: Subsidia*, 2 (1979).

[60] Tolmie, *Triumph of the Saints*, 4, 37; W. Beck and T.F. Ball, *The London Friends' Meetings* (1869), 32.   [61] Tolmie, *Triumph of the Saints*, 28 ff.

[62] R. Thaxton, 'The World Turned Downside Up', *Modern China*, iii (1977), 214.

China, but what he says would make equal sense of seventeenth-century England. Still, there is little doubt that the Revolution was (to steal a phrase from George Rudé) a forcing-ground for ideology.[63] True, ideas were not just plucked out of thin air in the early 1640s, but we should never forget that the Revolution was a tremendous generator of radical thought.[64]

The questioning and revaluation of the 1640s took many forms. Despite the acts mentioned earlier, there was a deluge of pamphlet literature. The London bookseller, George Thomason, it is well known, collected over 700 publications in 1641, 2,000 in 1642; in all some 22,000 items (tracts and news-books) during the Revolution. In 1646, in his famous tract *Gangraena*, Thomas Edwards catalogued the range of opinions found during the opening years of the decade. 'You have made a Reformation', he told Parliament, 'but with the Reformation have we not a Deformation, and worse things come in upon us than ever we had before?'; and he proceeded with his list of errors. The Scriptures are 'but humane', 'not able to discover a divine God'; they are allegories and should be tested by reason; they are 'writings only probably to be believed as the Story of Henry the Eighth'; there are so many 'contradictions and lyes in them, that they are no better then a Ballad' (i. 18, 19, 82, 38). 'Every creature in the first estate of creation was God, and every creature is God, every creature that hath life and breath being an efflux from God, and shall returne into God again, be swallowed up in him as a drop is in the ocean' (i. 21). There is but one person in the divine nature: the doctrine of the Trinity is 'a Popish tradition' (i. 21). We do 'look for great matters from one crucified at Jerusalem 16 hundred years ago, but that does us no good, it must be a Christ formed in us, the deity united to our humanity' (i. 21). Christ died 'for the damned in hell as well as the Saints in Heaven', for Turks and Pagans as well as Christians (i. 22). 'There is no hell, but in this life' (i. 27). There is no certainty in religion save the necessity for liberty of conscience (i. 28). 'All the earth is the Saints, and there

[63] G. Rudé, *Ideology and Popular Protest* (1980), 81.
[64] Cf. A. Woolrych, 'Political theory and political practice', in C.A. Patrides and R.B. Waddington (eds.), *The Age of Milton* (Manchester, 1980), ch. 2.

ought to be a community of goods, and the Saints should
share in the Lands and Estates of Gentlemen, and rich men'
(i. 34). Finally, horror of horrors, black puddings are 'un-
hallowed meat'; the eating of black puddings is 'a barbarous
custome' (ii. 2). Ironically the mere act of cataloguing such
errors must have helped with their dissemination. Nor can we
dismiss all this as the waking nightmare of a conservative.
For, black puddings excepted, the ideas reported by Edwards
all reappear in the pages which follow — in the doctrines of
Levellers, Diggers, Baptists, Fifth Monarchists, Ranters,
Seekers, Quakers, and with the various popular messiahs and
prophets who occasionally make an appearance. All were
products of Edwards's milieu.

V

Bernard Capp warns against 'imposing rigid categories on the
mid-century flux of ideas' and provides an example of a
royalist, radical, episcopalian millenarian![65] Inconsistency and
eclecticism there certainly was; but the fact remains that
there are detectable radical themes. Christopher Hill deals
with them in chapter 8, so they need not detain us long.
Elsewhere he has traced some continuities — geographical
and ideological — between the heretics of the sixteenth century and the radicals of the seventeenth.[66] Michael Mullett
has argued that there was consistency in what he terms the
'lay religious impulse'.[67] An emphasis on immediate contact
with the divine, either through the Scriptures or by means of
visions or the spirit within; a stress on experienced truth
against established, given truths; a rejection of the distinction
between the priest and layman and of the whole notion of an
established church; hostility to tithes; a refusal to recognize
orthodox teachings on the Trinity; speculation about the
existence of Heaven and Hell; an advocacy of human effort as

[65] See p. 184 below.
[66] C. Hill, 'From Lollards to Levellers', in M. Cornforth (ed.), *Rebels and their Causes* (1978).
[67] M. Mullett, *Radical Religious Movements in Early Modern Europe* (1980), 65.

a means to salvation, or at least an attempt to control if not to reject completely the influential Calvinist doctrine of pre-destination; a call for liberty of conscience: these are just some of the connecting themes. There are others. A recurring theme of this volume is that Revolution radicalism took a predominantly religious form; contestation took place within a religious framework. Bernard Capp's chapter on millenarianism demonstrates popular expectations of some vague age of bliss and equality. God or his agents would provide a new world 'freed from the in-security of the seventeenth century': 'The worker alone, liberated from taxes, tithes, and rent, would benefit from his labour.'[68] The Levellers were able to formulate a programme for secular parliamentary and legal reform, but their radical-ism was still firmly bound to religion as Brian Manning shows in chapter 3:

The Levellers throughout sought both religious liberty and political liberty. Their political aims were influenced by their religion and their religion was influenced by their political aims. The interrelation be-tween their religion and their politics was determined by their recog-nition of the divisions and conflicts in their society, and of the fact that both the church and the state were instruments of class.[69]

In his book *The Triumph of the Saints* Murray Tolmie has demonstrated the close links between London separatism and the Leveller movement during the years 1647-9. The sects provided a 'popular base' for the Levellers and 'shaped their aspirations and polemic'. (They also, Tolmie argues, helped to break the movement when influential separatist figures spoke out against it in 1649.)[70] In another seminal piece which deals with the Levellers, Colin Davis has stressed the importance of the fight for liberty of conscience in the early history of the movement.[71] Although their emphases are sometimes different, the work of Tolmie, Davis, and Manning meshes together nicely. Religion was important. The commu-nism of Winstanley, writes Christopher Hill, was 'indissolubly linked' to his radical theology. 'Landlords, kingly power and

[68] See p. 189 below. [69] Below, chapter 3, concluding paragraph.
[70] Tolmie, *Triumph of the Saints*, 144, 148-9, 182, 184.
[71] J.C. Davis, 'The Levellers and Christianity', in B. Manning (ed.), *Politics, Religion and the English Civil War* (1973), 247.

priests will be overthrown together as Christ rises in sons and daughters: there is no distinction between economic freedom, political freedom and spiritual freedom.'[72] Gerald Aylmer makes a similar point in chapter 4 below. Clearly Winstanley was not 'the first secular saint of the modern world'; C.H. George will have to look for another candidate for canonization.[73] Finally, to come back to the importance of the Christian milieu, it is almost impossible to talk of atheism for the period with which we are concerned: even irreligion took a religious form.[74]

This is not to negate intellectual change, to deny the importance of the Revolution in the development of secularism or indeed that it pointed towards the Age of Reason.[75] Nor — from the opposite point of view — is it to stress the importance of some kind of simplistic, compartmentalized 'religious' influence over and above the 'political' and 'economic'.[76] It is merely to make the point that it is impossible to consider the radicalism of the mid-seventeenth century without being aware of the religious factor. If the work of J.F.C. Harrison and Eileen Yeo is any indication, the radical–religious connection was still important in England in the nineteenth century.[77]

Another aspect of radical thought which is worth mentioning is the noticeable theme of practical morality, the importance of the golden rule 'to do unto others as you would have them do unto you'. For the Levellers it was 'that Principle which we professe' and accordingly found a place in the preface to the second *Agreement of the People*.[78] The 'golden

---

[72] C. Hill, *The Religion of Gerrard Winstanley* (P. and P. supplement 5, 1978), 53.

[73] C.H. George, 'Gerrard Winstanley: A Critical Retrospect', in C.R. Cole and M.E. Moody (eds.), *The Dissenting Tradition* (Athens, Ohio, 1975), 191.

[74] See chapter 8 below; also G.E. Aylmer, 'Unbelief in Seventeenth-Century England', in D. Pennington and K. Thomas (eds.), *Puritans and Revolutionaries* (Oxford, 1978), 22–46.

[75] See Hill, *Religion of Gerrard Winstanley*, 53–4; idem, *Change and Continuity in Seventeenth-Century England* (1974), ch. 4; WTUD (1972), 299–301, 313–19, 336; and ch. 8 below.

[76] See the latest offering by L. Mulligan, 'The Religious Roots of William Walwyn's Radicalism', *Journal of Religious History*, xii (1982).

[77] J.F.C. Harrison, *The Second Coming. Popular Millenarianism 1780–1850* (1979); E. Yeo, 'Christianity in Chartist Struggle 1838–1842', *P. and P.* 91 (1981).

[78] See p. 71 below; and also Davis, 'Levellers and Christianity', 228–9.

rule' theme can be detected in most radical writing: in the Digger or near-Digger pamphlets from Buckinghamshire, for example, or in the work of the radical John Warr.[79] The Quakers looked to a new age in which the light or spirit within would lead men to 'do unto all men as they would be done unto'.[80] Winstanley's God, 'pure Reason', tells men and women 'Is thy neighbour hungry and naked to-day, do thou feed and clothe him; it may be thy case tomorrow, and then he will be ready to help thee.'[81] There are tantalizing similarities here with nineteenth-century working-class Christianity as described by Hugh McLeod: Christianity as ethics, as 'decent behaviour'.[82] 'Do unto others . . .' was to be a favourite text for Chartist sermons.[83] The golden rule was part of an emphasis on what Richard Overton called 'Practical Christianity'.[84] Action against oppression in its various forms was vital for Levellers, Diggers, Quakers, and some Ranters. By your actions you are 'brought to the touch-stone', wrote the Quaker William Tomlinson, '*Your works, Your works*, they are your discovery.'[85] Or as Winstanley put it, 'action is the life of all, and if thou dost not act, thou dost nothing'.[86]

Linked to all this was the strong sense of community which is to be found in all the radical literature — including that of the Levellers. We can see it in popular millenarianism. We can see it in the Quakers: the light in your conscience tells you to 'deal the bread to the hungry'; it is 'equity'. The 'unity of heart among those about Jerusalem', explained the Quaker Francis Howgil in a gloss on Acts 4:34, 'was such that all was in common, and none wanted; And as many as were possessors of lands and houses, sold them, and brought the price of that which was sold, and laid it at the Apostles feet, and it was distributed to every man according as he had need.'[87] For

---

[79] Hill, *Religion of Gerrard Winstanley*, 8, n. 37, 19.

[80] T. Adams and R. Farnworth, *An Easter-Reckoning* (1656), 31; J. Crook, *An Apology for the Quakers* (1662), 2.

[81] Hill, *Religion of Gerrard Winstanley*, 8.

[82] H. McLeod, *Religion and the People of Western Europe 1789-1970* (Oxford, 1981), 125.

[83] Yeo, 'Christianity in Chartist Struggle', 112, 120.

[84] See p. 72 below; and Davis, 'Levellers and Christianity', 234-6.

[85] W. Tomlinson, *A Word of Reproof* (1656), 6.

[86] Winstanley, *Works*, 315.

[87] G. F[ox]., *A Warning from the Lord* (1654), 1; idem, *This is to all Officers*

Winstanley God was the 'great Leveller' who would 'bring in true community; and destroy murdering propriety'.[88] William Walwyn the Leveller said that practical Christianity would 'empty the fullest Baggs; and pluck downe the highest plumes'.[89] The Ranters Abiezer Coppe and Laurence Clarkson expected a new age of universal freedom. God would 'make the low and poor equal with the rich'.[90]

Fifth Monarchists and Levellers (and the occasional Quaker) attacked monopolies and merchant oligarchies. All the groups in the pages which follow wanted law reform and most were, to say the least, critical of the monarchy, nobility, and gentry.[91] Yet despite the rhetoric of men like Howgil, and with the notable exception of the Diggers, the radicals were not out to overthrow property. As I explain later of the Quakers, they seem to have had in mind a nation of small producers, with some limitations on the distribution of wealth. Richard Overton's interpretation of the golden rule implied the protection of private property no less than it implied compassion.[92] The Quaker Richard Hubberthorne condemned tithes because they prevented him from free enjoyment and use of his property.[93] In other words, the radicals' general political and economic outlook seems to have reflected their social support: in the towns, independent craftsmen and small traders; in the country, the same groups plus husbandmen and yeomen.[94] The ideologists and leaders of the radicals and sectaries were quite often men (or women) of substance, alienated merchants, the sons of lesser gentry,

(1657), 1; G. Fox the younger, *This is for You* (1659), 3; F.H[owgil]., *The Great Case of Tythes* (1665), 12.

[88] Winstanley, *Works*, 391, 453.
[89] Davis, 'Levellers and Christianity', 236, n. 47.
[90] A. Coppe, *A Fiery Flying Roll* (1649), 2. For Clarkson, a fascinating figure, see B. Reay, 'Laurence Clarkson: An artisan and the English Revolution', in C. Hill, B. Reay, and W. Lamont, *The World of the Muggletonians* (1983), ch. 6.
[91] B.S. Capp, *The Fifth Monarchy Men* (1972), chs. 6–7; Manning, *English People*, chs. 9–10.
[92] See p. 72 below.
[93] Reay, 'Quaker Opposition to Tithes', 109.
[94] See Capp, *Fifth Monarchy Men*, ch. 4; B. Reay, 'The Social Origins of Early Quakerism', *Journal of Interdisciplinary History*, xi (1980); idem, 'The Muggletonians: An Introductory Survey', in Hill *et al.*, *World of the Muggletonians*, 49–53; and pp. 36–9 below.

wealthy yeomen.[95] But the rank and file was firmly of the 'middle sort of people'; the less illiterate sections of the population; those who would have been included in a Leveller franchise. In one of the visions of George Foster, God appeared as a 'mighty Leveller', cutting down all those who 'were higher than the middle sort' and raising up 'those that were lower than the middle sort'.[96] Foster's God personifies the social preoccupations of the revolution radicals.

Radical groups and movements rose and fell with amazing rapidity during the 1640s and 1650s. In an attempt to impose some kind of pattern on the events of that period, some historians have detected a high-water mark of radicalism in the years 1647-9. Undeveloped political consciousness, 'inchoate protest' in the form of religious sectarianism, underwent a secular and political transformation: the Levellers and Diggers were the result. But radicalism was crushed. The Levellers were finally defeated in 1649, the Diggers in 1650. Then followed a retreat into mysticism and sectarianism in the shape of the Ranters (1649-51), and the Fifth Monarchy Men and Quakers of the 1650s. 'The Revolution, which man has been unable to complete, must and will be completed by a miracle.' 'The angels may enter where men may not venture to tread; and what political activity had failed to achieve, Divine intervention would surely effect.'[97]

There is a lot of truth in this picture. Certainly the late 1640s, with Leveller democracy and Digger agrarian communism, witnessed a 'tendency towards secularization'.[98] Certainly the radical religious pamphlet literature of 1649 and the following decade shows a feeling of betrayal at the hands of those in power: generals, parliaments, and Oliver Cromwell. The Fifth Monarchists and Quakers were movements of

[95] G.E. Aylmer, 'Gentlemen Levellers', *P. and P.* 49 (1970); R.T. Vann, *The Social Development of English Quakerism* (Cambridge, Mass., 1969), ch. 2.

[96] G. Foster, *The Sounding of the Last Trumpet* (1650), 17. For a good short biography of Foster, see *The Biographical Dictionary of British Radicals in the Seventeenth Century*, ed. R.L. Greaves and R. Zaller (Brighton, 1982), i: George Foster.

[97] See D.W. Petegorsky, *Left-Wing Democracy in the English Civil War* (1940), 115-16, 237; P. Zagorin, *A History of Political Thought in the English Revolution* (1954), 105; A.L. Morton, *The World of the Ranters* (1970), 16-19.

[98] Olivier Lutaud, quoted by Hill, *Religion of Gerrard Winstanley*, 54.

protest against the retreat from revolution by the Rump
Parliament (1648-53) and the Protectorate (1653-9). Yet we
have seen — and shall see — that the relationship between
religion and politics in radical thought and action was not
simply one of movement towards and away from secularism.
It is not the case (*pace* Perez Zagorin) that millenarianism replaced Levellerism;[99] it is more accurate to think of parallel
and perhaps in some respects conflated ideologies, the one
outliving the other. 1649 *was* a turning-point but so too was
the fall of Barebone's Parliament in 1653: as far as millenarians were concerned, the calling of the Parliament of Saints
in July 1653 (it was dissolved in December) was the high
point of radicalism. Nor would the Quakers have seen themselves as apolitical nonconformists, part of a new stage in the
retreat from revolution.[100] Indeed they picked up the somewhat dusty radical banner and became the conscience of the
radical republican cause, 'the Good Old Cause'. For them
1659 was a high-water mark, as we shall see in chapter 6.

The chronology of the significant radical groups is easy to
establish. The 1640s were dominated by the Levellers. They
were replaced by the Fifth Monarchists of the early 1650s,
for a short time the 'only significant radical group',[101] until
they were in turn eclipsed in the mid-1650s by the Quakers.
While the Baptists, a kind of common denominator of
radicalism, survive the whole period 1640-60. Rather than
thinking in terms of a decisive high-water mark of radicalism,
then, it is perhaps better to talk of a continual ebb and flow.
Radical hopes fluctuated with the various changes in regime.

VI

The radicals have achieved a place in the British socialist
pantheon. To quote Tony Benn, they 'raised and fought over
. . . many of the basic questions which we still debate to-
day'.[102] But still more important — and I think that the
contributors to this volume would agree — is their resistance,

---

[99] Capp, *Fifth Monarchy Men*, 89-90.
[100] See Morton, *World of the Ranters*, 18-19.   [101] See Capp, p. 174 below.
[102] Foreword to F. Brockway, *Britain's First Socialists* (1980), x.

the very fact that they questioned. Ordinary people thought about the great issues of life and death; they speculated. They did not necessarily believe everything they were told. They shared a healthy distrust of the orthodoxies of the clerical and lay élite. And, quite often, they acted to change their situation.

When held up to the harsh light of political reality, religious radicalism was a failure. Radicalism impinged on English politics throughout the 1640s and 1650s. Fear of radicalism was important in the crystallization of parties in the early 1640s. During the years 1647-9 radicalism in the Army forced the Revolution in a direction which it would not have otherwise taken. But the sectaries never triumphed, despite the fears of many an Anglican and a Presbyterian. Their main effect was to terrify the men of property and to reinforce religious conservatism. In 1642, in 1648, in 1653, in 1657, and most important of all in 1659, radicalism stimulated reaction. As Alexis de Toqueville once said of the Revolution sects, 'they were able to alarm and trouble their century but not to subdue or lead it'.[103]

[103] *Tocqueville and Beaumont on Social Reform*, ed. S. Drescher (NY, 1968), 197.

2 The Baptists: Fount of All Heresy

J. F. McGregor

I

The title of this chapter is a rough paraphrase of that given by Robert Baillie, a Scottish Presbyterian minister, to a tract which he published early in 1647.[1] Baillie was one of the Scottish representatives at the Westminster Assembly, a committee of clergy and laymen convened by the English Parliament in July 1643. Although distracted by the problems of waging civil war against their king, the parliamentarians were anxious to establish a reformed Protestant church to replace the episcopal system which had collapsed with the calling of the Long Parliament in November 1640. Baillie and his countrymen had assumed that in accordance with the conditions of the Solemn League and Covenant of September 1643, the military alliance between Scotland and the English Parliament, their mission would be to supervise the imposition on England of the Scottish, Presbyterian version of Calvin's Genevan church. But a saving clause in the Covenant, requiring any religious settlement to be 'according to the Word of God' as well as 'the example of the best reformed Churches', allowed members of both the Assembly and Parliament to subject Baillie's cherished example of reform to detailed and protracted revision. The Scottish Presbyterian insistence on the autonomy of the church in relation to the state, and on the *jure divino* authority of its ministry, found little sympathy in England. Lay demands to participate in and ultimately, through Parliament, to control religious affairs was one of the principal dynamics of English Puritanism. The pretensions of the Presbyterian clergy more than

[1] R. Baillie, *Anabaptisme, the true Fountaine of Independency, Brownisme, Antinomy, Familisme, and most of the other errours which for the time doe trouble the Church of England* . . . (1647).

matched those of the old bishops, for they were reinforced by an efficient system of parochial discipline.[2]

In January 1647, when Robert Baillie published the latest of his periodic expressions of frustration at the slowness of reform, the legislation to establish a national, compulsory Presbyterian church, a pragmatic compromise described by Baillie as a 'lame, Erastian Presbyterie', was still emerging, in piecemeal fashion, from Parliament.[3] As a result of this tardy progress, lamented Baillie, the English people had for years been deprived of strict church discipline. They had, for want of action, been given a dangerous liberty which had resulted in a profusion of heretical opinions which seriously threatened the prospects of godly reformation. The unprecedented variety of this radical religious speculation had been described in great detail the previous year by Thomas Edwards, a London Presbyterian minister. Edwards laboured to demonstrate that the agitation of popular, unlettered preachers was flouting the authority of the national church and the prestige of the professional clergy. No fundamental doctrine of the Christian faith, no ordinance or practice of the reformed church was free from their attacks. Their claims to the liberty of true Christians was inevitably overflowing into moral libertarianism and demands for political liberty. Popular heresy was a dangerous threat to all lawful authority.[4] Baillie did not seek to augment Edwards's comprehensive catalogue but to establish the origins of these heresies. He blamed the Anabaptists; a sect particularly strong in London, increasingly prevalent in the Army, and spreading its influence throughout the country. They rejected the uniform, national church for voluntary communities of lay believers; the infant baptism of the state church for the immersion of spiritually regenerated saints. From their principles all heresies flowed. The sect was a convenient and credible scapegoat since these baptized believers were described by Baillie as Anabaptists, a name they consistently rejected, in order to emphasize that

[2] W. Haller, *Liberty and Reformation in the Puritan Revolution* (NY, 1955), chs. 4, 7.

[3] *Letters and Journals of Robert Baillie*, ed. D. Laing (Edinburgh, 1841-2), ii. 326; Baillie, *Anabaptisme*, dedicatory epistle.

[4] *Gangraena*, i. 61-76.

they were no new heresy but the re-emergence of a dangerous menace to authority and social order.

The original Anabaptists were the radical wing of the sixteenth-century Reformation. They were profoundly sectarian in their insistence that true Christians must separate themselves from the degenerate society in which they lived. Pacifists in principle, they regarded civil authority, dependent on the power of the sword, as irredeemably corrupt. It was unlawful to swear oaths, bear arms, or hold civil office. In their rejection of the authority of the established churches, which were inevitably corrupted by both the inclusion of the wicked and their dependence on the coercive power of the magistrate, the Anabaptists argued for liberty of conscience, religious toleration, and the total separation of church and state. Their restriction of baptism, the seal of entry into the church, to adult believers most dramatically signified their rejection of a comprehensive or compulsory ecclesiastical system. Catholics, Lutherans, Anglicans, and Calvinists alike regarded Anabaptism as dangerously subverting the authority of church and state. From the later 1520s the movement was persecuted with great ferocity. With one notable exception, the Anabaptists remained faithful to their pacifist principles. In 1534, however, in the north German city of Münster, that stubborn pacifism turned to violent revolution. The Anabaptists seized control of the city government, expelled all those who would not be rebaptized, and declared Münster the site of the New Jerusalem. Under the leadership of Jan Bockelson (John of Leiden), a mentally deranged tailor, the Anabaptists introduced communism and polygamy. For over a year the city was beseiged by the forces of the local princes. When it eventually fell, the population was put to the sword.[5]

For well over a century, Münster and John of Leiden remained potent images of anarchy; vivid examples of the dangers of popular religious heresy and justification for the stern suppression of all its manifestations. It is hardly surprising that the emergence of the English Baptists in the early 1640s inspired the publication of a spate of polemical histories

[5] N. Cohn, *The Pursuit of the Millennium* (1957), ch. 12.

of the Münster affair.[6] The considerable similarities of doctrine encouraged the fear that the new movement likewise
threatened the sanctity of family and private property, as
well as the authority of the magistrate. Given the uncertain-
ties of civil war and the emergence of popular agitation supporting the parliamentary cause in 1641, the fear that London
might become another Münster did not seem too fanciful.
Every Baptist leader was a prospective John of Leiden. As
the Baptists claimed in their defence, there were radical
differences between old and new Anabaptism. The continental movement had spread to southern and eastern England
from the Netherlands but it had taken the brunt of Mary
Tudor's campaign against heresy. The remnants may have
merged with Lollardy in a popular heretical tradition which
was to surface in the forms of radical Puritanism during the
English Revolution. But it is unlikely that organized Anabaptism survived Elizabeth's reign.[7]

While continental Anabaptism did have some influence on
the English Baptists, the movement which emerged in the
early 1640s was essentially a product of native English Puritanism. The Baptists were part of a separatist tradition which
saw little prospect of Christian reformation in a national
church tainted with relics of popery and too lax in its admission of the ungodly to communion. The saints, those
confident of their election to salvation, must withdraw to form
their own churches. From the 1580s official persecution led
many separatists to seek refuge in the more tolerant climate
of the Netherlands.[8] The antecedents of the Revolution
Baptists can be found in one such group of Puritan separatists
from the lower Trent valley which emigrated to the Netherlands in 1608. Either shortly before or after departure, it
divided into two parties led by deprived clerics, John Smyth
and John Robinson. Smyth's group was immediately influenced by Dutch Anabaptism. Its members were convinced
that they must reject not only the authority of the Church of

---

[6] e.g. *A Short History of the Anabaptists of High and Low Germany* (1642);
*A Warning for England especially for London in the Famous History of the
Frantick Anabaptists* (1642).

[7] M.R. Watts, *The Dissenters* (Oxford, 1978), 7–14.

[8] Ibid. 14–34; B.R. White, *The English Separatist Tradition* (Oxford, 1971).

England but also the validity of its ordinances, including their own baptism. So Smyth rebaptized himself, then his followers.[9] Equally significantly, the Smyth church rejected the orthodox Calvinism of English Puritanism (that Christ died to save only particular men and women) for the Anabaptist belief in the potential of all to be saved. This doctrine of general redemption, offering saving grace to all who would accept it through faith, was more intrinsically optimistic in its view of the moral qualities of humanity.[10] By rejecting Calvinist predestination and infant baptism, Smyth's exiled church was well on the way to absorption into Dutch Anabaptism. But the majority, led by Thomas Helwys, a Nottinghamshire gentleman, refused to surrender the remainder of their Puritan principles. In particular they found Anabaptist belief in the natural corruption of worldly power incompatible with Puritan faith in the ability of a godly magistracy to reform both church and state according to the true Christian model. Helwys accepted the logic of his position and in 1612 returned to England to found in London the first General Baptist church. By 1626 there were five such congregations scattered around England but their subsequent histories are generally obscure.[11]

The other part of the original migration, led by John Robinson, remained untouched by the influence of Anabaptism. It held to a kind of semi-separatism which expressed the *émigré* ideal to return home reconciled with a reformed national church. Henry Jacob, the most influential exponent of the semi-separatist principle, did return in 1616 and established a congregation in the London suburb of Southwark. Having renounced the option of emigration, many of the Southwark congregation reacted to the Laudian persecution of the 1630s by adopting increasingly extreme separatist

[9] Watts, op. cit. 41–50; M. Tolmie, *The Triumph of the Saints* (Cambridge, 1977), 69–71.

[10] The term 'general redemption' is used in preference to 'radical Arminianism' to describe Anabaptist doctrine in order to avoid confusion with Anglican high-church Arminianism which was equally radical in rejecting the conventional theology of English Protestantism. For the clerical Arminianism of the 1620s and 1630s see N. Tyacke, 'Puritanism, Arminianism and counter-revolution', in C. Russell (ed), *Origins of the English Civil War* (1973).

[11] White, *English Separatist Tradition*, chs. 6–8.

doctrines. The most radical seceded to form congregations practising believers' baptism. These were the first Particular Baptist churches; so called because, unlike the General Baptists, they remained true to Calvin's doctrine that Christ had died to save only particular individuals, the predestined elect. In 1644 seven London congregations of Particular Baptists published their own confession of faith.[12]

Between 1640 and 1642 both Particular and General Baptists further demonstrated their exclusive separatism by adopting the dramatic ritual of baptism by total immersion. Henceforth they were known by their opponents as Dippers as well as Anabaptists. The consequences of this innovation were both to draw popular attention to the strange practices of the new sect and to exaggerate the impression that the Baptists were a church apart from the rest of Puritan separatism. Most contemporaries failed to grasp the distinction between General and Particular Baptists, regarding their doctrinal differences, along with their internal disputes over church ordinances, as evidence that the Baptist sect lacked discipline and order. In fact, these differences in redemption theology so outweighed common rites of church entry that co-operation, even friendly communication between the two sorts of Baptists, was practically impossible during the Revolution. The Particular Baptists condemned general redemption as heresy: the General Baptists tended to regard this doctrine, rather than believers' baptism, as the foundation of their faith. Strictly they were distinct churches with many common, sectarian attitudes and practices. In the context of the early 1640s, however, they are better regarded as two autonomous elements of an amorphous movement of radical Puritanism.

The dispute between Presbyterians and Independents over the true model of a reformed church allowed the Baptists and other separatists to flourish with relative impunity in the first years of civil war. Presbyterian opposition to the Independents' doctrine of the church as autonomous congregations of saints, under the patronage of the magistrate,

---

[12] Tolmie, *Triumph of the Saints*, chs. 1–3. For the original record of the emergence of the first Particular Baptist churches, see *TBHS* i (1908–9), 203–56; ii (1910–11), 31–52.

pushed the Independents into alliance with the separatists and obliged them reluctantly to defend liberty to worship of all Puritan saints, including Baptists.[13] The growing influence of the Independents, in both Parliament and its armies, protected religious radicals from the punitive actions of hostile magistrates and clergy. The dynamic energy of separatism, which had previously been absorbed in surviving the rigours of persecution, was increasingly channelled into evangelism. Since the acceptance of believers' baptism was a principal mark of separatist zeal in the early 1640s, it is not surprising that the Baptists proved the most successful disseminators of radical religious ideas until the rise of the Quakers in the 1650s. During the first years of civil war, when much of the country was in the hands of the royalists, their missionary efforts were necessarily confined to London and the surrounding counties. Initially the Particular Baptists sought their converts in the Independent congregations: 'They gather members out of other Churches in whose conversion they were not at all instrumental', was a common complaint.[14] As Independent resentment and Baptist exclusiveness widened the divisions among the London saints, the Particular Baptists looked outwards for new converts.

The General Baptists were 'looser in organisation, more radical in outlook, and more fluid in membership' than the Particular Baptists.[15] Largely isolated by doctrinal differences from the radical Calvinist coalition, they appear to have found their support in a lower stratum of the London population, less touched by Puritan influence. Like the Quakers a decade and the Methodists a century later, they demonstrated that the doctrine of general redemption, with its emphasis on human dignity, could have greater appeal to the lower orders than the harsh determinism of Calvinism. The missionary campaigns of the London General Baptists have been described as the first of the modern revivalist

[13] Watts, op.cit. 94–105. For the debate on the political significance of the religious denominations see S. Foster, 'The Presbyterian Independents exorcised', *P. and P.* 44 (1969) and the replies, ibid. 47 (1970).

[14] S. Winter, *The Summe of Diverse Sermons* (1656), 168.

[15] Tolmie, *Triumph of the Saints*, 80.

movements.[16] Their most celebrated evangelist, Thomas Lambe, a soap-boiler, ran open meetings where allcomers could exercise their spiritual gifts in lively discussions of the mysteries of religion, much to the disgust of Presbyterian ministers such as Thomas Edwards:

This man and his Church are very Erroneous, strange Doctrines being vented there continually, both in Preaching and in way of Discoursing and Reasoning, and strange things also done by them both in the time of their Church meetings, and out of them. Many use to resort to this Church and meeting, the house, yards full, especially yong youths and wenches flock thither, and all of them Preach universal Redemption. In their Ch. meetings and Exercises there is such a confusion and noise, as if it were at a Play; and some will be speaking here, some there; yong youths and boyes come thither, and make a noise while they are at their Exercises, and them of the Church will go to make them quiet, and then they fight one with another . . . they have many Exercises, in one meeting two or three, when one hath done, theres sometimes difference in the Church who shall Exercise next, 'tis put to the Vote, some for one, some for another . . . in this Church 'tis usual and lawful, not only for the company to stand up and object against the Doctrine delivered when the Exerciser of his gifts hath made an end, but in the midst of it, so that sometimes upon some standing up and objecting, there's *pro* and *con* for almost an hour, and falling out among themselves before the man can have finished his Discourse.[17]

Lambe's theatrical methods had considerable success. They bear, however, more resemblance to Quaker evangelism than the usual style of the London churches. The Particular Baptists developed the practice of challenging parish ministers to public debate. Such meetings were often banned by local authorities for fear of tumults. When they took place, the issues were rarely satisfactorily resolved. Most Baptist preachers insisted on extempore argument; their learned opponents preferred the formal procedures of debate. The Baptists, one complained, 'utter old broken notes taken from other mens Sermons'.[18] They were too ignorant to understand Scripture and incapable of logical discourse. Such

[16] M. Tolmie, 'Thomas Lambe, soap-boiler, and Thomas Lambe, merchant, General Baptists', *BQ* xxvii (1977–8), 7.
[17] *Gangraena*, i. 92–5.
[18] T. Thacke, *The Gainsayer Convinced* (1649), 64. See A.S. Langley, 'Seventeenth-century Baptist disputations', *TBHS* vi (1918–19), 216–43.

disputes often overflowed into pamphlet warfare which served to spread radical ideas to a wider audience. Baptist publications were not particularly well designed as propaganda. They were more concerned to counter the attacks of their opponents than to develop an effective polemical style. Nevertheless they were the first radical, popular movement able to take advantage of the freedom and relative cheapness of the printing press in the unique conditions of revolution to appeal to an increasingly literate population.

In the first years of the civil war, the London Baptists refined their evangelical techniques: revivalist meetings, public debates, and printed propaganda. The victories of the parliamentary armies in 1644 and 1645 allowed them to expand their missionary activities into most of England. In the vanguard were the many saints who had volunteered for military service. The Anabaptist principle of pacifism found little sympathy with either wing of the Baptists, both of which were prepared to fight for a just cause and serve in the armies of a godly regime. They shared the Puritan conviction that Parliament's forces, and particularly the New Model Army, were God's instrument for the destruction of popery and tyranny. Military service in a regiment with sympathetic senior officers gave considerable scope for lay evangelism. Many Baptists became unofficial preachers in companies dominated by zealous Puritans. In June 1645 two captains of the New Model Army, one of them Paul Hobson, a prominent London Particular Baptist, were arrested by Sir Samuel Luke, governor of the garrison at Newport Pagnell, Buckinghamshire, for unlicensed preaching under a parliamentary ordinance passed two months previously. Having dispatched them to London for examination by Parliament, Luke was furious to find them returned several weeks later to resume their preaching with a safe conduct from their colonel, Charles Fleetwood, a radical Independent. Hobson's case became a *cause célèbre* among the London radicals.[19] It also brought home to local authorities the futility of attempting to suppress military preachers when they had the support of sympathetic

---

[19] *Original Letters*, ed. H. Ellis, 3rd ser., iv (1846), 254-5, 260-6; *Gangraena*, i. 90-1.

Independents such as Fleetwood and General Oliver Cromwell. Objecting a year before to a fellow general's cashiering
of one of his officers for Anabaptist principles, Cromwell
claimed that 'the State, in choosing men to serve it, takes
no notice of their opinion; if they be willing to serve it, that
satisfies'.[20]

Civilian preachers also relied on military support to protect them from local hostility. For Baptist evangelists, complained a beleaguered clergyman, 'it is ordinary to come
with a gang of soldiers, and prate on a tombstone, while the
Minister preacheth in a pulpit'.[21] Despite the hostility which
they aroused among the political nation, there were relatively few cases of Baptist preachers being apprehended by
local authorities. A fair proportion were the result of a drive
by both wings of the movement in 1645 to evangelize the
eastern counties, an area strongly, but conservatively, Puritan.
Samuel Oates, a disciple of the General Baptist Thomas
Lambe, adopted his mentor's techniques of mass revivalism
in an energetic missionary campaign through the east Midlands in 1647 and 1648. The magistrates of Rutland charged
him with 'filling the Countie with divers sects and Schismes,
withdrawing them from theire owne Ministers into mutinous
assemblies, weeklie and almost dailie, and perverting wholl
ffamilies, working divisions even betweene nearest relations'.[22] Oates jumped bail and continued his preaching un-
molested. Local magistrates were generally uncertain of the
law and lacked confidence in their power to deal with lay
preachers. Long before Colonel Pride's purge of Parliament
in December 1649 ended any lingering hopes of Presbyterian
domination, the rulers of the counties had realized the
futility of proceeding against Baptist evangelists.

II

Baptist preachers stressed the duty of their converts to gather

---

[20] *The Writings and Speeches of Oliver Cromwell*, ed. W.C. Abbott (Cambridge, Mass., 1937–47), i. 278.

[21] F. Fullwood, *The Churches and Ministery of England* (1652), sig. C.

[22] Quoted in A. Betteridge, 'Early Baptists in Leicestershire and Rutland',
BQ xxv (1974), 207.

together as churches of Christ practising the true gospel ordinances. By 1660 there were more than 250 such churches, about 60 per cent of them Particular Baptist.[23] There is some indication that the General Baptist congregations were usually larger so that the numbers of the two wings may have been roughly equal. The size of the congregations ranged so widely, from 18 to 261 according to the surviving evidence, that any average is meaningless.[24] Most rural churches would have subdivided long before the larger number was reached. 25,000 would be a generous estimate of Baptist strength by 1660. Although this represents but one-half of 1 per cent of the population, Baptist influence was obviously much wider. The estimate does not allow for the considerable number expelled from the movement, many for the profession of more radical heresies. It is impossible to estimate the number of those more casually influenced by Baptist religious and social attitudes.

Independent churches were founded on a covenant subscribed to by the congregation, each therefore being an independent branch of the true church.[25] While they respected congregational autonomy, the Baptists' belief that they were 'fellow members of one body though in distinct congregations',[26] united by their commitment to a common model of the true church, enabled them to organize the random fruits of their evangelism into larger units. Seven London Particular Baptist churches had joined in association by 1644. During the 1650s groups of Particular Baptist churches in the West Country, the Midlands, south Midlands, the counties immediately north and west of London, south Wales, and the garrisons of the army of occupation in Ireland formed themselves into regional associations.[27] The London leaders attempted, with limited success, to develop a rudimentary, national organization. They encouraged visiting delegates and correspondence between associations but their attempt to

---

[23] *TBHS* ii (1910-11), 236-54.

[24] *AR* 196; *BQ* xiii (1949-50), 153.

[25] G.F. Nuttall, *Visible Saints, the Congregational Way, 1640-1660* (Oxford, 1957), 70-81. [26] *AR* 77.

[27] B.R. White, 'The Organisation of the Particular Baptists, 1644-1660', *Journal of Ecclesiastical History*, xvii (1966); G.F. Nuttall, 'The Baptist Western Association, 1653-1658', ibid. xi (1960).

establish a national fund for missionary work came to nothing.[28] The limited evidence for the General Baptists suggests that their regional organization was more fluid. They retained much of the characteristics of the first London churches when they colonized the provinces; a relatively informal, mass evangelical movement. Though poorer than the Particular Baptists, they nevertheless financed full-time evangelists, or messengers, serving neither congregation nor association but the whole movement. By 1654 these messengers had established a national assembly in London.[29] Social homogeneity, their relatively informal structure, and their theological isolation from the rest of radical Puritanism gave the General Baptist movement a cohesiveness which the Particular Baptists could not achieve. Their model of a mass movement served by itinerant messengers was to have considerable influence on the Quakers.

Much of the business of the associational meetings concerned doubtful or controversial issues of doctrine and church discipline referred by the constituent congregations.[30] The associations also organized missionary programmes and undertook welfare commitments beyond the resources of particular churches. Some associational system was necessary for the more efficient use of the limited financial resources and administrative experience at the sect's disposal. Many of the smaller rural churches could not have survived even the peaceful climate of the 1650s without the organized support of their neighbours. The more socially prominent and the better educated of saints inevitably assumed a disproportionately dominant role in associational proceedings. Nevertheless the leaders and delegates were largely of the middling sort whose administrative experience would have been confined to the minor offices of the parish, manor, or guild. Yet they were able to create a system of democratic, representative assemblies with no previous parallel, at least in English history. Limited resources required the Baptists to devise efficient systems of intercongregational government beyond anything achieved by the Presbyterians or conceived

[28] *AR* 111-18, 173-5.   [29] *Thurloe*, ii. 582-3.
[30] G.F. Nuttall, 'Association records of the Particular Baptists', *BQ* xxvi (1975-6), 21.

by the Independents. Their associational system was not matched until the Quakers, moved by the greater imperative of persecution, established their local and national meetings in the 1660s.

The rise of regional associations indicates the Baptists' geographical distribution. Their main strength was in the south, west, and Midlands. There were no more than a handful of churches in the six northern counties. Both Particular and General Baptists flourished in London and the Midlands, their relationship usually one of mutual indifference. The General Baptists were particularly strong in the Weald of Kent, the Lincolnshire Fens, and the Chiltern Hills of Buckinghamshire, areas with a tradition of popular heresy. Native Lollardy still flourished in Buckinghamshire and Kent in the first half of the sixteenth century. In Kent this tradition was augmented by the influx of Dutch Anabaptist refugees in the 1530s and 1540s. Lincolnshire also had a history of Lollardy but the major source of popular heresy in this area was probably the Anabaptists among the Dutch engineers imported to drain the Fens in the first half of the seventeenth century.[31] The Fens, the Weald, and the Chilterns were non-fielden regions where parishes covered large areas and manorial authority was weak. It has been suggested that the 'masterless men', squatters and cottagers, in these relatively underdeveloped areas, were attracted to heretical ideas that the remote and ineffective authority of parson and squire found difficult to suppress.[32] General Baptists may have found fertile ground in marginal areas with similar heretical attitudes but equivalent conditions can account for the concentration of Particular Baptists in the moors and hills of the West Country.[33] Some of these areas were also the centres of the cloth industry, a traditional source of heresy. Generally the Particular Baptists appear to have met a better reception in areas subject to some Puritan influence. Where it was particularly strong among the local gentry, as in the eastern counties, they made little headway. There is no

---

[31] G.F. Nuttall, *The Puritan Spirit* (1967), 74.
[32] *WTUD* (1972), ch. 3; A. Everitt, 'Nonconformity in country parishes', *Agricultural History Review*, supplement, xviii (1970).
[33] Watts, op. cit. 282-4.

general explanation of the relative distribution of the two wings of the Baptists or the movement's particular strength in some parts but not others. Much depended on the successful qualities of local evangelists such as Thomas Collier in the West Country, Samuel Oates and Henry Denne in Kent and the north Midlands.

The Baptists' critics, especially the professional clergy, dismissed the new evangelists as a pack of 'mechanick' preachers: rude, uneducated, barely literate tradesmen and artisans. 'Russet Rabbies, and Mechanick Enthusiasts, and profound Watermen, and Sublime Coachmen, and illuminated Tradesmen', they were described by Daniel Featley, a moderate Anglican, in 1645.[34] The known occupations of Baptists largely substantiate Featley's comments. Small craftsmen and tradesmen predominate: weavers, shoemakers, tailors, ironmongers, bakers, glovers, and buttonmakers. They comprise those 'middling sort' whose independent or itinerant patterns of work and vulnerability to market forces had traditionally attracted them to popular heresies. There is no doubt, however, that the surviving evidence underestimates the number of rank and file Baptists wholly or partly engaged in agriculture. While the movement had its first strength in the metropolis, by 1660 it was also well established in the countryside. Congregations were usually named after towns and large villages but these were often geographically convenient centres, sites of suitable meeting places or sympathetic army garrisons. Congregations recruited members from villages more than a good day's walk from the principal place of meeting. Porton church covered twenty villages and hamlets in south Wiltshire and north Hampshire within a radius of twelve miles. Fenstanton in Huntingdonshire had members from thirty villages covering an even wider area.[35] The rural base of the Baptists before the Restoration must have been considerable. The leadership may have been predominantly tradesmen and artisans but there were others such as John Onley, a notable Warwickshire General Baptist, who 'painfully follows Husbandry all the Week dayes'.[36]

---

[34] D. Featley, *The Dippers dipt* (1645), sigs. C3–C3^V.
[35] *TBHS* i (1908–9), 57; Watts, op. cit. 287.
[36] J. Ley, *A Discourse of Disputations* (1658), 85.

The evidence for Baptist occupations comes largely from hostile observers who are concerned to emphasize the leaders' mean status but make no allowance for wealth, power, or prestige. There were prosperous merchants and manufacturers among the Baptists. John Tomkins, an Abingdon maltster, left £6,000 in his will.[37] The London Particular Baptists had the greatest concentration of wealthy merchants. While it was more usual for such men to join the Presbyterians or non-separatist Independents, believers' baptism does not appear to have imposed restraints on capitalist enterprise. Samuel Moyer, a merchant of considerable wealth, was active in the City government during the 1640s and in the revolutionary regimes of the early 1650s. William Kiffin, a founder of the London movement and perhaps its most influential leader, amassed a large fortune as an interloper, flouting the Merchant Adventurers' official monopoly of the wool trade.[38] Moyer was a radical millenarian: Kiffin, however, is more representative of the cautious, restraining influence which the bourgeois saints of the capital exercised on the affairs of the movement. A small number of gentry also went beyond Independency to believers' baptism. Most prominent was Henry Lawrence of Huntingdonshire, President of the Protectorate Council of State. Socially conservative, he was nevertheless a useful lobbyist for Baptist interests at Cromwell's court. The minor gentry of Baptist persuasion, such as Henry Danvers of Staffordshire, Robert Bennett of Cornwall, and John Rede of Wiltshire, were of more radical temperament. Rising to power in county government from the late 1640s, they provided patronage and protection for the local congregations.

The presence of two other elements among the Baptists of the Revolution further qualifies the model of the sect as a church of the 'middling sort'. The professional soldiers were the most powerful and disruptive force within the movement. A considerable number of saints of humble origin had risen through zeal and competence to ranks of command by the 1650s. Handsomely paid, officers had special opportunities

[37] *AR* 207, n. 16.
[38] For Moyer, see G.E. Aylmer, *The State's Servants* (1973), 214-16; for Kiffin: *DNB*.

to acquire confiscated lands in England and Ireland. William Packer, Cromwell's major, joined with other Baptist officers to purchase the royal manor of Theobalds. Jerome Sankey, intended for a career as a rural parson before the outbreak of war, rose to command a regiment and founded a gentry family in Ireland.[39] They constituted part of a revolutionary gentry whose survival depended upon the maintenance of the Army's capacity to influence political events to its advantage. Their sectional interests and their radical republican *esprit de corps* were not always easily reconciled with the more cautious approach of the civilian saints to the affairs of the world.

The professional clergy, about twenty in number, converted to believers' baptism were also a mixed blessing for the movement.[40] Some clerical renegades, such as Samuel Fisher who gave up a living in Kent worth £240 a year, fully embraced the Baptists' sectarian ethos. He became a farmer and an energetic leader of the General Baptists until his conversion to Quakerism in 1655.[41] Other clerical converts, however, retained many of the attitudes of Independent pastors. The most eminent, Henry Jessey and John Tombes, refused to deny communion to separatist saints who could not accept rebaptism.[42] Their model of open membership was followed by more than a dozen congregations, the most famous being the Bedford church which recruited John Bunyan in the early 1650s and Broadmead, Bristol, whose early history has survived.[43] The mixed communion principle was a commendable example of tolerance towards all saints contrasting with the legalistic exclusiveness of the Baptist mainstream, which

---

[39] I. Gentles, 'The management of the crown lands, 1649-60', *Agricultural History Review*, xix (1971), 36 (Packer); R.T. Dunlop, *Ireland under the Commonwealth* (Manchester, 1913), 27, n. 1 (Sankey).
[40] W.T. Whitley, *A History of the British Baptists* (1923), 70.
[41] *Biographical Dictionary of British Radicals in the Seventeenth Century*, ed. R.L. Greaves and R. Zaller (Brighton, 1982), i. 285-6.
[42] For Jessey and Tombes see *DNB*.
[43] *The Minutes of the First Independent Church (now Bunyan Meeting) at Bedford, 1656-1766*, ed. H.G. Tibbutt (Bedfordshire Historical Society, 1976); *The Records of a Church of Christ in Bristol, 1640-1687*, ed. R. Hayden (Bristol Record Society, 1974). See B.R. White, 'Open and closed membership among English and Welsh Baptists', *BQ* xxiv (1971-2).

regarded it as 'going out of Babylon by half'.[44] Tombes's learning in particular raised the academic level of Baptist polemic and earned the movement some respectability. The particular willingness of some renegade clergy to accept maintenance from a godly magistrate associated the Baptists with the reforming policies of the revolutionary regimes. But these clerical attitudes also compromised and confused the sect's simple doctrines of the uselessness of formal learning and the ungodliness of a national ministry. They were the cause of internal conflict and ammunition for the attacks of more stubbornly separatist movements such as the Quakers. The presence of influential groups of prosperous bourgeoisie, radical gentry, professional soldiers, and former clergy diluted the homogeneity of the Baptists. With such diversity of political interests and social attitudes, it was difficult to establish common aims or unite in common action. While the mass of their followers consisted of the middling sort, the Baptists' leaders were a loose coalition united by the doctrine that the true church was a community of saints practising believers' baptism.

III

Each Baptist congregation was a voluntary association of free and equal members, united in opposition to the doctrine, practices, and moral discipline of the national church and, by implication, of the social system whose values that church expressed. This fellowship of true Christians sought to reconstruct the primitive, apostolic church according to the law of the Gospels. In the words of the General Baptist Edmund Chillenden:

The Churches of Christ are a holy people called out of the world by the good word of his grace, they being begotten againe, purged and cleansed from all uncleanness and unholiness, made pure by the washing of water by the word . . . called to be Saints . . . a spiritual house, a holy priesthood to offer up spiritual sacrifices . . . a holy nation, a chosen

[44] *Records of the Churches of Christ gathered at Fenstanton, Warboys and Hexham, 1644–1720*, ed. E.B. Underhill (1854), 368. The reference is to the Hexham records.

generation, a royal priesthood, a peculiar people . . . and they may not suffer any unclean or unholy person to come in and be of fellowship with them . . . a little leaven leveneth the whole lump.[45]

The Baptist church was a gathering of those whom the Lord had sanctified by his grace, called out of the ungodly world into the fellowship of saints. As a voluntary association of God's chosen, the church was necessarily an egalitarian, democratic, and consensus society. The sect allowed for no distinction between clergy and laity. In the vast majority of Baptist congregations, the ruling ministry consisted of lay elders who exercised the functions of both pastor and teacher as well as the disciplinary duty 'to oversee the lives and manners of men'.[46] They were supported by deacons whose principal concern was the organization of poor relief. Elders were chosen by the congregation from those brethren gifted in preaching and teaching the gospel. They were then ordained by their fellow elders, evangelists, or other gifted brethren: but the legitimacy of church office came from the vote of the congregation. Ordained officers acquired no special status. Elders were expected to emulate the apostles by continuing their secular callings and 'work with their hands at all seasonable times', and the congregation to recompense its leaders if the demands of office affected their material welfare.[47] Elections and congregational business were decided by consensus. But since the purity of the church was determined by its strict adherence to the correct model of apostolic Christianity, the principle of consensus in practice required uniformity. The churches were urged to distinguish between the scruples of those with tender consciences and those whose stubborn opposition betrayed a lack of faith.[48] But tender conscience had ultimately to be amenable to loving persuasion. There was no provision for principled dissent from the will of the congregation except for defection or expulsion. The tension between sectarian collectivism and its voluntary, egalitarian principles continually disturbed the domestic peace of the Baptist churches. Nevertheless their

[45] E. Chillenden, *Nathans Parable* (1653), 8.   [46] *AR* 11.
[47] BL, Add. MS 36, 709 (Speldhurst and Penbury Churchbook), fo. 32.
[48] *AR* 67-8.

inchoate model of a contract society of free individuals represented a radical alternative to traditional social values.[49]

The guiding principles of the Christian sect have been described as the fulfilment of Christ's law set out in the Gospels and the expression of that law in the high ethical conduct of its members.[50] Obedience to Gospel law was interpreted by the Baptists as strict adherence to apostolic ordinances, the foundation principles of the true church.[51] Believers' baptism, the most characteristic of the sect's ordinances, was the 'visible way of profession by which they are distinguished from the world'.[52] It was the seal of the covenant of grace confined to those in receipt of that grace through conversion. Infant baptism was meaningless, as indeed was the ideal of a Christian society outside the churches of the saints. Orthodox Puritans, to whom baptism was a birth privilege, a condition of the federal covenant between God, his people, and their heirs, complained that Baptist doctrine made even 'infants of best believing Parents' little better than pagans.[53] Believers' baptism was imaginatively compared with Herod's massacre of the innocents and the practices of witchcraft since 'witches after conviction say that the Devil persuaded them to deny their first Baptisme'.[54] The innovative practice of baptism by total immersion, symbolizing both the death and resurrection of Christ and the washing away of the believer's sin, provoked even greater hostility. The necessity during the early 1640s to avoid discovery by baptizing converts at night, in whatever stream or pond was convenient, associated the ritual in the popular imagination with promiscuous practices reminiscent of the Münster Anabaptists. As late as 1647 Samuel Oates was charged by the Rutland magistrates: 'Hee dipps women naked, in ye night, fitt for workes of darknes.'[55] Dipping,

---

[49] C. Hill, *Society and Puritanism in Pre-Revolutionary England* (1964), 493–5.
[50] E. Troeltsch, *The Social Teaching of the Christian Churches* (NY, 1960), 748.
[51] Hebrews, 6:1-2. Paul's bare list of the principles or fundamentals of the Christian religion represents the nearest the Baptists came to a common creed.
[52] *AR* 64.   [53] J. Stalham, *Vindiciae Redemptionis* (1647), sig. A4^V.
[54] P. B[arbon]., *A Defence of the Lawfulnesse of Baptizing Infants* (1645), sig. A2^V; N. Stephens, *A Precept for the Baptisme of Infants* (1651), 38.
[55] Quoted in Betteridge, 'Early Baptists in Leicestershire and Rutland', 209.

particularly in winter, was claimed to be a hazard to life, especially for gentlewomen. There were frequent anecdotes of death following immersion. Mass dipping would spread contagious diseases, inevitably rife among promiscuous Anabaptists.[56] The most eminent of divines contributed to this polemical dross which undoubtedly had some success in characterizing the saints as deviant, immoral menaces to society.

Believers' baptism did not endow sainthood: faith had to precede baptism but baptism should proceed from faith. The Baptists did not deny that their fellow Puritans were true Christians, only that they were deficient in their obedience to Christ's precepts. Non-Baptist saints were compared with 'a man that having served an apprenticeship . . . is not yet made free of the company of which his Master is, neither servant, nor freeman in the interim'.[57] Such assumptions of superiority provoked considerable hostility. Among their most vocal critics, John Goodwin, the celebrated pastor of a London separatist congregation, bitterly condemned the Baptists as 'heady, rash, fierce, despisers of others (yea of good men) self-conceited, arrogant, quarrelsome, clamorous, captious, vain boasters, unjust defamers of men dissenting in judgement from them'. These unchristian qualities, he informed them, were the result of 'the simple conceit that you are, by means of your new Baptisme, gotten nearer to God, and deeper in his favour than other men, how holy or worthy soever otherwise above your selves'.[58] The mark of the true believer, he claimed, was faith expressed in commitment to the Commandments, not to gospel ordinances. The Baptists, wrote another critic, 'laid up their religion in little things: in certain washings'.[59] In other words their petty obsession with religious forms neglected the spiritual substance of Christian life. The Baptists' treatment of the foundation principle of the laying on of hands adds weight to this criticism. Its use in

---

[56] A. Houghton, *An Antidote against Hen. Haggars poysonous pamphlet* (1658), 241; T. Bakewell, *The Dippers plunged* (1650), 7; idem, *Doctor Chamberlain visited* (1650), 14; J. Goodwin, *Catabaptism* (1655), 56.

[57] W. Allen, *An Answer to JG his XL Queries* (1653), 52.

[58] Goodwin, op. cit. sigs. B3^V-4^V.

[59] R. Ballamie, *The Leper Clensed* (1657), 31.

the ordination of ministers was a general Christian convention. During the civil war, however, there developed
among the General Baptists the innovation, probably derived
from Anglican confirmation, of laying hands on all believers
after baptism.[60] The new practice disrupted and divided
congregations and turned church against church. For decades
there were acrimonious disputes about the validity of the
practice. Churches which held to the principle established it
as a test of orthodoxy equal to believers' baptism. General
Baptists were especially affected by the controversy: Particular Baptists suffered less because they were more solidly
against the innovation. The Baptists' preoccupation with
building the true church on the firm foundations of scriptural
ordinances easily lapsed into narrow intolerant legalism. The
apparent obsession with formal observance to the detriment
of spiritual experience alienated fellow Puritans and pushed
many dissatisfied Baptists into enthusiastic movements such
as the Quakers which denied all external ordinances. For the
majority, however, the security of élite fellowship according
to the true law of Christ was the principal attraction of
the sect.

The high ethical conduct demanded of the sect's members
emphasized its detachment from the corrupt, materialistic
world. Baptist asceticism was routine, a denial of superficial
pleasures. The churches and associations seriously debated
the lawfulness of playing musical instruments and the appro-
priately modest dress for saints.[61] The moral responsibilities
of sainthood were generally expressed in concern for the
material welfare of sect members: 'the poor Saints belonging
to the Church of Christ, are to be sufficiently provided for by
the Churches, that they neither want food or rayment, and
this by a free and voluntary contribution, (and not of necessity, or by the constraint or power of the Magistrate)'.[62]
Following gospel precept the deacons raised a fund and distributed aid at the direction of the elders. Small sums were
routinely doled out for the immediate relief of poverty. In

---

[60] See *BQ* xv (1953–4), 203–15.   [61] *AR* 56, 59.
[62] *A Brief Confession or Declaration of Faith* [General Baptist] (1660), 8.
See Watts, op. cit. 336–40.

1653 the elders of the Fenstanton church were authorized to find a house for a destitute widow, to provide her with trading stock worth twenty shillings, and to give security that she would not be a burden on the parish.[63] Churches were prepared in principle to provide more than basic relief and were particularly concerned to manage members' debts to avoid public scandal. When Brother John Wilson lost thirty pounds' worth of crops and farm buildings in a fire, Fenstanton attempted to recompense him with the aid of local congregations. They raised only six pounds.[64] Generally the churches could guarantee only basic provision of food and clothing; even this commitment being beyond the resources of small, rural congregations which were dependent on the assistance of their associations.

The saints had inevitably to define, with increasing strictness, their charitable obligations. The church's duty was confined to its members who were obliged to seek provision, from the magistrate if necessary, for their non-believing families. In 1656 the General Baptists voted to refuse aid to those whose poverty was the result of their leaving their proper callings and undertaking 'such dealings as far exceeds their abillity to mannage'.[65] The western churches required prospective members to declare their debts and urged deacons to investigate those members threatened by poverty to establish the causes of their condition.[66] The general assumption was that most cases of indigence were the result of financial irresponsibility. The implicit association of poverty with inferior moral conduct justified the sect in tailoring its charitable duties to fit its financial resources while promoting economic prudence as a quality of sainthood.[67] Nevertheless the Baptists probably offered their followers more reliable insurance against destitution than the parish system. It is not unreasonable to assume that, particularly during the economic troubles of the later 1640s, this promise of material security was to many the principal attraction of Baptist membership.

---

[63] *Fenstanton Records*, 82-3, 86.   [64] Ibid. 103-5, 108-9, 113-14.
[65] Speldhurst and Penbury Churchbook, fo. 30ᵛ.
[66] *AR* 57.   [67] See *WTUD* 304.

The necessity to reduce their charitable obligations was an incidental if pressing incentive for the Baptists to limit sect membership to a hard core of committed saints. The strength of the church came from the moral superiority of its members while lax conduct exposed the saints to scandal in the eyes of the world. The preservation of the church's purity required a rigorous disciplinary system.[68] The routines of church membership — long sabbath meetings for prayer, fasting, and exercising of spiritual gifts; regular visitations by elders to members' households — kept the saints' conduct under close observation. Apostolic precept allowed for two stages of admonition of erring members, first privately, then before the congregation. Obstinate sinners were excommunicated, or 'delivered to Satan'. The cases of admonition and excommunication in church records illustrate the moral regime which the Baptists sought to impose on their members. Heresy, defined as 'an error directly contrarie to any fundamental doctrine of the Gospell'[69] could cover a multitude of sins: general redemption to the Particular Baptists, predestination to the General Baptists; acceptance or rejection of laying on of hands on all believers. The most common heresies in the Fenstanton records are denying external ordinances and the literal meaning of Scripture. With the most frequent offence, attending the services of the parish churches, religious error merged with disorderly conduct. The latter category of sins covered the usual activities of frail humanity: drunkenness, swearing, gambling, fornication, keeping unseasonable hours, and 'unwarrantable sports', such as dancing. Church discipline also covered relations with family and servants, the beating of whom was frowned on, and the general dealings of the saints with the world. The Baptists were more successful than the national church in imposing Christian discipline on their members because they rigorously purged from their ranks all but the most committed of saints. They also ejected many an independent-minded enthusiast, common during the heady days of revolution, who would not conform to the collective will of the sect.

---

[68] See T. Dowley, 'Baptists and discipline in the seventeenth century', *BQ* xxiv (1971-2); Watts, op. cit. 319-36. [69] *AR* 133-4.

Some aspects of church discipline, particularly the relative claims to loyalty and obedience of sect and family, brought the saints into conflict with the world. They were vulnerable to charges that they sought to undermine both the cohesiveness of the family, the fundamental unit of society, and the quasi-religious authority of its patriarchal head. It was assumed that because they defined true Christians as adult believers only, they were indifferent to the spiritual and moral welfare of their children, as well as any unbelievers among their family and servants.[70] While they emphasized the conventional Christian duties of saints towards those under their charge, the Baptists were committed to the sectarian principle that their ultimate allegiance was to the sect. Marriage with unbelievers was a sin against God and grounds for excommunication. Mixed marriages were spiritually dangerous to the saint: 'how great difficulties there must needes be found in ruling or being ruled by a yoke-fellow in whom Satan rules.'[71] Charged with following their Anabaptist predecessors in rejecting mixed marriages as null and void, the Baptists protested that they did not expect married converts either to cast off their unbelieving spouses or to refuse them natural obedience except when it conflicted with the obligations of sainthood. The Fenstanton congregation would not accept her husband's opposition as sufficient grounds for a sister's absence from church.[72] The Baptists also flouted traditional ideas of the sanctity of marriage when they demanded repentance of a saint who married an unbeliever against the advice of the church. The General Baptists ruled that 'for those so married yet to live together as man and wife when repented of, is a sin'.[73] In such a situation, the conflicting demands of loyalty to sect and spouse must often have proved intolerable.

The Baptists' critics frequently described them as false prophets 'which creep into houses, and lead captive silly

---

[70] Ballamie, op. cit. 4, 23; R. Wastfield, *An Equall Ballance* (1659), 20.

[71] *AR* 141. The western churches were prepared to allow marriage with 'such as may be judged godly': ibid. 55.

[72] *Fenstanton Records*, 242.

[73] *Minutes of the General Assembly of the General Baptist Churches in England*, ed. W.T. Whitley (1909), i. 23.

women laden with sins'.[74] However, the conventional
assumption that women tended to be attracted in greater
numbers than men to sectarian movements is not supported
by Baptist evidence. Keith Thomas has described the appeal
of the sects to women as 'spiritual equality, the depreciation
of educational advantages, and that opportunity to preach
or even to hold priestly office which they were otherwise
denied . . . self-expression, wider spheres of influence and an
asceticism which could emancipate them from the ties of
family life'.[75] The act of joining any sect was an assertion of
spiritual independence which rejected the orthodoxy that
female identity was subsumed into that of the male head of
the household. The Baptists, however, were the most conservative of the radical Puritan movements in their attitudes
to women. They 'may not speake as that their speaking shall
shew a not acknowledging of the inferioritie of their sexe and
so be an usurping authority over the man'.[76] Baptist biblical
literalism bound them to Paul's commands against women
preaching, teaching, or exercising formal authority in the
church. Sectarian organization probably allowed them many
informal ways of influencing the affairs of the congregation.
Baptist membership certainly gave many women a taste for
religious self-expression which encouraged them to defect to
more enthusiastic movements which denied the literal validity
of Paul's precepts. But whatever the limitations of women's
participation in congregational life, the Baptists' critics could
still claim with some justification that the duties of sainthood conflicted with family obligations, 'alienating the
affections of members of the family towards each other, and
worst of all, rending the bonds of obedience which held them
together'.[77] Commitment to the sect could effectively be
expressed as the right of religious self-determination, the
assertion of individual independence by wife, child, or servant
within the household. It was in conflict with patriarchal
authority of father, husband, or master, the traditional basis

[74] 2 Timothy 3: 6.
[75] K. Thomas, 'Women and the civil war sects', in T. Aston (ed.), *Crisis in
Europe, 1560–1660* (1965), 330. See also C. Cross, ' "He-Goats before the Flocks",
a note on the part played by women in the founding of some Civil War churches',
Studies in Church History, viii (1972).
[76] *AR* 185.   [77] Thomas, op. cit. 333.

of political authority, that the Baptist ideal of a free association of saints was most dramatically revealed as a radical, alternative social model.

The Baptists conform closely to the sociological model of the religious sect as an alternative society.[78] In rejecting the authority of the established church, the sect freed itself from the dominant culture whose values were largely expressed in conventional religious terms. Its superior ethics set it apart from the mundane morality of society: its charitable impulses strengthened the bonds of fellowship between members. It thrived on a sense of alienation: solidarity was fuelled by a siege mentality: the saints were despised, slandered, if not actually persecuted by the world. The antipathy was expressed in millenarian beliefs which in the Christian tradition are derived from the prophetic books of the Bible. Differences between the sect and the world were part of the cosmic struggle between good and evil, the chosen people and the powers of the Antichrist, rapidly approaching its eschatological climax. Tensions both within the sect, and in its relations with society, could be accommodated when the triumph of the saints was thought to be imminent.[79] Sect membership offered élite spiritual status, Chillenden's 'royal priesthood', to compensate for an inadequate or insecure social position. Millenarianism provided the bonus of power and respect in the world when Christ returned. The sects' constituency has therefore been defined as the dispossessed, the underprivileged, and the disinherited; somewhat melodramatic descriptions of the Baptists' social appeal. Thomas Lambe's London crusades would undoubtedly have appealed to the rootless urban migrant, the classic sect recruit, offering self-esteem, fellowship, social discipline, and economic aid. By 1660, however, the Baptists were, as we have seen, largely a movement of the middling sort of the small towns and villages. The economic changes which increased the number of tradesmen, craftsmen, and yeomen also destroyed much of the vitality of the traditional institutions through which they had exercised local power and asserted their social

[78] See B. Wilson, *Religious Sects* (1970).
[79] See S.L. Thrupp (ed.), *Millennial Dreams in Action* (The Hague, 1962).

interests. The craft and trade guilds were increasingly dominated by large capitalists: enclosure undermined the manorial
system: Protestantism was antagonistic towards much of the
community activity of the medieval parish.[80] While the
Baptists' official blueprint was the first Christian churches,
they were undoubtedly influenced by these traditional
models of communal discipline and communal welfare. In
the unique, *de facto* freedom of the 1640s and 1650s, the
Baptists were able to gather many of these victims of economic and social change into a mass evangelical movement.

IV

The Baptist saints had come out of the world into Christ's
spiritual kingdom but they were neither willing nor able to
divorce themselves from the revolutionary events of their
time. While they shared the sectarian principle of the Anabaptists that the national church was unchristian, they also
held to the Puritan ideal that reformation of society and its
institutions was possible through the action of godly men.
Radical zeal, however, was frequently constrained by sectarian
interest. To the Baptists the foundation of Puritan reformation was the guarantee of liberty of worship for the saints
and in defence of this liberty they made a substantial contribution to the cause of toleration. They argued that the
true church was the creation of divine grace, not of man.
Since it was not of this world, it must necessarily be completely separate from the state. The magistrate therefore had
no power in religious matters: the state must allow total
liberty of religious opinion and worship. 'No man ought to be
forced in matter of religion, the Gospell being spirituall and
requiring only spiritual worshippers who cannot be made so,
but by the Word and Spirit of God, which breatheth where
and when it listeth, and not where and when mens lawes and
statutes pleaseth.'[81] Baptist arguments for toleration were

[80] Hill, *Society and Puritanism*, 483 f.
[81] E. Barber, *An Answer to the Essex Watchmens Watch-word* (1649), 17. In
practice the Baptists were never so committed to unqualified freedom of religious
expression as their statements of principle suggest.

founded in 'common sense, necessity, and the requirements of human dignity'.[82] Devoid of theological sophistication, they reflected the pragmatic attitudes of their lay exponents. Religious persecution promoted political strife, not civil order: it was also bad for trade.[83] In support of their principle of the separation of church and state, much of the Baptists' propaganda was directed against the foundations of the traditional ecclesiastical system: a professional clergy financed by a compulsory tithe.

> It was alwaies Gods way, (or for the most part) to chuse his Prophets out of unlearned men, and honest labouring men, that knew what it was to get their living by the sweat of their brows; and not such as were brought up idly, so that they cannot dig, and are ashamed to beg: and therefore prove unjust stewards. They are not fit to be Ministers of Christ, because they must preach for hire, or else they cannot live; therefore they must please men, and have mens persons in admiration because of advantage, as Jude saith, ver. 16 or else men will give them little or no wages.[84]

Clergy, like lawyers, used their professional monopoly to line their own pockets. They were 'only brought up in the schools of humane learning, to the attaining humane arts and variety of languages . . . seeking rather the gain of large revenues, then the gain of souls to God'.[85] Baptists shared the general radical criticism of the university as 'a factory of divines'.[86] But the corrupt foundation of the state church was 'that Jewish and Antichristian yoke of tythes . . . an intolerable burden, inconsistent with the liberty of conscience unto all'.[87] Once liberty of worship was achieved in practice, the abolition of tithes became the principal platform of godly reformation.

In their contributions to the religious controversies of the 1640s, the Baptists developed from their fundamental

---

[82] W.K. Jordan, *The Development of Religious Toleration in England*, iii (1938), 45.

[83] S. Richardson, *The Necessity of Toleration in matters of Religion* (1647), 9.

[84] H. Haggar, *The Foundation of the Font Discovered* (1653), 127-8.

[85] *Brief Confession . . .* (1660), 4.

[86] C. Hill, 'Radical critics of Oxford and Cambridge in the 1650s', in his *Change and Continuity* (1974), 132.

[87] *A Further Testimony to Truth* (1659), quoted in Betteridge, 'Early Baptists in Leicestershire and Rutland', 280.

doctrine of the separation of church and state the elements of a radical reform programme. The general expectation of the movement, however, was that change would come about through the chosen instruments of the Lord, whether Parliament, Army, or Protector, rather than the direct action of the saints themselves. The political circumspection of most Baptist leaders illustrates the movement's concern to overcome the popular prejudice that it was the heir of the Münster Anabaptists. The confession of faith produced in 1644 by the London Particular Baptists reflects their cautious conservatism but it is generally representative of official Baptist statements of their relationship with the state. The confession avoided direct reference to the Anabaptists but rejected the distinctive doctrines of the General Baptists. Its principal emphasis was on obedience to the civil magistracy, 'an ordinance of God set up by God for the punishment of evill doers, and for the praise of them that doe well'. Defined as 'King and Parliament freely chosen by the Kingdome', it was to be 'acknowledged, reverenced and obeyed, according to godlinesse; not because of wrath onely but for conscience sake'.[88] In presenting themselves as moderate, orthodox Puritans differing only on questions of church organization, the London Particular Baptists aimed to cement that alliance with the Independents which offered them the best chance of achieving their reform programme.[89] In the process, however, they were drawn into political activity which could be difficult to reconcile with their sectarian principle that the saints were apart from the world.

The London leaders were content with the Independents' strategy of discreetly lobbying their sympathizers in government as they feared that any attempt at popular agitation would only provoke cries of Münster and John of Leiden. Their timidity allowed the Levellers to mobilize from 1646 the discontent of the rank and file separatists, turning the principle of religious liberty into a secular theory of natural rights. The Leveller party built its ideology and organization on the foundations of London separatism. It is likely that

---

[88] *The Confession of Faith* (1644), 17, 19.
[89] See Tolmie, *Triumph of the Saints*, ch. 6.

Leveller egalitarianism owed much to General Baptist theology, with its greater emphasis on human accountability and
the innate goodness and equality of all mankind. General
redemption 'gave free reign to the individualist and democratic logic of Protestantism: if all men could be saved, then
the priesthood of all believers was an essentially democratic
doctrine'.[90] If all mankind were even potentially of the elect,
then there could be no practical distinction between the
spheres of grace and nature, the civil rights of saints and
citizens. To guarantee the liberty of the saints it was necessary to seek freedom for all. Furthermore, the General
Baptists' fluid membership, mass meetings, evangelical campaign tactics, and wider social appeal provided the Levellers
with the basis of a popular political organization.[91]

Murray Tolmie has persuasively argued that for most of its
short but dramatic life as an influential force in Revolution
politics, the Leveller movement was greatly dependent on
the support and organizational structure of the separatists,
and particularly.the Baptists, both in London and the Army.
The movement, however, 'cannot be regarded simply as a
kind of sectarian pressure group' for it never enjoyed the real
confidence of the radical Calvinist leaders, who had little
sympathy for its secular ideology but who were obliged to
contain their disquiet while the conservative threat remained.[92] Only after the Independent revolution of 1648-9
could they openly express their theocratic distaste for
Leveller democracy. They blocked access to the separatist
network thereby hastening the movement's demise. Many
General Baptists remained sympathetic to Leveller ideals but
they lacked the strength to sustain the movement by themselves. The London Particular Baptists publicly broke with
the Levellers in April 1649. They compared the Levellers'
agitation in their congregations with the civil disturbances of
the old Anabaptists. Parliament was urged to satisfy the just
grievances of the people and relieve 'the languishing condition of the poor' but also to produce laws against whoredom,

---

[90] C. Hill, *Milton and the English Revolution* (1977), 273. See N.T. Burns,
Christian Mortalism from Tyndale to Milton (Cambridge, Mass., 1972), 91-4.
[91] Tolmie, *Triumph of the Saints*, 151.   [92] Ibid. 148.

drunkenness, cheating, and all such like abominations (of civil cognizance) in whomsoever'.[93] The Levellers' secular ideology of universal freedom, for the reprobate, immoral, and idolaters alike, severely strained the Particular Baptist principle of toleration. Ultimately they regarded liberty not as a right of nature but as a gift of grace. The Independent ideal of godly rule more closely resembled the interests and guaranteed the privileges of the saints.

The destruction of the monarchy and the declaration of a republic seemed to herald the New Jerusalem in which the true church would prosper. The Baptists looked forward to the early achievement of their more mundane goals: legal toleration and the end of tithes. The Commonwealth gave the Baptists practical toleration by abolishing compulsory attendance at parish churches, but the four years of the Rump Parliament produced little else in the way of godly reform. While the Baptists prospered under the benign regime, they celebrated its dissolution by Cromwell in April 1653 and the prospect of true government by the saints. The events of 1653 — the high expectations that Barebone's Parliament would effect the saints' most cherished reforms; its abdication of power when the abolition of tithes seemed imminent; the establishment of the Cromwellian Protectorate in December of that year — placed the Baptists in a dilemma similar to that posed by the Levellers.[94] Pressure among the separatists for radical change had produced another political movement, the Fifth Monarchy Men, whose activities could jeopardize the Baptists' comfortable relations with the ruling powers.[95] The theocratic millenarianism of the Fifth Monarchy Men was more palatable to many saints than Leveller ideology. Militant Baptists, particularly the Irish Army officers, shared their belief that Cromwell had usurped the role of King Jesus in adopting rule by a single person. ' 'Tis a day of darknes and confusion, verry unlike that day of

[93] *The Humble Petition and Representation* (1649), in *Confessions of Faith*, ed. E.B. Underhill (1854), 289, 290, 291.
[94] A. Woolrych, *Commonwealth to Protectorate* (Oxford, 1982). See also M. James, 'The political importance of the tithes controversy in the English Revolution, 1640-60', *History*, n.s. xxvi (1941-2).
[95] See below, ch. 7.

the glorious reign of Christ, soe much, I feare, on mistaken grounds expected by Christians', lamented William Allen, adjutant-general and one of the Protector's most vocal critics.[96] Army opposition attracted the earnest counsels of the cautious, pragmatic leaders of the London Particular Baptists. They feared that any indication of support for the Fifth Monarchy cause would encourage the prejudice 'that we deny authority, and would pull downe all Magistracy'. The dissolution of Barebone's Parliament had been necessary 'for the prevention of dishoner which was like to fall upon the profession of the gospell, if things had gone on in that way they weare going'. Most inappropriately the military saints were instructed that 'though wee are in the flesh, wee doe not warr after the flesh'.[97] This principle determined the response of the General Baptists. The saints had no promise that they would inherit the world before the appearance of Christ: they must not try to anticipate the millennium by violent action.[98] The tone of Baptist apologies for the Protectorate ranged from resignation to enthusiasm. Samuel Richardson urged his brethren 'to bee content with this Government, and quietly to sit down under it, and to thanke God that things are not worse than they are'.[99] Thomas Tillam of Hexham described the Instrument of Government as 'the Saints civill Magna Charta' and Cromwell as the 'wise, valiant, faithful Joshuah' whose mission was to suppress all profanity, idolatry, atheism, and blasphemy.[100]

In general the Baptist movement rejected the hazardous prospect of reform through militant action for the tangible benefits of toleration under the Protectorate. The most active and consistent advocates of this policy were the London saints led by William Kiffin, a prosperous merchant. Eschewing confrontation for the cultivation of the favour of the magistrate, he was condemned by the Fifth Monarchy Men as a Cromwellian courtier.[101] With other London leaders

---

[96] *Thurloe,* ii. 215.
[97] *Original Letters and Papers of State . . . of John Milton,* ed. J. Nickalls (1743), 159-60.
[98] B.S. Capp, *The Fifth Monarchy Men* (1972), 101.
[99] S. Richardson, *An Apology for the Present Government* (1654), 15.
[100] *Original letters . . . of John Milton,* 134-5.   [101] *Thurloe,* v. 755-9.

he worked to mollify discontented saints and counter radical agitation in the Baptist congregations.[102] In May 1658 he appears to have been successful in blocking an attempt by Fifth Monarchy Men and former officers to win over the western churches to their cause.[103] Baptist acquiescence in the Protectorate survived Cromwell's flirtation with the offer of a crown and his acceptance in May 1657 of a revised constitution which not only gave him many of the trappings of monarchy but also rejected many of the radicals' most cherished ideals. The Humble Petition and Advice provided for a national preaching ministry, with no alternative to tithes, and imposed considerable restraints on liberty of worship.[104]

The end of stable rule with Cromwell's death in September 1658 left Kiffin's policy redundant. By February 1659 he was lobbying for a republic.[105] The disintegration of the Protectorate revived radical hopes but the saints were unable to agree on which of the ephemeral regimes of 1659 would best serve their interests. The Baptists acquired unprecedented influence as the political factions vied for their support. Such prominence, however, served only to encourage rumours of Münster-like risings of Anabaptists and increase pressure for the return of the monarchy. In December 1659 the Baptists anticipated the imminent defeat of the radical cause when the two wings collaborated for the first time to declare it their consistent policy 'to be obedient to Magistracy in all things Civil, and willing to live peaceably, under whatever Government is, and shall be established in this Nation'.[106] The joint declaration was followed by a series of confessions and petitions in the months before and after the restoration of the monarchy in May 1660. Their aims were hardly different from those of the first confession of 1644: to deny that the Baptists were for anarchy and communism. John of Leiden's ghost still haunted the saints.

---

[102] L.F. Brown, *The Political Activities of the Baptists and Fifth Monarchy Men in England during the Interregnum* (1911), 69-102.
[103] *AR* 96-7.
[104] J.P. Kenyon (ed.), *The Stuart Constitution* (Cambridge, 1966), 350-7.
[105] Brown, op. cit. 174.
[106] *A Declaration of Several of the People called Anabaptists* (1659).

Despite the best efforts of the London saints, the Baptists remained a dramatic exemplification of the dangers of popular religious radicalism which served to unite the political nation in support of the restored monarchy. The militant army saints rather than the sober bourgeoisie determined popular conceptions of the Anabaptist. Yet despite their not inconsiderable numbers, sectarian discipline, and elaborate associational organization, the Baptists played a minor role in the political events of the English Revolution. Their ineffectiveness is explained in part by the doctrinal antagonism between the two wings which, in the case of the Levellers, also expressed itself in conflicting political sympathies. The disparate elements comprising the leadership of the Particular Baptists, the more powerful wing, were also unable to subordinate their special interests to the promotion of the common principles of the separatist reform programme. There were, however, more fundamental ambiguities in the Baptists' attitude to the world which inhibited them from effective political action either independently or through their influence on the pressure groups, the Levellers and Fifth-Monarchy Men, originally formed to prosecute the separatist cause. The social egalitarianism implicit in the Baptist model of a free and voluntary community was qualified, especially among the Particular Baptists, by the conviction that sainthood brought with it élite privileges. Although they promoted the general theory of the freedom of speech and association, they could not ultimately conceive those liberties as secular, natural rights. But the Baptists' predominantly theocratic temperament proved no more incentive to determined political action. The sectarian sense that the saints were apart from the world, exacerbated by popular notions of Anabaptism, encouraged a passive response to the events of the Revolution. The consistent policy of the London leaders was to court the favour of whatever power seemed best able to guarantee them their liberty of worship. Such pragmatism was rarely compatible with the millenarian impulse to conquer and purge, rather than withdraw from, the world. The Baptists were both sectaries and Puritans: only half out of the world. By joining the Independents' coalition of radical Puritan interests, they secured their immediate goal of toleration but were obliged to defer to leaders such as Cromwell whose commitment to social reform was at best ambiguous. Yet as the cautious voices of William Kiffin and his associates constantly urged, the Baptists had no choice but to follow the lead of the Independents. Standing alone they were too vulnerable to repression inspired by fears of another Münster.

V

The necessary qualification for Baptist membership was 'a declaration of an experiential work of the spirit upon the heart'.[107] The saints' subsequent spiritual experiences were, however, strictly constrained by the sect's doctrine and discipline. Members' spiritual gifts were to be cultivated under the supervision of the elders: the church was to judge such gifts; gifted members could not preach to the world without the consent of the congregation. During the 1650s public evangelism was increasingly confined to official messengers.[108] Private revelation had to be subordinated to Baptist doctrine, ordinances, and discipline, justified by the literal word of Scripture. Such constraints were understandable but frequently counter-productive. In the climate of revolution, with unprecedented liberty of expression, the Puritan principle of the supremacy of individual conscience, instructed by Scripture and guided by grace, inevitably developed into less restrained claims to enthusiasm: direct inspiration by the divine spirit. No congregational system could possibly have accommodated the resulting confusion of enthusiastic speculation. Enthusiasm was intrinsically anarchic: the authority of the divine light within was supreme, autonomous, and self-sufficient. But the Baptists so elevated the status of the saint blessed by grace, and so rigidly and formally restrained free expression of the effects of that grace, that they encouraged and exacerbated enthusiastic sentiment which could only flourish outside the movement.

---

[107] *AR* 56.
[108] *AR* 24–5, 34, 55; Speldhurst and Penbury Churchbook, fo. 32.

To a considerable extent the doctrines of enthusiasm were developed in reaction to the contradictions between the saint's liberty and the sect's authority. The problem of enthusiastic dissent fills the pages of the records of the Fenstanton church, the most comprehensive for the revolutionary period.[109] The opinions recorded are sufficiently varied to be attributed to the main movements of enthusiasm described by contemporaries: Seekers, Ranters, or Quakers.[110] The basic principles, however, do not vary. The enthusiast is subject to no external religious authority. The Scripture, by appeal to which the elders sought to assert their authority, is an inferior source of revelation to the inner light. Baptist ordinances, justified by Scripture, are the dry husks, the carnal forms of religion appropriate only for the uninspired. These fundamental tenets of enthusiasm, stubbornly held by Midland rustics in debate with Fenstanton's elders, were subject to much more radical interpretation by more imaginative minds.

The rise of enthusiasm confused and disturbed both Baptist leaders and more conservative commentators. Many divines followed Robert Baillie in describing it as an offshoot of Anabaptism; an inevitable consequence of the Baptists' undermining of the clergy's authority. Samuel Rutherford, Baillie's Scottish colleague at the Westminster Assembly, defined the component heresies of enthusiasm as Familism and antinomianism.[111] By Familism he meant the doctrine of the defunct continental sect, the Family of Love, that the divine spirit could raise man to a state of permanent perfection, beyond the occasion of sin. The antinomian is defined as 'one who maintains that the moral law is not binding upon Christians, under "the law of grace"'.[112] The conventional usage of the term emphasizes the rejection of all external moral guides, above all the Law of Moses, for the supremacy of the divinely enlightened conscience. Many hostile critics like Rutherford applied the term with its full

---

[109] *Fenstanton Records, passim*; *WTUD* 302-6.
[110] See below, chs. 5 and 6.
[111] Baillie, *Anabaptisme,* 96-106; S. Rutherford, *A Survey of the Spirituall Antichrist, opening the secrets of Familisme and Antinomianisme* (1648).
[112] *Oxford English Dictionary.*

pejorative implications to the more restrained doctrine of free grace not uncommon among radical Puritans. Free grace was a reaction against the qualification of the strict determinism of Calvinist doctrine by late Elizabethan Puritan casuists, most notably William Perkins. Their federal covenant theology allowed the desire for grace as evidence of sainthood, suggesting that faith preceded grace, but obliged the saint to demonstrate the gift of grace through Christian conduct. Free grace was a rigorous restatement of the simple logic of predestined election. It was free in being unearned and unconditional: prior worthiness and subsequent conduct were irrelevant. The consequence of sin was effectively removed since while the saint might transgress in the flesh, he remained one of the elect.[113]

Baptist doctrine neither naturally nor usually led to perfectionism and antinomianism. Baptists held that the saints could not achieve perfection in this world. The principal source of Familist perfectionism was the writings of continental spiritualists, on the fringe of the Anabaptist movement, translated during the 1640s and 1650s.[114] The perfectionist doctrine that scriptural ordinances were merely figurative representations of higher spiritual experiences was totally offensive to Baptist literalism. Before 1640 free grace was 'but the fancy of solitary vicars musing to themselves'.[115] During the civil war it was taken up most enthusiastically by radical Army preachers, including such prominent Baptist leaders as Thomas Collier and Paul Hobson. Free grace offered a secure, uncomplicated relationship with God, which inspired self-confidence in times of crisis. Restrained by sect discipline and literal obedience to scriptural precepts, it was neither immoral nor anarchic in its consequences. In 1650, however, the Ranters reduced Scripture to a dead letter and revealed the antinomian implications of free grace. Inspired by the divine spirit, they could not sin, for then it were God sinning. What was sin to the unredeemed creature was to the Ranter an act of pure holiness.[116] The London Particular

---

[113] L.F. Solt, *Saints in Arms* (1959), 25–38.
[114] See below, p. 192, n. 2.
[115] G. Huehns, *Antinomianism in English History* (1951), 66.
[116] See below, ch. 5.

Baptists rushed into print to dissociate themselves from the activities of the most notorious of the Ranter prophets, Abiezer Coppe, who had been a notably successful evangelist for the movement. They roundly condemned all doctrines which undermined the literal and historical significance of Christ. Enthusiasm was personified in a conventional Puritan phrase as the Devil transforming himself into an angel of light. Ranter doctrines strained the limits of toleration, being 'against civil societies, violating the bonds of marriage, and Laws of families, against the very principles and light of nature, which common justice (remaining among the heathens) would soon adjudj to merit severe punishment'. Coppe was not, however, compared with John of Leiden. The London saints argued, less than accurately, that 'many, if not most of them, were never members with us'.[117] A good proportion of Ranters, and enthusiasts generally, served their religious apprenticeship in a Baptist congregation.

The theological doctrines of antinomianism, saving grace liberating the saint from the guilt of sin, and Familist perfectionism, the divine spirit emancipating the adept from the occasion of sin, easily merged in the mass of enthusiastic speculation. The basic tenets of the Fenstanton dissenters were usually justified by a spiritual millenarianism: Christ's coming was not in the flesh but in the hearts of men: his return was not imminent but current. There was a mystical tendency to interpret Christian revelation as a series of metaphors of spiritual experience. Inevitably not only religious orthodoxy but the political and social conventions which it supported were exposed to the subjective judgement of the inspired saint. Enthusiasm was capable of infinite variety: the mystical ideals which influenced Gerrard Winstanley's Utopian communism as well as the eccentric activities of an assortment of religious prophets and messiahs: both the amoral antinomianism of the Ranters and the ecstatic evangelism of the early Quakers.

Quakerism was the most influential expression of enthusiasm and the most substantial threat to the Baptist movement during the Revolution. The vanguard of the early

---

[117] *Heart-Bleedings for Professors Abominations* (1650), 8, 12.

Quakers came from the northern counties where Baptist influence was minimal. But their principal leader, George Fox, appears to have come under the influence of the Nottinghamshire General Baptists in the late 1640s.[118] Much of Quaker doctrine is a radical extension of general redemption: the expression of true Christianity as moral conduct; the potential of all humanity to know the spirit of God. The simple doctrine of the supremacy of the indwelling light purged antinomianism and perfectionism of their mystical and introspective tendencies to produce a dynamic ideology of spiritual regeneration and social protest. From 1654 the Quakers made considerable inroads into the ranks of the Baptists, both General and Particular. Ordinances were rejected as dead forms; believers' baptism as a carnal representation of the true baptism of the spirit. The Baptists were accused of 'crying up sin' for denying that divine grace could make them perfect in this world. Quakerism consciously proclaimed itself a revival of the pure ideals of separatist evangelism. The Baptists, it was claimed, had grown worldly and lax in comfortable toleration, corrupted by the privileges which they had received from the powers of the world. Not only had some of their adherents betrayed the radical cause against tithes but their general opposition in theory was not matched in practice. The Quakers' routine refusal to pay tithes was for the Baptists a counsel of excellence, 'if any have faith to expose themselves to sufferings'.[119] Modesty of dress and manner among Baptist leaders had disappeared with the acquisition of wealth and power, particularly in Ireland. The impromptu leadings of the spirit had been stifled by the imposition of set times and formal procedures for prayer and prophecy. Worst of all, the Baptists, formerly the great advocates of toleration, had joined the ranks of the persecutors by calling on the magistrate to prevent Quaker demonstrations of the living faith at their dead, formal meetings.[120]

The Quaker campaign to revive the original spirit of sectarian radicalism, purged of carnal forms and legalistic

[118] *Journal of George Fox*, ed. J.L. Nickalls (Cambridge, 1952), 25.
[119] *AR* 69.
[120] For the substance of this paragraph, see C.W. Horle, 'Quakers and Baptists, 1647–1660', *BQ* xxvi (1975–6).

discipline, and of all compromises with the powers of the world, supports Robert Baillie's claim that the Baptists were the fountain of all sects and heresies during the Revolution. The new movement was conscious of assuming the Baptists' role as the vanguard of popular evangelism. The subsequent chapters of this book are largely concerned with men and movements, doctrines and ideals which derived much of their inspiration from the principles of the early Baptists but could only find uninhibited expression outside their church order. The variety of radical ideas developed from separatist doctrine, particularly of the Baptist kind, demonstrates as much the strengths as the deficiencies of the movement, especially during the 1640s when evangelical and reforming zeal was less inhibited by introspective concern for collective solidarity than in the 1650s. A great number of religious radicals acquired their revolutionary education through exposure to Baptist propaganda against religious persecution, the state church, the professional clergy, and compulsory tithes. Baptist membership gave them practical experience of an alternative social model; a voluntary association of equal individuals.

No religious movement could have accommodated more than a fraction of the wealth of speculative variations on the themes of Puritan separatism during the Revolution. Furthermore it is the nature of the sect to lose the more open informality of its early days as it regulates its doctrine and discipline in order to consolidate the fruits of its evangelism. Eventually millenarian anticipation declines and the church modifies its antagonism towards the world, thereby ceasing to be an effective instrument of radical change. The primitive evangelical spirit reappears as new revivalist movements. With the Baptists the transition from sect to denomination was accelerated in the 1650s by the challenge of such enthusiasts as the Quakers and the advantages of accommodation with the revolutionary state. However, the effectiveness of the Baptists as a radical religious movement was always limited by the conflicting demands of egalitarian individualism and theocratic élitism, sectarian introversion and millenarian action, spiritual autonomy and collective discipline.[121] They

[121] For a discussion of such polarities in radical Puritanism generally, see Solt, op. cit. 3-5, 99.

were capable neither of expressing their political aims as a practical programme nor of effective support for those radical movements, the Levellers and Fifth Monarchy Men, which filled the vacuum left by their indecision. The Baptists' fundamental weakness was their inability to attract leaders of the quality necessary to resolve the ambiguities in their relations both with the world and with their fellow radicals. Their mentality was shaped in the hostile environment of the late 1630s and early 1640s when submission to collective discipline, rather than imaginative leadership, best served the elementary cause of survival. The early congregations of the middling sort established solid mediocrity as the primary criterion for leadership. They lacked the dynamic inspiration of the clerical renegades so influential among their separatist precursors. Imaginative talent, lay or clerical, was usually either suppressed or alienated by the sect's narrow legalism and claustrophobic discipline.[122] The most original of radical minds, William Walwyn the Leveller, Gerrard Winstanley the Digger, Abiezer Coppe the Ranter, and George Fox the Quaker, flourished outside the ranks of the Baptist saints.

[122] Among the few exceptions, Samuel Fisher, the clerical renegade, defected to the Quakers: *WTUD* 208-15. Thomas Lambe, the great 'mechanick' preacher, disappeared into virtual oblivion after joining the losing side in the dispute over laying on of hands: Tolmie, 'Thomas Lambe, soapboiler', 11.

3 The Levellers and Religion

Brian Manning

The Levellers were the left wing of the parliamentarian party
which won the English civil war. They became increasingly
disillusioned with the outcome of victory. They sought to
explain the cause for which they thought they had been
fighting and why they felt it was being betrayed. At the same
time the Levellers sprang from the radical religious groups of
the period and the major problem for historians has been to
identify and analyse the relationship between their religious
beliefs and their political thinking. The question has been
whether the movement remained religious in its primary
inspiration and ultimate aims or became wholly secular in
ideas and objectives. The Levellers did not all hold exactly
the same views on religion, but this essay is concerned with
those aspects of Christianity which they all tended to stress
and with the attitude towards religion which they had in
common, when they formulated and developed their political
philosophy and programme.

The Levellers believed that the essential points of religion
were simple and within the grasp of all men. The people did
not have to depend on the teachings of clergymen or the
judgements of learned men but they could discover for themselves all they needed to know. In tracts published in 1643
and 1644 William Walwyn put forward the view that everything necessary 'either for the enlightning of our understandings, or the peace of our mindes' had been set forth so
plainly in the Bible 'that the meanest capacity is fully capable
of a right understanding thereof'. It was not inevitable that
the explanation and interpretation of the Scriptures should
be left to the clergy and scholars, for 'if the people would but
take boldnes to themselves and not distrust their own understandings, they would soon find ... that all necessary

knowledge is easie to be had, and,by themselves acquirable'.[1]
The people could ignore the clergy and 'come to a good and
right understanding' of the Bible for themselves.[2] Indeed,
they would sooner and more easily grasp the essential truths
of Christianity than the learned men because God revealed
his message not to the educated and great scholars, not to
the rich and powerful, not to the ruling classes of the world,
but to the poor and humble and uneducated: 'God . . . made
not choise of the great, or learned men of the world, to be
his Prophets and publishers of the Gospell; but Heards-men,
Fisher-men, Tent-makers, Toll-gatherers, etc. and . . . our
Blessed Saviour thought it no disparagement to be reputed
the Sonne of a Carpenter.'[3]

Although the people can understand the Bible better than
the scholars, the clergy has conspired to divert them from
recognizing this and to keep them in darkness. The clergy
makes out that the Scriptures are hard to understand and
difficult to interpret. 'When they treate upon some very
plaine place of Scripture . . . yet in handling thereof they
make it difficult, and darken the cleare meaning thereof with
their forced and artificiall glosses.' But they prefer to concentrate 'upon some hard texts' and to dispute 'upon some
nice and difficult questions', ever raising, and starting new
Questions, and new Opinions'. They 'frame long methods and
bodies of Divinity, full of doubts and disputes, which indeed
are made of purpose difficult'. They pretend that years of
study of arts and languages in the university are necessary in
order to be able to understand the Bible. But they say this in
order to justify their own existence, their superior status, and
the wealth they extract from the labours of the people to
support themselves in rich livings and benefices. They establish themselves as a separate and superior order of men by
securing a monopoly of interpreting the Bible, teaching
religion, and performing spiritual functions, but their real aim
is not to inform, enlighten, and help the people but to dominate and exploit them. The people are accustomed to defer

---

[1] Haller, ii. 282-4; iii. 77. I have benefited from the comments of my colleague
Dr S.J. Connolly on an earlier draft of this essay.
[2] Haller and Davies, 262, 265, 273.
[3] Haller, iii. 345; Haller and Davies, 383.

to the clergy, but Walwyn urges them to shake off their awe and to realize that the clergy hinders them from discovering 'the true Gospell of Jesus Christ'. They should ignore the clergy, study the Bible for themselves, and rely on their own understandings and judgements.[4]

The implications of Walwyn's argument extended beyond religion. The Levellers saw a parallel between the capacity of all men to discover for themselves true principles of religion and the demand that the laws of the land should be accessible to all citizens.[5] Although the Bible had been translated into English, making it possible for ordinary people to find out the truths of Christianity for themselves, the laws of England were 'lockt up from common capacities in the Latine or French tongues'. It was a constant demand of the Levellers that the laws should be translated into English 'that so the meanest English Commoner that can but read written hand in his owne tongue' may fully understand the laws by which he is to be governed.[6] The laws had become so numerous and been made so complicated that only lawyers could understand them. The Levellers claimed that just as the clergy made religion difficult and uncertain in order to monopolize it and to dominate and exploit the people, so the lawyers made the law complex and confusing in order to keep the exclusive control of it by which they grew rich and powerful. Just as the clergy obstructed the people from knowing the truth of religion, so the lawyers 'juggle, and put false glosses upon the Law' and concealed and evaded the plain rules of 'Justice, Equity and Conscience' which were the essence of true law.[7] The Levellers argued that if the laws were translated into English, reduced in number, and simplified, and legal proceedings made easier, people would be able to conduct their own cases, and have them heard and decided by their neighbours: lawyers and professional judges would become redundant.[8]

---

[4] Haller, ii. 283; iii. 76-83; Haller and Davies, 262, 263, 265-7, 269, 270.

[5] A.E. Barker, *Milton and the Puritan Dilemma 1641-1660* (Toronto, 1942), 149; C. Hill, *Change and Continuity in Seventeenth-Century England* (1974), 161.

[6] Haller, iii. 266; J. Lilburne, *The Just Mans Justification* (1646), 11-13; Wolfe, 139-40, 192, 266-7.

[7] Haller, iii. 266.

[8] Lilburne, *Just Mans Justification,* 15; *Regall Tyrannie discovered* (1647), 15,

The Levellers wanted to reduce the laws to 'express and plain Rules',[9] which would 'be comprized in one volume in the English tongue', 'to bee kept in every Church throughout the Land; and to be read over at several appointed Times and Seasons, in open Congregation', so that 'every free Commoner might understand his own proceedings'.[10] This would be possible if the laws were 'reduced to an agreement with common equity, and right reason',[11] or, and this amounted to the same thing, 'to the nearest agreement with Christianity'.[12] The simple rules and basic principles which lay behind, or ought to lie behind, the laws, were the same as those which were the essence of Christianity as the Levellers understood it, and were similarly within the capacity of all men to understand. The rules and principles which they had in mind are revealed therefore in their notion of true religion.

The foundation of true religion in the view of the Levellers was 'doing good'. 'The great end wherefore God sent man into the world was, that he should do good in his generation, and thereby glorifie God in his generation', declared John Lilburne.[13] 'No man showes forth any lustre of the image of God in him, unless by doing good', wrote John Wildman, 'and its made the Character of a man of worth or excellency, or a man approved of God, that he serveth God in his generation.'[14] Walwyn maintained in a tract which Joseph Frank regards as most clearly revealing 'the inner sources of his political idealism',[15] that the true Christian was known by 'his good Workes': faith showed itself in works, and faith

25; Wolfe, 303; *The humble Petition and Representation of the Officers and Souldiers of the Garrisons of Portsmouth* (1649).

[9] Wolfe, 303.

[10] Ibid. 216; *The Declaration of Divers Well-Affected Inhabitants of the Cities of London and Westminster* (1648), 5; *The Humble Representation of the Desires of the Officers and Souldiers in the Regiments of Horse, for the County of Northumberland* (1648).

[11] Wolfe, 124.

[12] Ibid. 139; J.C. Davis, 'The Levellers and Christianity', in B. Manning (ed.), *Politics, Religion and the English Civil War* (1973), 236; Haller, iii. 194-5.

[13] J. Lilburne, *An Impeachment of High Treason against Oliver Cromwell* (1649), 23.

[14] J. Wildman, *Truths triumph, or Treachery anatomized* (1648), 4.

[15] J. Frank, *The Levellers* (Cambridge, Mass., 1955), 116-18.

without works was 'as sounding brasse, or as a tinckling
cymball'.[16] Francis White, a Leveller sympathizer amongst
the officers of the Army, at least until 1649, believed that
'Religion is not a name, but a thing; not a forme, but a power
. . . Religion consisteth in faith, and workes of righteousnesse'.[17] Christopher Hill observes that it was a radical
tradition to attach 'greater value to works than to faith', thus
emphasizing human effort and the capacity of all men to
choose to do good. He calls this 'Arminianism of the left'. It
involves a rejection of the Calvinism of the dominant element
in the parliamentarian party and its doctrine of predestination, by which only a small minority was assured of
salvation; and also a rejection of 'Arminianism of the right',
which assumed that salvation was possible only through the
church and its ceremonies. 'Arminians of the left' repudiated
the church and formal ceremonies in favour of acts of love
and charity.[18] Whatever differences there were in their
religious opinions, the Leveller leaders could join together in
a common statement of belief that they did not value 'the
formall and Ceremonial part of [God's] Service' but they did
care about 'the practicall and most reall part of Religion'.[19]
This doctrine of 'practical Christianity' shifted the emphasis
in religion away from devotion and virtue towards concern
for mankind — not that, of course, the Levellers would have
seen this in any other light than that of obeying God's commands and worshipping him by doing good. Perez Zagorin
and J.C. Davis miss the significance of what the Levellers are
saying when they conclude that the Levellers locate the
essence of true religion in conduct.[20] Don M. Wolfe discerns
correctly that the Levellers moved the stress from 'personal
virtues' to 'social action'.[21]

[16] D.M. Wolfe, *Milton in the Puritan Revolution* (1941; hereafter cited as
Wolfe, *Milton*), Appendix ii, 370, 374; Haller and Davies, 262, 381.
[17] F. White, *The Copies of Several Letters Contrary to the Opinion of the
Present Powers* (1649), 10.
[18] C. Hill, 'From Lollards to Levellers', in M. Cornforth (ed.), *Rebels and their
Causes,* (1978), 58-9; C. Hill, *Milton and the English Revolution* (1977), ch. 21.
[19] Wolfe, 393; Haller and Davies, 231.
[20] P. Zagorin, *A History of Political Thought in the English Revolution*
(1954), 25; Davis, 'Levellers and Christianity', 234.
[21] Wolfe, *Milton*, 167; Haller and Davies, 230-1.

The individualism of the Levellers, A.S.P. Woodhouse notes, was 'balanced by a . . . sense of community'.[22] 'Its the command of God', wrote Wildman, 'that every man should seek the good of his neighbour.'[23] 'I was not born for my self alone, but for my neighbor as well', said Richard Overton, 'and I am resolv'd to discharge the trust which God hath repos'd in me for the good of others.'[24] 'No man is born for himself only', repeated the Leveller leaders in a joint statement, but he is required by God and nature to seek the 'communitive Happinesse' of all men.[25] His neighbours were all mankind: 'God is love . . . and . . . love is good and seeketh the good of all men', wrote Walwyn.[26] But most commonly the Levellers identified their sphere of moral action specifically with the English nation.

'Its the command of God', declared Wildman, 'that every man should seek the good of his neighbour, and consequently much more the good of the Nation.' 'Have God united people into a body or society, or Nation? is it not for this? that every one should be helpfull each to other and endeavour one another's good mutually.' 'And . . . hath not God commanded us to relieve and help our neighbours oxen or Asses in any distresse, or being sunk down under any burthen and doth he not much more command us to endeavour the relief of the people of our Nation, whose backs are bound down under heavie burthen?'[27] 'As I am an individual, I am a part of the whole Nation', wrote Lilburne, and so bound up with the fate of the whole nation.[28] 'For what is done to any one, may be done to every one: besides, being all members of one body, that is, of the English Commonwealth, one man should not suffer wrongfully, but all should be sensible, and endeavour his preservation.'[29]

It was the sense of personal responsibility for the good of their fellow men and of the society to which they belonged —

---

[22] A.S.P. Woodhouse (ed.), *Puritanism and Liberty* (1938), introduction, 100; D.B. Robertson, *The Religious Foundations of Leveller Democracy* (NY, 1951), 105-9.

[23] Wildman, *Truths triumph*, 4.

[24] [R. Overton], *A Defiance Against All Arbitrary Usurpations* (1646), 5.

[25] Wolfe, 388.   [26] Haller, iii. 348.

[27] Wildman, *Truths triumph*, 4.

[28] Lilburne, *Impeachment of High Treason*, 24.   [29] Haller and Davies, 455.

the English nation — that provided the Levellers with the religious and philosophical justification for defying the tradition that private individuals did not pronounce on public affairs and for campaigning for the political rights and liberties of all Englishmen. 'I esteem it a high part of true religion to promote common justice', said Walwyn.[30] True religion, wrote Francis White, manifested itself 'in acts of Justice and mercy'.[31] Justice and righteousness were attributes of God and in standing up for them the Levellers were standing up for God.[32] True Christians were the most valiant defenders of their country's just liberties because the love of God led men to oppose whatever was contrary to God and so to defend their brothers and neighbours from oppression and tyranny.[33] Christopher Cheesman or Chisman, a rank-and-file Leveller, felt that he had been inspired directly by God to take up arms for Parliament against principles of injustice and acts of unrighteousness.[34] 'And thus in every age', commented Lilburne, 'sometimes upon a religious, and sometimes upon a civil account, and very often upon both in one and the same persons: the most faithful servants of Christ in every country where they lived' have been 'ever the greatest enemies to tyranny and oppression, and the most zealous maintainers of the known laws and liberties of their Country.'[35] The good work required of true Christians was the liberation of the commonwealth 'from all Tyrants, oppressors and deceivers'.[36]

The principle which linked the religious beliefs of the Levellers to political action was the 'golden rule' — 'to do unto others as you would have them do unto you'.[37] In the introduction to the second *Agreement of the People* Lilburne called it 'that Principle which we professe'.[38] It was a divine law, confirmed by Christ.[39] It was central to Lilburne's personal religious experience. In 1649 he described how thirteen

---

[30] Haller, iii. 325.   [31] White, *Copies of Several Letters*, 10.
[32] Lilburne, *Impeachment of High Treason,* 15-16.
[33] Haller, ii. 297-9.
[34] C. Chisman, *The Lamb contending with the Lion* (1649).
[35] Haller and Davies, 405-7, 452-5.   [36] Ibid. 272.
[37] Davis, 'Levellers and Christianity', 228-30.   [38] Wolfe, 294.
[39] G.E. Aylmer (ed.), *The Levellers in the English Revolution* (1975), 72; Haller, iii. 325; Winstanley, *Works,* 611.

years earlier God had made known to him 'his eternall, everlasting and unchangable loving kindnesse' and that he had
'washed and clensed my soul with the precious bloud of Jesus
Christ, and had caused the grace of God to appear in my
soul . . . Ingraving with his Spirit upon my heart as with a
point of a Diamond those Divine Laws, viz. to doe to all men
as I would they should do to me'.[40] But this was not just a
scriptural law binding only upon Christians, it was also a
natural law binding upon all mankind and upon all secular
authorities. At the creation God had 'ingraved by nature in
the soule of Man, this goulden and everlasting principle, to
doe to another, as he would have another to do to him'.[41]
All men were endowed with reason which taught them this
rule.[42] Overton saw it as the basic principle which made
civil society possible.[43] As it was a natural as well as a scriptural law it required all men 'to doe good unto all the Sons
of Adam'; and to Lilburne it meant that a man was obliged
to stand up for the civil rights and liberties of all the people.[44]
Overton described it as directing him to do 'whatsoever my
understanding tels me is for the good of mankind, for the
safety, freedom, and tranquility of my Country'. He associated it with 'practical Christianity' as the 'spirit of love' and
'brotherly charity' which imposed on him the duty to seek
the 'happinesse and prosperity of my Neighbours, to do to
my neighbor as I would be done by', and also with the defence of private property so that a man may 'injoy the fruit
of his own labour, industry, and sweat of his brow, and freedom of his Conscience and estate, his own naturall right, and
property, and have none to invade or intrench upon the same,
more then you would have upon your own'.[45]

The religion of the Levellers directed them not only to
fight against political oppression but also against poverty.
The 'good works' 'most pleasing to God' were 'fully and
plainly set forth in Scripture'. These were stated again and
again by the Levellers to be 'Feeding the hungry, Cloathing

---

[40] Haller and Davies, 402-3.　　　　　[41] Aylmer (ed.), Levellers, 71.
[42] Davis, 'Levellers and Christianity', 229; Woodhouse (ed.), Puritanism and
Liberty, introduction, 91; Winstanley, Works, 627.
[43] Wolfe, 182, 183.　　　　　　　　　[44] Aylmer (ed.), Levellers, 73.
[45] Haller and Davies, 230-1; [Overton], A Defiance, 5.

the naked, visiting and comforting of the sicke', 'the Farther-
lesse, the Widdowes', 'releeving the aged, weake and im-
potent', 'supporting of poore families', and 'delivering of
Prisoners': 'thereby manifesting our universal love to all mankind . . . doubtlesse there were no way like unto this, to
adorne the Gospel of Christ.'[46] The principle of mercy was
at the heart of the nature of God, wrote Overton, and 'greater
love and mercie cannot be amongst men then to take compassion, over the helplesse and destitute'.[47]

The corollary to this was that those who did not seek to
help the poor and the oppressed were not truly religious. The
Levellers were fond of declaring 'that he who hath this worlds
goods, and suffereth his brother to lack, hath not the love
of God in him, yea though he have never so great parts of
knowledg, zeale, tongues, miracles'.[48] Thus their doctrine of
'practical Christianity' was directly related to their attacks
on the rich and the powerful in general, and on those groups
which had come to power as a result of the civil war in particular.[49] Concern for the poor and the oppressed, which
seemed to the Levellers the message of Christianity and the
substance of religion, was lacking in the ruling classes, which
could not therefore be truly Christian and religious. More
especially the well-to-do of the parliamentarian party, both
laity and clergy, who claimed to be the godly people, were
hypocrites by the Levellers' test. The opposition of Presbyterians, Independents, and some members of sectarian congregations to the political programme of the Levellers was
interpreted as evidence that they did not understand or
practise true religion. These self-styled saints, said the
Levellers, were more concerned to combat opinions of which
they disapproved than to relieve their poor neighbours.

As for his body, or estate, thats no part of his care, hee is not so hasty
to runn into his poor neighbours house, to see what is wanting there,
hee may ly upon a bed, or no bed, covering or no covering, be starved

---

[46] Wolfe, *Milton,* Appendix, 369–70; Haller, iii. 329, 348; Haller and Davies,
263, 266, 272, 381–2; Wildman, *Truths triumph,* 4; Chisman, *Lamb contending
with the Lion*; White, *Copies of Several Letters,* 10; Winstanley, *Works,* 111.
[47] Wolfe, 179–80.
[48] Haller, ii. 274–5; Haller and Davies, 266–7, 382, 435–6.
[49] Davis, 'Levellers and Christianity', 235.

through cold and hunger, over burthened with labour, be sick, lame, or diseased . . . he may through want and necessity goe into what prison he will, and ly and rott and starve there . . .

and none of this troubles these 'Christians' nor moves them.[50] Addressing the members of Parliament, in the first of their manifestos, the Levellers declaimed:

Yee are Rich, and abound in goods, and have need of nothing; but the afflictions of the poore; your hunger-starved brethren, ye have no compassion of . . . Nay, yee suffer poor Christians, for whom Christ died to kneel before you in the streets, aged, sick and cripled, begging your halfe-penny Charities, and yee rustle by them in your Coaches and silkes daily, without regard, or taking any course for their constant reliefe, their sight would melt the heart of any Christian, and yet it moves not you nor your Clergy.[51]

Lilburne observed:

how many men in the Parliament, and else-where of their associates (that judge themselves the onely Saints and godly men upon earth) that have considerable (and some of them vast) estates of their own inheritance, and yet take five hundred, one, two, three, four, five, six thousand pounds *per annum* salaries, and other comings in by their places, and that out of the too much exhausted Treasury of the Nation, when thousands, not onely of the people of the world, as they call them, but also of the precious and redeemed Lambs of Christ, are ready to sterve for want of bread, I cannot but wonder with my self, whether they have any conscience at all within them or no . . . .[52]

Addressing the rich merchants of London on behalf of the poor artisans, the Levellers cried out: 'O you . . . that are at ease, and drink Wine in Bowls, and stretch your selves upon Beds of Down . . . Will no man amongst you regard, will no man behold our faces black with Sorrow and Famine? Is there none to pity?'[53] The Levellers reserved their bitterest condemnations for the well-to-do 'saints' who formed the leading element in the parliamentarian party and came to power after the defeat of the King.

Judge then by this rule who are of Gods family; looke about and you will finde in these woefull dayes thousands of miserable, distressed,

---

[50] Wolfe, *Milton*, Appendix, 369.   [51] Wolfe, 125.
[52] Haller and Davies, 435.
[53] Wolfe, 275; *Englands Troublers Troubled* (1648), 6-7.

starved, imprisoned Christians: see how pale and wan they looke: how coldly, raggedly, and unwholesomely they are cloathed; live one weeke with them in their poore houses, lodge as they lodge, eate as they eate, and no oftner, and bee at the same passe to get that wretched food for a sickly wife, and hunger-starved children; (if you dare doe this for feare of death or diseases) then walke abroad, and observe the generall plenty of all necessaries, observe the gallant bravery of multitudes of men and women abounding in all things that can be imagined: observe likewise the innumerable numbers of those that have more than sufficeth. Neither will I limit you to observe the inconsiderate people of the world, but the whole body of religious people themselves, and in the very Churches and upon solemn dayes: view them well, and see whether they have not this worlds goods; their silkes, their beavers, their rings, and other divises will testifie they have; I, and the wants and distresses of the poore will testifie that the love of God they have not.[54]

'These authors complain', replied Walwyn to his critics,

I am ever harping upon the hard-heartednes and uncharitablenes of professors; and those that are religious men, how grinding they are in bargines: how penurious, base, and back-ward in works of charity, and mercy; how undermining, and over-reaching they are in buying, in selling; how having and craving in things of this life; how hardly any work of mercy, and charity comes from them; how they let their · brethren starve, and dy, and perish, rather than help them; . . . and herin . . . I speake too true . . . .[55]

Christopher Cheesman, cornet in Captain Bray's strongly Leveller company in Colonel Reynolds's regiment, may be regarded as representative of the rank and file of the Leveller party and as expressing their consciousness of the social divisions within which religion and politics operated. He wrote in a pamphlet of 1649, which was praised by Overton:[56]

The Religion of the great Ones of our Age, is a meer shadow, and all their pulpit-pratling is nothing; They are onely Wolves in Sheeps-clothing; they are Devils transformed into Angels of light: but pure Religion and undefiled, is to visit the fatherless and widow, and to keep our selves unspotted of the world; which the great Professors of our times will not do I am sure; for they add house to house, land to land, nay thousands to ten thousands; whiles the poor of the Kingdom are ready to starve . . . .[57]

---

[54] Haller, ii. 274–5; Haller and Davies, 264. [55] Haller and Davies, 380–1.
[56] A.L. Morton (ed.), *Freedom in Arms* (1975), 290.
[57] Chisman, *Lamb contending with the Lion.*

At the heart of the Levellers' perception of religion lay their awareness and experience of social differences, and their conclusion was that the religion of the rich and powerful was a 'false religion' and that the religion of the poor and the powerless was the 'true religion'.

The rule 'to do unto others as you would have them do unto you' could lead to very radical conclusions.[58] Like Overton, Gerrard Winstanley, the leader of the Diggers, associated it with 'practical Christianity' and doing 'all acts of love to his fellow creatures; feeding the hungry; cloathing the naked; relieving the oppressed; seeking the preservation of others as well as himselfe; looking upon himselfe as a fellow creature . . . to all other creatures of all kinds; and so doing to them, as he would have them doe to him'.[59] It could be employed to attack the existing distribution of property and it meant to the left-wing Levellers of Buckinghamshire that none was 'to lord or force any arbitrary power one over another, or to assume any priviledge above his brethren', and 'that every man hath a right and propriety in the creatures, one as well as the other', so that it was wrong 'for any to inclose them wholly from his kind, to his own use, to the impoverishment of his fellow creatures, whereby they are made his slaves' or 'forced to beg or starve for want'.[60] But the Leveller leaders drew back from such conclusions.

The profound distress of leading Levellers at the plight of the poor is clear enough, as is their sensitivity to the extremes of wealth and poverty in their society. It is also clear enough that they blamed the rich for the state of the poor, and indeed for the existence and continuance of poverty, which they regarded as the greatest evil of their society. But it is not so clear why their programmes of reform paid so little attention to this problem and its cure. The Levellers declared that it was 'a shame to Christianity' that so many people lived in such poverty that they had to beg their bread. They believed that it was the duty of government to do something about it: 'truly . . . I do think it one main end of

---

[58] C. Hill, *The Religion of Gerrard Winstanley*, (*P. and P.* supplement 5, 1978), 8, 19, 23.
[59] Winstanley, *Works*, 111.   [60] Ibid. 627.

Government, to provide, that those who refuse not labour, should eat comfortably', wrote Walwyn.[61] But the positive proposals they put forward were few and did not have the central place in their programmes that 'practical Christianity' had in their philosophy. The reason for this was that they looked mainly to a change of heart on the part of the rich and conversion to the true religion of 'practical Christianity' to solve the problem of poverty. They denounced the luxury, covetousness, and hard-heartedness of the rich.[62] Lilburne condemned the 'pomp, superfluities, and debauchery' of the wealthy.[63] Walwyn constantly harped on the silks, beavers, jewels, and plate of the people who had 'more than sufficeth'.[64] He criticized the spending of money on luxury foods from foreign parts, on fine clothes, expensive furniture, and grand houses. He condemned the pursuit of 'vaine superfluous things' as carnal and unchristian. He praised those who lived simply and abandoned 'all kindes of superfluities'.[65] He believed that if the rich spent less on luxuries there would be more for the relief of the poor who were unable to work, more for the payment of better wages to poor artisans and labourers, and more for investment in the expansion of production and employment.

It would be much more profitable to society and good neighbourhood that there were a more exact accompt taken by every man of his own wayes; it is verily thought most men neede not goe abroad for want of work, if either pride, covetousnesse, backbiting, unreasonable jealosy, vanity of minde, dotage upon superfluities: with hard heartedness to the poore: were thought worthy of Reformation.[66]

The religion of the leaders of the Levellers led them to be sympathetic towards the poor, but it did not provide them with an ideology of social change. It operated within the traditional notions of good neighbourliness held by the people they represented — the small producers (craftsmen and peasants). There was a tension between their concern for

---

[61] Wolfe, 137, 140, 270, 288; Haller and Davies, 384; *Englands Troublers Troubled,* 10; D.W. Petegorsky, *Left-Wing Democracy in the English Civil War* (1940), 109.

[62] Wolfe, 275-6.   [63] Haller and Davies, 435-6.

[64] Haller, ii. 274-5; Haller and Davies, 264.

[65] Haller, ii. 279-82.   [66] Wolfe, *Milton,* Appendix, 372.

the poor and their position as representatives of the small property owners. They defended private property and accepted inequalities of wealth. They could not advocate confiscation of property or compulsory redistribution of wealth and so confined their hope for the abolition of poverty to urging the rich to give voluntarily more of their wealth to the poor.

Central to the Leveller programme was the demand for religious liberty — for each individual to be free to hold what opinions in religion his reason told him to be true and to worship God in the way his conscience told him to be right, without interference from the state or state-church. This involved carving out for the individual an area of autonomy beyond the reach of any human power. Walwyn distinguished between 'things naturall', which came under the jurisdiction of the civil government, and 'things supernaturall', which came under the jurisdiction only of God. The rules relating to the former were knowable by all men by the light of nature and were binding upon all men, but the rules relating to the latter were knowable only by those to whom God had so far revealed them and were binding only upon such. Therefore the state could compel men in relation to 'things naturall', but it could not compel them in relation to 'things supernaturall', for in the latter sphere the truth came directly from God to the individual who had to obey only God.[67] Overton distinguished between 'the outward man' and 'the inward man'. God reserved entirely to himself the government of 'the inward man', which was responsible to no human authority. God delegated the government of 'the outward man' to the civil rulers, who had no authority over 'the inward man'. This meant that 'matters of conscience or opinion about Religion or Worship . . . doth not fall under the power of the Magisteriall sword, either for introduction and setlement, or for extirpation and subversion'.[68] Lilburne made the same point by saying that Christ had a kingdom in this world amongst believers, who obeyed only his laws in matters relating to that kingdom. Neither kings, parliaments, magistrates, nor even ecclesiastical authorities had any jurisdiction in

[67] Haller, iii. 340-1.   [68] Wolfe, 180-2.

Christ's kingdom, where the individual was responsible only and directly to God.[69] The conclusion was that in matters of religion each man must make up his own mind, neither being compelled by the state, nor accepting on trust the opinion of another, whether layman or clergyman, whether parliament or church.[70] But it was not easy to determine exactly where the dividing line ran between 'things supernaturall' and 'things naturall', or between 'the inward man' and 'the outward man', and to distinguish between opinions or acts properly in the religious sphere and those properly in the civil sphere. This was the main issue in the debates at Whitehall between the Levellers and the chief officers of the Army about a new constitution to replace the monarchy. Who was to judge whether an opinion or act was properly in the one sphere or the other? If the autonomous individual, then he would be free in anything he chose to call religious, and the freedom would be unlimited. If the civil authority, then it could punish anything it chose to call an offence against the state, which might be so interpreted as to swallow up the whole sphere of religion.[71] The Levellers did not intend the freedom of the individual to be unlimited, and that meant restriction on it by the civil power.[72]

The Levellers accepted the need for government, with power to compel people to obey it and to use force to maintain public order and to protect the nation.[73] Although the sphere of religion was exempted from its jurisdiction, the civil government was commissioned by God. Civil society was bound by natural law which itself was derived from God.[74] Thus civil government and civil society had a moral function.[75] Lilburne declared that 'the end of the institution of all Magistracy in the world, is for a terror to evill doers, and for a praise to those that doe well'. Walwyn maintained that the purpose of government was 'to promote virtue,

[69] Haller, iii. 183-4, 185.

[70] Ibid. ii. 277, 300; iii. 67, 195, 196, 199, 325; Wolfe, 121-2, 227.

[71] Woodhouse (ed.), *Puritanism and Liberty*, 143, 144, 146-7, 149, 153-4, 154-6, 157-9, 159-60, 160-1, 162, 164-5, 166, 167-8, 168-9.

[72] Ibid., introduction, 81.   [73] Haller, iii. 240-3; Wolfe, 391.

[74] Wolfe, 180-2; Davis, 'Levellers and Christianity', 230; Frank, *Levellers*, 93; W. Schenk, *The Concern for Social Justice in the Puritan Revolution* (1948), 30.   [75] M. Tolmie, *The Triumph of the Saints* (Cambridge, 1977), 144.

restraine vice, and to maintain to each particular his owne' (i.e. to protect private property).[76] The Levellers agreed that the freedom they advocated in religion should not extend to opinions which were 'destructive to humane society', 'dangerous to the State', or contrary to belief in Jesus Christ.[77] Thus in making liberty of conscience one of the natural rights of man they also subjected it to the jurisdiction of natural law. If a man claimed that his opinion in religion permitted him to commit theft, or adultery, or murder, that would not be allowed by the civil laws, by which he would be punished.[78] Such acts were punishable by the secular authorities, not because they were contrary to scriptural law, but because they were against natural law, and therefore legitimately under the jurisdiction of the civil government. As Overton explained, they were against natural law because destructive to human society. This concept of what was 'destructive to human society' extended much further and embraced open and public profaneness, licentiousness, and looseness, which were punishable by the civil authority, which had the duty and the power to 'preserve publike modesty, comlines, and civility' and to ensure that the 'carriage and publicke demeanours' of the citizens were 'rationall, regular, and comely'.[79] A.S.P. Woodhouse holds that the Levellers, in placing the state in the sphere of nature, strictly segregated the sphere of nature from the sphere of religion. But this was not so, because natural law embraced much of the moral law of the Bible.[80] The Levellers' demand that the laws be reduced 'to the nearest agreement with Christianity', their conviction that the Christian should 'do good in his generation' and oppose tyranny and injustice and fight for the rights and liberties of all Englishmen, their statement that it was 'a shame to Christianity' that any should beg their bread,

---

[76] Haller and Davies, 406; Haller, iii. 74-5, 97-8, 199, 200.
[77] Haller, ii. 277, 300; iii. 67; Wolfe, 180-2; *The Declaration of Divers Well-Affected Inhabitants of the Cities of London and Westminster* (1648), 3; Woodhouse (ed.), *Puritanism and Liberty*, introduction, 81; Zagorin, *History of Political Thought*, 16.
[78] Haller, iii. 74-5, 97-8, 199, 200.   [79] Ibid. iii. 240-3.
[80] Woodhouse (ed.), *Puritanism and Liberty*, introduction, 57-60, 68, 87-91; Zagorin, *History of Political Thought*, 28-9.

and their belief that the state was bound by the obligations of 'practical Christianity' to relieve the poor, all pointed to an assumption that the society about which they were talking was a Christian one, and its state and its laws were Christian.[81] The Levellers permitted the state to perform religious functions. It was allowed to set up a state-church and to see that the people were instructed in religion, providing that — and this was all-important — it was not made compulsory to attend and conform to that church.[82] The Levellers may have had in mind the distinction made by John Saltmarsh between the 'policy of Christ' and the 'government of Christ'. A Christian magistrate should pursue the 'policy of Christ' and encourage 'moral virtues, as prudence, temperance, obedience, meekness, love, justice, fortitude', and seek to reform 'the outward man', but he should not usurp the 'government of Christ' over the opinions and consciences of men in religion.[83] But the Levellers evaded in the end the problem of defining what was properly religious and what was properly civil by shifting the issue from limiting the freedom of the people in religion to limiting the power of the state.[84] The *Agreement of the People* laid down what Parliament could not do, and most importantly it could not 'continue in force or make any Laws, Oaths, and covenants, whereby to compel by penalties or otherwise, any person to any thing in or about matters of Faith, Religion or Gods Worship, or to restrain any person from the professing his Faith, or exercise of Religion according to his conscience'.[85] The provisions limiting the central government and decentralizing power reduced the capacity of the state to invade religious freedom. But the shifting of the issue shows that restricting the power of rulers was as important to the Levellers as establishing liberty of conscience.

It may be argued whether the Levellers' ultimate aim was religious liberty, for which political liberty was the means, or

---

[81] See above, pp. 67–78.

[82] Haller, iii. 187; Wolfe, 122, 227, 287, 300; Haller and Davies, 144; Wolfe, *Milton,* 98; W. Haller, *Liberty and Reformation in the Puritan Revolution* (NY, 1955), 325–6.

[83] Woodhouse (ed.), *Puritanism and Liberty,* 184–5.

[84] Haller, *Liberty and Reformation,* 325–6.   [85] Wolfe, 227, 300, 405.

whether their overriding objective was political liberty, for which religious liberty was the means.[86] But the Levellers would have remained buried amongst the mass of the religious radicals and the sects if they had not differentiated themselves by the nature and scope of their political programme, and by their political organization and campaigning. For many religious radicals religious liberty was the ultimate aim and it could be separated from political liberty; for the Levellers political liberty was the overriding objective but it could not be separated from religious liberty.[87]

Overton maintained in 1645 that it would not be possible to establish political liberty so long as persecution for religion continued, and that religious liberty was necessary in order to prevent political tyranny.[88] The people in control of the state and the church called heretical or blasphemous opinions or practices which threatened their positions or interests. The laws against heresies and blasphemies were 'generally invented . . . to affright men from that liberty of discourse by which Corruption & tyranny would be soon discovered'.[89] The Buckinghamshire Levellers identified the tyranny of kings, lords, and lawyers with the power of the Devil, and argued that it could be overcome only by giving godly men freedom to preach against it in public.[90] Freedom of the press was desired at least as much for political as for religious reasons.[91] Lilburne held that freedom of the press was essential for the establishment and the preservation of political freedom, it being the means 'whereby all trecherous and tyranical designes may be the easier discovered, and so prevented'.[92]

For what-ever specious pretences of good to the Common-wealth have bin devised to over-aw the Press, yet all times fore-gone will manifest, it

---

[86] Davis, 'Levellers and Christianity', 246-50; Haller, i. commentary, 87.
[87] Haller, i. commentary, 86-7; Haller and Davies, introduction, 16, 21-2, 23-4, 49.
[88] Haller, iii. 241.
[89] Wolfe, 137-8, 289; *The Moderate*, 28 (16-23 Jan. 1649); Morton (ed.), *Freedom in Arms*, 129.
[90] Winstanley, *Works*, 637-8.   [91] Wolfe, 121, 128.
[92] Haller, iii. 268-9; Haller and Davies, 167, 184; Haller, *Liberty and Reformation*, 286.

hath ever ushered in a tyrannie; mens mouth being to be kept from making noise, whilst they are robd of their liberties, So it was in the late Prerogative times before this Parliament, whilst upon pretence of care of the publike, Licensers were set over the Press, Truth was suppressed, the people thereby kept ignorant, and fitted only to serve the unjust ends of Tyrants and Oppressers, whereby the Nation was enslaved: Nor did any thing beget those oppressions so much opposition, as unlicensed Books and Pamphlets.

Liberty of the press was 'so essential unto Freedom, as that without it, its impossible to preserve any Nation from being liable to the worst of bondage; for what may not be done to that people who may not speak or write, but at the pleasure of Licensers?' The least constraint on the press was inconsistent with the good of the commonwealth and dangerous to the liberties of the people.[93]

The Levellers believed that compulsion in religion and the punishment of people for religious opinions caused divisions and conflicts in society and threatened the stability of the state.[94] Overton attributed the rising of the Scots, the rebellion in Ireland, and the civil war in England, to religious intolerance: 'One would compell the other to their faith, and force them from their owne, and that will not be borne, they had rather dye, then deny their faith; and therefore is it, that a considerable party rebelleth . . . yet both (as they suppose) fight the Lords battell.' Religious intolerance 'occasioned the feares and jealousies betwixt his Majesty and the two Houses of Parliament, and unhappily drew them into the Feild of Blood, neither party would be oppressed in Conscience, or deprived of their Religion'.[95] The Levellers recognized the genuineness and strength of religious beliefs amongst the people, but the perception which formed their attitude towards religion and towards the relationship between religion and politics, was that religion meant one thing for the ruling groups and another thing for the subject groups, and that the ruling groups in their own interests exploited the religious beliefs of the people. Walwyn argued that the clergy divided into parties and sowed discords and divisions amongst the people in order to win support for quarrels in which only

[93] Wolfe, 326-30.   [94] Ibid. 289.   [95] Haller, iii. 221-3.

the interests of the clergy were involved and not at all the
interests of the people. The interests of the clergy were in
truth opposed to the interests of the people, for the clergy of
all factions sought in the end to maintain their dominance
over the people and their power to tax them to support their
'covetous, ambitious, and persecuting spirit'.[96] Neither party
in the civil war had the interests of the people at heart, and
neither fought really intending to free the people from
oppression and injustice. The clergy were 'the cheife causers'
and 'the grand Incendiaries' of the troubles in England.

Although the Episcopall Clergie pretend to strive for the Regall Prerogative on the one side, and the Presbiterian Prelacy for Reformation,
and Liberty of the Subject on the other side; yet both of these mainely
intend their owne respective profits and advancements; so that which
sd. soever prevaile (if such may have their wills, both aiming at their
own greatnesse and Dominion over the consciences of their Brethren)
extreamest miserie, and basest kind of slavery will unavoydably
follow . . . .[97]

The people had been deluded by religion into fighting for
causes which would not make them free but keep them slaves.
But behind the clergy stood the nobility and gentry, who had
fallen out amongst themselves in the pursuit of power and
office and had divided into parties, which exploited the
clerical quarrels and employed pretences of religion to win
support and get the people to fight their battles for them.[98]

And to this end . . . they have their Juglers, who can play the Hocus
Pocus, and invent a thing they call Religion . . . they quickly juggle
them together with Oaths, Covenants, Etc. then they do as the lowbel-
men amongst Larks, carry a false light and gloss of Scripture, and with
their preaching and noises, thumping and bumping the Pulpit cushions
. . . then like so many Beagles they open their mouths, and with full
cry, having the scent of such a great benefit, Etc. lay on like Thatchers:
Oh rise, help your King, help your Parliament: Oh your Lives, Liberties
and Religions lyeth at stake: Thus were the poor men made murder
each other . . . .[99]

Both sides pretended to fight for religion and liberty but
their real aims were the oppression and exploitation of the

---

[96] Haller, iii. 80–1.   [97] Ibid. 81–2.   [98] Wolfe, 117–24.
[99] Winstanley, *Works*, 632–3. A 'lowbel' is a bell used to frighten birds into
a net.

people, and the same applied to both the factions into which
the victorious parliamentarian party had split, the Presbyterians and the Independents.[100] 'What else but your Am-
bition and Faction continue our Distractions and Oppressions?
Is not all the Controversie whose Slaves the poor shall be?
Whether they shall be the Kings Vassals, or the Presbyterians,
or the Independent Factions?'[101] 'To be short, all the quarrell
we have at this date in the Kingdome, is no other then a
quarrel of Interests, and Partyes, a pulling down of one
Tyrant, to set up another.' 'The King, Parliament, great men
in the City and Army, have made you but the stairs by which
they have mounted to Honor, Wealth and Power. The only
Quarrel that hath been, and at present is but this, namely,
whose slaves the people shall be.'[102]

The Levellers escaped from exclusive dependence on
religion for their critique of society by adopting and deve-
loping a secular theory — the myth of the Norman Yoke:
the people had been free in Anglo-Saxon England but they
had been deprived of their liberty by the Norman Conquest,
from which came the ruling class and all the oppressions and
injustices of which the Levellers complained.[103] This enabled
them to express and explain the divergences between, on the
one side, the people, and on the other side, kings, lords,
gentry, clergy, lawyers, merchants. It facilitated their insight
that what they called 'false religion' was a cloak for class
interests and disguised from the people their true interests or
'true religion'. This led the Levellers to see the ending of
compulsion in religion and the leaving of each individual free
to follow his own judgement, together with the reduction of
the power and influence of the clergy, as the way both to
promote true Christianity and to diminish the opportunities
for the ruling class to exploit religion in its own interests
against those of the people. Their aim in both religion and
politics was the same and that was to reduce the power of the
ruling class.[104] This is shown by the fact that alongside the
ending of compulsion in religion they gave equal importance

---

[100] Haller and Davies, 262-3, 271.
[101] Wolfe, 276; *Englands Troublers Troubled*, 2.
[102] Haller and Davies, 136-7, 140, 142-3, 144-5.
[103] C. Hill, 'The Norman Yoke', in his *Puritanism and Revolution* (1958);
Haller and Davies, introduction, 41, 46-7.   [104] Haller, i. commentary, 87.

to the ending of compulsion in military service. The main purpose of the *Agreement of the People* was to establish things which Parliament could not do, and in all three versions the Levellers laid down that it could not impress men to serve in the Army or Navy.[105] The reason for this was the same as the reason for freedom from compulsion in religion: each individual had to decide freely for himself what was right and just. 'You must note that you are a free people, and are not to be pressed and enforced to serve in Wars like horses and bruit beasts, but are to use the understanding God hath given you, in judging of the Cause, for defence whereof they desire you to fight.'[106] The *Agreement of the People* prohibited compulsory military service because 'every mans Conscience' had 'to be satisfied in the justness of that cause wherein he hazards his own life, or may destroy an others'.[107] It was only legitimate to fight for a just cause. A soldier who killed, or ordered others to kill, without a just cause, was guilty of murder. In the end he would have to account to God for his actions, and he would not be allowed to plead that he merely did what he was told or followed unquestioningly the judgements of others. He would have to accept responsibility for his own actions, and so he must be convinced by his own understanding and conscience of the justice of the cause for which he fought.[108] Thus the Leveller doctrine of individual freedom of judgement embraced politics as well as religion. The belief of the Levellers in the capacity of the common people to understand the principles of the Christian religion and of political justice, and to form their own judgements independently of their social superiors, and to act upon them, underlay both their religious and their political philosophy.

In order to arrive at such a belief the Levellers had to escape from the conclusions derived traditionally from the Fall of Man and the depravity of human nature. They did not deny original sin and 'the corrupt nature of man'.[109] Govern-

---

[105] Wolfe, 125-6, 227, 287, 300, 405; Petegorsky, *Left-Wing Democracy*, 59.
[106] Haller and Davies, 142; Winstanley, *Works*, 633.
[107] Wolfe, 300, 405.
[108] Haller and Davies, 135, 136, 140, 141, 142; *The English Souldiers Standard to Repaire to, for Wisdome and Understanding* (1649), 6, 10-11.   [109] Wolfe, 159.

ment was necessary because 'the pravity and corruption of mans heart is such that there could be no living without it'.[110] The law of nature required the existence of government.[111] But Christopher Hill observes that the Levellers built upon the doctrine of the sinfulness of human nature the principle that power corrupts. Thus they shifted the focus of original sin from the wickedness of the mass of mankind, which required that they be kept under the rod of the magistrate, to the wickedness of the men in power, which required a form of constitution which reduced and checked their ability to do harm.[112] They based their constitution on the knowledge learnt from history and experience that power corrupts. John Wildman said in the Whitehall debates that 'the magistrate must be conceived to be as erroneous as the people whom he is to restrain, and more probable to err than the people that have no power in their hands, the probability is greater that he will destroy what is good than [that he will] prevent what is evil'.[113] Lilburne wrote in a marginal note, which H.N. Brailsford rightly sees as giving the clue to much of his political thinking:[114]

It hath been a maxime amongst the wisest Legislators, that whosoever means to settle good Laws, must proceed in them with a sinister, or evil opinion of all mankind; and suppose that whosoever is not wicked, it is for want of opportunity, & that no State can be wisely confident of any publick minister continuing good longer then the Rod is over him.[115]

The laying down of restrictions on the power of Parliament was the consequence of 'having by wofull experience found the prevalence of corrupt interests powerfully inclining most men once entrusted with authority, to pervert the same to their own domination, and to the prejudice of our Peace and Liberties'.[116] Lilburne learned the lesson that men who remained too long in office or power became corrupt, and used

---

[110] Ibid. 391; Robertson, *Religious Foundations*, 93-6; Schenk, *Concern for Social Justice*, 28.
[111] Robertson, *Religious Foundations*, 64-70, 93-6.
[112] *WTUD* (1972 edn.) 132-3.
[113] Woodhouse (ed.), *Puritanism and Liberty*, 161.
[114] H.N. Brailsford, *The Levellers and the English Revolution* (1961), 322.
[115] Wolfe, 270 n.   [116] Ibid. 405.

their position to further their own ends rather than the people's good: 'for standing water will speedily corrupt . . . though it were never so pure at the first.'[117] From this it followed that parliaments should be elected biennially or annually.[118] 'And above all things', warned the Surrey Levellers, 'avoid the perpetuation of Command, Trust, or Office, in the hand of any person or persons, it having proved by the sad experience of all Ages and Countries, and of our own in particular, the means of Corruption and Tyranny in those that are trusted, and of bondage to the people.'[119] The Leveller leaders concluded:

> that the experimentall defections of so many men as have succeeded in Authority, and the exceeding difference we have hitherto found in the same men in a low, and in an exalted condition, makes us even mistrust our own hearts, and hardly beleeve our own Resolutions of the contrary. And therefore we have proposed such an Establishment, as supposing men to be too flexible and yeelding to worldy Temptations, they should not yet have a means or opportunity either to injure particulars, or prejudice the Publick, without extreme hazard, and apparent danger to themselves.[120]

Joseph Frank observes that the Leveller conviction that power corrupts shifts the emphasis from acceptance of the depravity of human nature to faith in the potentialities of the common man.[121] The people were capable of understanding and implementing the true principles of government, and a system based on the consent and participation of the people would be less liable to corrupt than one run by and in the interests of the rich and the powerful. The Levellers moved the focus from defects in human nature to defects in laws and institutions: if the former could not be changed, the latter could be remedied.[122] In the end it was not human nature which defeated them but the social order.

The emphasis on corruption by power was nevertheless an evasion of the problem of original sin, and there remained an

---

[117] Haller, iii. 291; J. Lilburne, *The Juglers Discovered* (1647), 10-11; idem, *The resolved mans Resolution* (1647), 22; Haller and Davies, 166-7.
[118] Wolfe, 226-7, 295, 403-4.
[119] *The Moderate*, 28 (16-23 Jan. 1649).
[120] Wolfe, 394.
[121] Frank, *Levellers*, 246.
[122] Haller, i. commentary, 37, 40, 44.

inconsistency between the Levellers' acceptance of the
depravity of human nature and their faith in the potentialities of the common man.[123] But that faith was from the
start qualified by their recognition that the habits of centuries and the pressures of the ruling order left the people
deferential towards their social superiors and diffident about
their own capacities. Walwyn warned the people in 1647:
'yee looke not into publike affaires your selves, but trust
wholly unto others; and . . . ye remain liable to be deluded
and betrayed by them.'[124] 'Such and so long hath been the
Arbitrary encroachments, usurpations, and invasions of the
naturall Rights, properties, and freedoms of the people of
this Nation, through the abused power, and machivilian
policy of the Kings, Lords, and Clergy-men thereof', wrote
Overton in 1646, 'that the spirits of this people . . . are even
vassalaged';

> the poore deceived people are even (in a manner) bestiallized in their
> understanding, become so stupid, and grosly ignorant of themselves,
> and of their own naturall immunities, and strength too, wherewith
> God by nature hath inrich'd them, that they are even degenerated from
> being men, and (as it were) unman'd, not able to define themselves by
> birth or nature, more then what they have by wealth, stature, or
> shape, and as bruits they'l live and die for want of knowledge, being
> void of the use of Reason for want of capacitie to discern, whereof,
> and how far God by nature hath made them free . . . .[125]

In 1649 these fears were realized when the people failed to
appear for the *Agreement*, and Overton explained that some
were preoccupied with their private affairs and with earning
a living, while others were 'cow'd out of' their 'abilities and
principles' by the power of the government and the Army.[126]
The significance of this was that the Levellers did not rely
wholly for their explanations on original sin but recognized
that the forces arrayed against them were social and historical.
    The Levellers throughout sought both religious liberty and

---

[123] G. Huehns, *Antinomianism in English History* (1951), 117-18; Schenk,
Concern for Social Justice, 46-7.
[124] Morton (ed.), *Freedom in Arms*, 123; Haller, iii. 269-70.
[125] [Overton], *A Defiance*, 1-2.
[126] Morton op. cit., 287-8, 291.

political liberty.[127] Their political aims were influenced by their religion and their religion was influenced by their political aims. The interrelation between their religion and their politics was determined by their recognition of the divisions and conflicts in their society, and of the fact that both the church and the state were instruments of class.

[127] Haller, *Liberty and Reformation*, 256.

4 The Religion of Gerrard Winstanley[1]

G. E. Aylmer

I

Gerrard Winstanley (1609-76) received little attention from historians until the end of the nineteenth century. One modern edition of his writings appeared in 1941, and another selection in 1944, and the most recent and accessible in 1973. More has in fact been written about him since 1960, perhaps even since 1970, than in the whole intervening period since his own lifetime.[2] There are a number of puzzles about Winstanley with which this chapter will be partly concerned; not all of them can be solved because of the lack of evidence, or in some cases its ambiguity; but at least they can be clarified and unnecessary difficulties resolved.

[1] I am grateful to Dr Timothy Kenyon of the University of Warwick for kindly giving me a copy of those chapters of his Ph.D. thesis (on English Utopianism) which are concerned with Winstanley; I hope that his work will be published before too long. Ms Mary James reawakened my own interest in Winstanley by her work in a special subject class at the University of York in 1965-6, though it may be thought by some that, as a pupil myself of Hill and Tawney, I should never have forgotten him. I am very grateful indeed to Dr John Morrill for having made many helpful suggestions to improve this chapter; neither he nor the editors can be held responsible for its shortcomings.

[2] References to Winstanley's writings are to the standard collection edited by G.H. Sabine (see List of Abbreviations), cited in this chapter as *Works*, and to the less comprehensive but more accessible edition by Christopher Hill, *Winstanley: The Law of Freedom and Other Writings* (Cambridge, 1983), cited as 'Hill'. I have also found helpful the following works not cited in the notes: L.H. Berens, *The Digger Movement in the days of the Commonwealth* (1906); C.Hill, *The Religion of Gerrard Winstanley* (*P. and P.* supplement 5, 1978); D.W. Petegorsky, *Left-Wing Democracy in the English Civil War* (1940); J. Sanderson, 'The Digger's Apprenticeship: Winstanley's early writings', *Political Studies*, xxii (1974). The fullest account, with much supporting material, is now Olivier Lutaud, *Winstanley: socialisme et Christianisme sous Cromwell* (Publications de la Sorbonne. Littératures 9, and Études Anglaises, no. 66, Paris, 1976). The introductions to Sabine's and Hill's editions of Winstanley's writings are also of fundamental importance. The latter of these and Lutaud contain the most up-to-date bibliographies.

Before we can decide where he got his ideas from, it is necessary to agree on what their most important features were. After this, we may then try to consider how and why his ideas changed; and finally to assess their significance both in his own time and for posterity. The sections which follow will deal with Winstanley's background and the context of his career, his early writings, his adoption of communism, the period of his 'Digger' activities, his disillusionment at its failure, his most elaborate programme for a new society, his later career, and finally his historical importance.

The extent of contemporary support for Winstanley is hard to estimate. We do know that, although very few copies of his pamphlets have survived, some at least were in sufficient demand to be reprinted and to go into more than one edition. On the other hand the total number of his companions and followers was to be reckoned in scores rather than in hundreds, let alone in thousands. Although his appeal was to the unprivileged, to the downtrodden masses, he was never to lead anything remotely like a mass movement. His following was small compared, for example, with that of the Leveller John Lilburne or the Quaker George Fox.

The real interest of Winstanley lies in the totality of his challenge to established beliefs and systems of values. He offered a considered, thought-out critique and a positive programme, even if — as will be seen — there are variations and perhaps inconsistencies within the structure of his thought. Some of the disagreements about him seem sterile and unreal. Whatever his starting-point as a religious thinker, he was not a normal kind of millenarian, still less a Fifth Monarchist; nor during the period of his published writings was he a Quaker, even if he became one after the Restoration.[3] Nor was he a complete materialist, a precursor of the eighteenth-century *Philosophes* or of Marx and Engels.[4] His

---

[3] L. Mulligan, J.K. Graham, J. Richards, 'Winstanley: A Case for the Man as He Said He Was', *Journal of Ecclesiastical History*, xxviii (1977). See also their attack on Christopher Hill's interpretation in *P. and P.* 89 (1980), with Hill's reply. For an earlier version of the same approach see W.S. Hudson's article in *The Journal of Modern History*, xvii (1946).

[4] G. Juretic, 'Digger No Millenarian: The Revolutionizing of Gerrard Winstanley', *Journal of the History of Ideas*, xxxvi (1975).

communism and his theology are literally inseparable in his writings from 1649 on, even though the emphasis varies in different pamphlets. His message is essentially about the human condition. And it is above all else a moral criticism of the existing social order, perhaps indeed of any conceivable social order. That is the real point of 'Utopian' idealists: not that they should persuade us of their particular panacea to solve humanity's problems, but that they compel us to re-examine the principles and the practices by which we live. They provide us with a moral yardstick by which to measure the imperfections of human nature, our own included.

II

Gerrard Winstanley was a Lancashire man, being born in or near Wigan in 1609. His father was a mercer there and was described as 'Mister' at his death in 1639, and so may have been on the edge of the gentry class, a member of what one modern historian has called the urban 'pseudo-gentry'. His parents were in trouble with the local church authorities for attending conventicles (Puritan nonconformist meetings) a few years before he was born. We know nothing of his schooling but some have suggested attendance at a grammar school on the grounds that he seems to have known some Latin. In 1630 he was apprenticed to a London merchant-tailor and he became free of that company in 1637. This meant that he could legally set up in business on his own. While no records have survived of his having done so, Winstanley himself tells us that he was driven out of business by the civil war, so presumably he did operate as a tradesman or merchant for a time. In about 1643 he moved from London to Surrey where his wife's family had property, and he was apparently reduced to acting as a herdsman for them or someone else. There is no direct evidence about his activities until his earliest pamphlets appeared in 1648. From then until 1652 his writings and his career were fused together. Almost everything of any consequence connected with him belongs to these few years, that is from the time of the second civil war to the last years of the Commonwealth under the rule of the Rump Parliament.

How much weight should be put on Winstanley's business failure in explaining his subsequent adoption of communism remains a matter of controversy. And much the same applies to the fact that he seems to have returned to commercial activities afterwards, despite his previous experience of free enterprise which cannot have fortified his belief in that system. He seems to have become a Quaker some time between 1660 and his death in 1676. Given the closeness of Fox's theological system and his own, this is not surprising; but there is no proof that either of them exercised any direct influence on the other. Setting aside both his earlier and his later career in business, Winstanley's ideas should surely stand or fall in their own right. Ideology-hunting, or reductionism, is an intellectual game at which we can all play — on other people and on ourselves. But the value, let alone the truth, of people's ideas does not depend upon the success or failure of their career or even on the conscious or unconscious motives which lead them to adopt such ideas.

As has been shown elsewhere in this book, the 1640s saw not only political and religious upheaval and military conflict but an exceptional ferment of ideas. The downfall of the episcopalian church of Archbishop Laud and of the personal rule of Charles I, followed by the virtual collapse of the censorship, led to a veritable outpouring, in pamphlets and sermons, of the most varied and often radical theories and viewpoints. So much so that by 1646, if not before then, some spokesmen for orthodox Calvinism and supporters of a Presbyterian church system were more worried about radical heretics and deviationists than about their old enemies the episcopalians. Thomas Edwards, whose extraordinary compendium *Gangraena*, published in three parts in 1646, is the fullest catalogue of the sects and their beliefs, saw religious toleration as the root of the evil, the hole in the dike through which the waters of error and heresy were pouring. The *Gangraena*, like Ephraim Pagitt's *Heresiography* and Daniel Featley's *The Dippers Dipt* (both 1645), appeared too early for Winstanley to be included in their respective excoriations. How they would have classified him is unclear. Although he tells us in one place that he had been rebaptized as an adult (presumably some time between 1640 and 1648), his theology bears little resemblance even to the minority sect of General (Arminian) Baptists, let alone to the mainstream Particular (Calvinist) Baptists. Nor is he what was normally meant by an antinomian, a believer that the recipients of divine grace were absolved from the observance of normal laws and restraints, which was the theological source of Ranterism. The term Seeker is used by Edwards and others to describe those who belonged to no organized sect but shared some tenets of belief with members of various radical groups (Edwards classified the future Leveller William Walwyn in this way). We cannot say that Winstanley belonged to the Seekers, only that he was initially less unlike them than any other group or sect.

III

Even in his earliest published works Winstanley's ideas are individual and distinctive. He accepts that the world and humanity were created by God, but despite frequent citations from the Bible his use of scriptural texts is loose, often symbolic, figurative or metaphorical. Man has fallen from his original state of grace and goodness, and lies under a curse or bondage. This is not, however, a matter simply of having inherited original sin from Adam, like some kind of genetic defect, as in so much Christian teaching of all ages. It is rather to be thought of as a defeat of good by evil, which is repeated in all of us, at least in all adults, and one which only a very few have so far overcome. Yet, with the help of Jesus Christ or the Holy Spirit within us, everyone has the potential to reverse the outcome of this battle: good can truly triumph over evil in all human beings. Hence he rejected the idea of an elect who alone would be saved, and so advanced instead the hope of universal salvation, in which the poor, the humble, and the downtrodden might well lead the way.

Winstanley uses millenarian images and scriptural texts to convey his sense of immediacy and crisis. Humanity — and the people of England in particular — is at a great turning-point. There is a sense of imminence and excitement, although he virtually never puts a date to any future happening. Indeed the victory of good, alias love or Christ or the Second Adam, over evil, alias the Beast or Serpent or First Adam, is a process which must take place within each of us, not an external event like the rule of the saints or the Second Coming. None the less there is a sense, as we shall see, in which he comes to envisage a kind of acceleration of the process, a 'domino theory' of human regeneration.

For Winstanley the dragon in the *Book of Revelations* is magistracy out of joint, the leopard represents what he calls 'gross Popery', and the horned Beast or monster is reformed episcopacy. But there is no question of any institutional church, Puritan, Baptist, or whatever, being other than a hindrance to salvation. His anticlericalism, indeed his opposition to any form of ecclesiastical organization and to all existing academic systems of universities and colleges, is firm and unwavering. None the less, as will be explained later, it is a mistake to call him anti-intellectual. The 'Saints' in his theology are simply those individuals in whom the Beast has been overthrown, and who thus act as pathfinders or examples for the rest of us. He is capable of producing the most ghastly puns, or maybe they are unintended ambiguities, between the Sun and the Son in his metaphors of human recovery and restoration to a pre-lapsarian state of love and virtue.[5]

In *The Saints Paradice* (1648), his third pamphlet, Winstanley internalizes the conflict of good and evil still more explicitly. The Devil is not a separate being but what he calls the spirit of flesh, or 'King Flesh', ruling in man. Although conventional theological descriptions seem inappropriate and may even be misleading, we might say that, at this stage, Winstanley's God is both transcendent and immanent. Another figure of speech, which is given much greater prominence in his next work, is also introduced here, namely the equation of God and Reason, although his idea of reason

---

[5] These paragraphs refer to Winstanley's first two published works: *The Breaking of the Day of God* (1648) and *The Mysterie of God* (1648), of which there are only brief summaries in *Works*. I have used the copies in the Library of Jesus College, Oxford (for access to which I am most grateful to Dr D.A. Rees, Fellow and Archivist) and in the British Library (but not in the Thomason collection of tracts).

is not some kind of vague cosmic principle as it is for some
eighteenth-century deists. To bring about the victory of the
spirit over the flesh, it is necessary, we are told: 'to know
that this spirit which is called God, or Father, or Lord, is
Reason: for though men esteem this word Reason to be too
mean a name to set forth the Father by, yet it is the highest
name that can be given him.' Once more there is a sense of
an intensifying conflict, but one which is by no means to be
confused with the military, political, or religious conflicts
which were taking place at the same time (we must remember that Winstanley was probably writing this during the
course of the second civil war, in which the Parliament's
old allies the Scots and some other ex-parliamentarians,
alarmed by the radicalism of the Army and the sects, supported the King). But there is less emphasis on waiting
patiently than in the two previous works, and more awareness 'that liberty is not far off'. As always in these early
writings, liberty or freedom is a process of spiritual and
moral emancipation; although the poor and unlettered may
well lead the way, nothing is yet said about the possible re-
ordering of society.[6]

His fourth work, *Truth Lifting Up Its Head*, dated October
1648 in the preface, but 1649 on the title page, carried further the identification of God and Reason. Winstanley is
also more explicit about the way in which he uses the Bible.
This time his citations are not distributed through the text
but listed together near the end, seeking to demonstrate that
his beliefs are truly founded on Scripture. This work was
apparently occasioned by the imprisonment of William
Everard, who had renamed himself 'Chamberlain the Redding
man'. He had been arrested by the bailiffs of Kingston-on-
Thames for alleged blasphemy, a serious offence under the
Long Parliament's recent legislation. It is specifically ad-
dressed: 'To the scholars of Oxford and Cambridge and to all
that call themselves ministers of the Gospel in city and
country.' And it is particularly hostile to priests and professors (in the same sense as George Fox was later to use that

---

[6] *The Saints Paradice* (1648), again only summarized in *Works*. I have used the
copy in the Bodleian Library.

word, meaning paid teachers or clerics who professed a particular doctrine).

Everard had served in the parliamentary army, and may even have been one of the Agitators in 1647. When the Diggers began their activities in the spring of 1649, he rather than Winstanley was at first described as their leader, but he seems soon to have faded out. He claimed to be a prophet (which Winstanley never did), and was regarded as a madman by at least one contemporary. In *Truth Lifting Up Its Head* there is for the first time an anticipation of a call for change in this world, in social relations between men, which was to be made fully explicit in his next publication:

Question.   Is his [the Father's or Reason's] time now come to rule the earth and fill it with himself?

Answer: Yes: and shall have as large a priviledge to fill the earth, as the first man had surely; and he will change times and customs, and fil the earth with a new law, wherein dwels righteousnes and peace.[7]

In his fifth work, *The New Law of Righteousness budding forth, in restoring the whole creation from the bondage of the curse*, Winstanley tells us that the message about digging, or communal cultivation, came to him in a trance. Even if we take this to mean some kind of spontaneous meditation, or what believers would call a mystical experience, it may seem strange to say that by the previous autumn he had already decided on the next stage in the development of his theories. But only the exhortation to go and dig in common is ascribed to the trance. The decisive fresh concept in *The New Law*, towards which his mind may well have been moving by late 1648, is that of the earth as a 'common treasury' for all mankind, a passionate conviction that private ownership and inheritance, the payment of rent, the buying and selling of the land and its products, and the system of hired labour must all be brought to an end in the process of spiritual regeneration and self-fulfilment within individuals.

IV

The New Law (Preface dated 26 January 1649, four days before the execution of Charles I) is one of the most difficult

[7] *Truth lifting up its head above scandals* (1649), in *Works*, 121.

but also among the most remarkable of all seventeenth-
century pamphlets. As has been suggested, in some ways it
marks a perfectly logical progression from Winstanley's
earlier writings. But it is novel and heterodox in other ways
besides its advocacy of communism. New metaphors for the
human conflict are introduced: the First versus the Second
Adam, Cain versus Abel, Esau versus Jacob,[8] the Dragon
('Gaffer Dragon' in one place!) versus Christ or the Lamb.

He was now a revolutionary in the sense that his ideas and
the policies which he advocated to achieve them were totally
incompatible with the existing order. But he was not one in
the sense of accepting the use of violence in order to attain
these ends. He never called for an outright attack on private
property, for the occupation and expropriation of people's
lands and estates, still less for the use of physical force against
the persons or possessions of the propertied classes. On the
contrary, he argued that the reoccupation and use of
commons and wastes and their cultivation by common
ownership and use, was fully justifiable at law and would
restore the historic freedom of the English people which had
been lost in 1066. And for an interim period he envisaged
what we should call the coexistence of two sectors in the
agrarian economy: individual or private, and communal or
public. None the less his condemnation of rent and of wage
labour, of people working for hire and being hired, would —
if ever translated into practice — have speedily reduced the
private sector to owner-occupiers and family holdings.

Another issue which has vexed students of Winstanley's
thought and has sometimes given rise to quite acrimonious
contention, is the relative priority which he gave to internal
regeneration and to external reform from this time on. From
the publication of *The New Law* through the whole of the
'Digging' phase of 1649-50 this seems to be what a famous
French historian of the earlier twentieth century would have
called *une question mal posée*; for the two kinds of change
are in reality only different aspects or facets of the same
phenomenon: 'when the earth becomes a common treasury
as it was in the beginning, and the King of Righteousnesse

---

[8] Hence, I assume, the title of David Caute's novel about Winstanley and
the Diggers, *Comrade Jacob* (1961).

comes to rule in every one's heart, then he kils the first Adam; for covetousnesse thereby is killed.'[9] And even in what might be called his most politically committed work, where he advocates subscription to the Commonwealth's loyalty oath or test, the Engagement, the same is true:

A. But doth none uphold, The power of Conquests, and Kingly power, but lords of Mannours, Tything-Priests, Impropriators, and Lawyers [?]

O. Yes, that everlasting covetous kingly power, is corrupt bloud, that runs in every man, more or lesse, till reason the spirit of burning cast him out. And as this kingly power is cast out from within, so it falls from without likewise.[10]

When we come on to his last published work the argument about priority is a more difficult one. I shall suggest that Winstanley did not reverse his fundamental position, although it has been powerfully argued that he did so.[11] Meanwhile the message given in the trance was to be translated into practice.

V

From April 1649 to March 1650 Winstanley's life and thought were dominated by his role as the leader of the Digger experiment in Surrey. This does not mean that all he wrote (still less all that he published) during this time was no more than a series of calls for support or appeals to the authorities for the Diggers to be left alone. But in several of them these are the main themes.

Following the revelation that this was the time and place intended, Everard, Winstanley, and a few others began to dig, manure, and plant the common at St George's Hill, in the parish of Walton-on-Thames, on April Fool's Day 1649. Their numbers grew, though never to more than forty or fifty. The local landowners quickly complained to the Council of

[9] *The New Law*, ch. 1 (*Works*, 159).

[10] *Englands Spirit Unfoulded. Or an Incouragement To Take the Engagement*, ed. G.E. Aylmer, *P. and P.* 40 (1968), 13.

[11] By J.C. Davis in his article, 'Gerrard Winstanley and the Restoration of True Magistracy', *P. and P.* 70 (1976).

State, the supreme executive body set up by the Rump Parliament; its President, John Bradshaw, lately President of the High Court to try the King, had recently himself acquired some ex-church property not very far away. The Council directed Sir Thomas Fairfax as Commander-in-Chief to look into the Diggers' activities, apparently seeing in them a threat to property and the social order. The officer in charge of the party sent to investigate thought Everard mad but the Diggers harmless. Subsequently the two leaders went to London and had an interview with Fairfax, in which they put their case in argument and also made a visual egalitarian point by anticipating the Quaker practice of refusing to doff their hats or caps in the presence of a social superior. A little later Fairfax himself visited them on St George's Hill, and it seemed that the Army would take no decisive action. Meanwhile it was the local landlords (and possibly lesser freeholders too) who began the use of force and violence. They embarked on a campaign of sustained and systematic harassment: trampling on the Diggers' crops, driving off their animals, pulling down their huts, and beating up individuals. Soon too some of the infantry soldiers stationed in the district joined in and behaved with needless brutality, but they seem not to have been acting on orders from headquarters. Making all allowance for some exaggeration in the Digger writings, the men of property certainly made a most unchristian exhibition of themselves. The law of trespass was also invoked against the Diggers. However, the civilian authorities were not satisfied; and both Bradshaw individually and the Council repeated their orders to Fairfax in October. In November some of the soldiers in the area once more joined in the attacks on the communal settlement. By this time — perhaps as early as August 1649 (the record is not clear) — the Diggers had moved their main site to another common in the neighbouring parish of Cobham. But to no avail. The local landowners, and especially the parson there, proved to be even more implacable and persistent opponents than those in the parish of Walton. The Diggers stuck it out, with remarkable courage and endurance, in the face of this repeated harassment, through a long hard winter, though what they lived on is far from clear. They were finally driven off and their site destroyed, while another legal action against them was still pending, at Easter 1650. Before that a forged circular letter in their names had been issued, either by their local enemies or by the government's tame journalists, after which they themselves sent out a genuine appeal for money and support, to sympathizers and like-minded groups else-where.[12] It is hard to know in how many other cases Diggers or similar groups actually occupied commons and wastes and began to practise communal cultivation. If publication of a manifesto be the test, then Wellingborough in Northampton-shire, and Iver in Buckinghamshire can definitely be added; the former was a populous township with an exceptionally large number of its inhabitants on poor relief. If passing references are any guide, there may have been at least seven other centres in five different counties. One historian has perceptively pointed out the parallel with the movement of squatters onto waste lands, usually in moorland and forest areas, which had been in progress for at least a century.[13] None the less there is no evidence that these settlers, squatters, or internal emigrants had in any previous cases practised common ownership and cultivation.

The other undertakings were too temporary and uncertain in their ways of operating for us to be able to equate them with the system which Winstanley envisaged in his writings and which he and his companions tried for about a year to practise in Surrey. Essentially this system involved common ownership of land, though not of all personal possessions and possibly not of dwellings and their furnishings, with the monogamous, nuclear family remaining as the basic unit of social life and (in some parts of Winstanley's writings) also as the unit for productive work; there were to be storehouses, where products were to be delivered and from which — pre-sumably when some families had a surplus to their needs and others fell short — they were to be drawn out, though the references to these storehouses are extremely scanty in the pamphlets of the Digger period proper.

[12] *Works*, 403, 440.
[13] See *A Declaration of the grounds and Reasons, why we the poor Inhabitants of the Parish of Iver in Buckinghamshire, have begun to digge and mannure the common and wast Land* (1 May 1650), ed. K. Thomas, *P. and P.* 42 (1969).

In these writings, not all of which seem to be exclusively of Winstanley's own composition, the justification for their action is threefold. First and foremost, as the argument had been developed in *The New Law*, human regeneration was held to require the restoration of the earth as a common treasury, which was incompatible with private ownership and with buying and selling (of land at any rate), and towards which their 'Digging' was seen as a small first step. The notion of some modern historians that they would have persisted for the best part of a twelvemonth in the face of such adversity if it was meant only to have 'symbolic' significance will not bear serious consideration.[14] Secondly, the measures of the Rump Parliament, abolishing the monarchy and then declaring England to be a free commonwealth, were held to have removed any possible legal or historical justification for control of private landowners and lords of manors over their tenants and over access to common lands. Manorial rights in particular were seen as part of the Norman Yoke which had been imposed after 1066 and which had originally rested on grants made by William the Conqueror and his successors to their captains and tenants-in-chief. Thirdly, the common people of England were held to be in need, not to say in acute want; common and waste land was being grossly under-utilized and its productive potential utterly neglected, and necessity knows no law. In different pamphlets, even in different passages within the same one, the emphasis is put on one rather than the others of these arguments. But there is no sign that Winstanley and his companions at St George's Hill and then at Cobham, or the other articulate Digger groups in Northamptonshire and Buckinghamshire saw any conflict, still less any incompatibility between these different justifications of what they were doing. Indeed at times purely tactical considerations seem to have dictated which one was given priority.[15]

[14] W. Schenk, *The Concern for Social Justice in the Puritan Revolution* (1948), ch. 6 (p. 102). This was a pioneering study; Schenk's tone is more moderate and his perceptions more acute than those of some more recent 'religious', anti-materialist interpretations of Winstanley.

[15] For a complete list of the known Digger writings, see Hill, 72–4. For the full titles of those not in Hill, see *Works*, 71–7, 607–8, also notes 10 and 13

The way in which the different arguments could be blended together by Winstanley himself may be illustrated by a single passage, chosen not quite at random but which is representative of many others:

Nay Covetousnesse is such a god, that where he rules he would have all the Earth to himself, and he would have all to be his servants, and his heart swels most against Communitie; calling Communitie a thief, that takes other mens Rights and Proprietie from them, but communitie will force nothing from any one, but take what is given in love, of that which others have wrought for; but no man yet hath bestowed any labour upon the Commons that lie waste; therefore the Diggers doth take no mans proper goods from them in so doing, but those that by force spoyls their labours takes their proper goods from them, which is the fruit of their own labours.[16]

As with the Bible, so with English history, Winstanley's apparent literalism can mislead us. At times he is capable of making statements about the Norman Conquest which almost suggest that he equated 1066 with the Fall of Man, and the free Anglo-Saxons with a pre-lapsarian state of grace in the Garden of Eden. It is clear that he did indeed share with other radicals of his time a fairly extreme anti-Normanism which may in turn have implied a somewhat roseate, over-idealized view of pre-Conquest society. But the conclusion of his letter to General Fairfax in June 1649 is quite explicit in distinguishing the two phenomena:

The Reformation that England now is to endeavour, is not to remove the Norman Yoke only, and to bring us back to be governed by those Laws that were before William the Conqueror came in, as if that were the rule or mark we aim at: No, that is not it; but the Reformation is according to the Word of God, and that is the pure Law of righteousnesse before the Fall, which made all things, unto which all things are to be restored: and he that endeavours not that, is a Covenant-breaker.[17]

above. The most important of them are generally reckoned to be: *The True Levellers Standard Advanced* (Apr. 1649); *A Watch-Word to the City of London, and the Army* (Aug. 1649); *A New-yeers Gift for the Parliament and Armie* (1 Jan. 1650); *An Appeale to all Englishmen, to judge between bondage and freedom* (26 Mar. 1650); 'The Diggers' Song' and 'The Diggers' Christmas Caroll' (no date, but the latter presumably Dec. 1649).

[16] *A New-yeers Gift* (*Works*, 383-4; Hill, 196).
[17] *A Letter to the Lord Fairfax, and his councell of war*, delivered on 9 June 1649 (*Works*, 292).

In spite of the second, again possibly unauthorized, intervention by members of the Army and the continued legal harassment, it was in the end physical violence by the local landowners and those whom they employed which brought the 'Digging' to an end. But Winstanley's disillusionment may have anticipated this event. For already, just before this, he had published what is perhaps the most obscure but possibly also the most important of his later writings.

VI

The tone if not also the content of *Fire in the Bush* (March 1650) seems to mark a return to his earlier pamphlets. It is a more obviously religious work than any of the Digger pamphlets. It could be said to take up more or less where *The New Law* left off, in its anticipation of a social order where the private sector had disappeared. According to the best authority there is no particular problem about its composition or dating.[18] On this view, Winstanley was perfectly capable of producing, during the final death agonies of the Digger experiment, a work concerned only with eternal verities, which looked forward to a wholly communist society, after what he describes elsewhere as 'the universal restoration of Mankind to the law of righteousness, from which he fell', and not so much as mentioning the activities of the Diggers, unless once very obliquely. It is true that *Englands Spirit Unfoulded*, which contains his argument in favour of supporting the Commonwealth for all its imperfections, seems to belong to the same stage in his career, and it only mentions the Diggers briefly in its anti-Ranter postcript. It is true too that other pamphlets from the Digger period, notably *A New-Yeers Gift for the Parliament and Army* and *An Humble Request, to the Ministers of both Universities, and to all Lawyers in every Inns-a-court*, do also contain quite lengthy sections of a general theological and social nature, not directly to do with digging. None the less it is odd that *Fire in the Bush* is incomplete, having thirteen

[18] K. Thomas, 'The Date of Gerrard Winstanley's *Fire in the Bush*', *P. and P.* 42 (1969), 160–2.

chapters listed in the table of contents but only seven printed in the text, and this in spite of the author saying that he had delayed it for a fortnight before having it printed and published.[19]

Other historians have suggested instead that it was written in 1649, in the interval between *The New Law* and the start of the 'Digging', laid aside for about a year, and then rather hastily prepared for the press in February–March 1650.[20] It is subtitled *The spirit burning, not consuming, but purging Mankinde. Or, the great battell of God Almighty, between Michaell the seed of life, and the great red dragon, the curse fought within the spirit of man.* After the usual prefatory letter, Winstanley sets out the three basic stages in his theology and view of mankind: the creation and man's perfect state; the Fall (which he normally calls the curse); and the restoration of mankind. Save for the Dragon and Michael replacing Cain and Abel, Esau and Jacob, there is nothing new here. Another anti-Ranter aside appears in passing.

Why did Winstanley so dislike the Ranters? It is clear that the primary reason was because of their actual or alleged belief in the community of women, that is sexual promiscuity, or – to put it more favourably – the multiparent family. And it was only secondarily because they were lazy, 'opters-out' who believed, or at least acted as if they believed, that a just and desirable society could be achieved without hard work. Much as Lilburne was concerned to dissociate the Levellers from the Diggers, alias the True Levellers, so Winstanley was likewise to dissociate the Diggers from the Ranters. But this was not just a matter of avoiding guilt by association. He really did believe, with almost suspicious

---

[19] In the prefatory letter, 'To all the several societies of people called churches in the Presbyterian, Independent or any other form of profession in the service of God' (*Works,* 445; Hill, 213).

[20] See Thomas, 'The Date of Winstanley's *Fire in the Bush*', for the argument that there is no problem to be explained, maintaining that 'Christ Levelling' (ch. 3: *Works,* 471; Hill, 242) and 'some of your brethren already, who are witnesses' (ch. 6: *Works,* 487; Hill, 262) are references to the Diggers. In *A New-yeers Gift,* Jesus Christ had already been described as 'the head Leveller'. I am sorry not to be persuaded by Mr Thomas. The passage attacking the very types of magistracy and government which upheld existing inequalities and injustices (ch. 4: especially *Works,* 472-4; Hill, 243-6) also seems to me harder than he allows to square with the 'half-a-loaf' pragmatism of *Englands Spirit Unfoulded.*

passion one might think, in monogamy and the individual family unit. And it is possible that his own premisses contained a contradiction. One man who attempted to practise communism earlier in the seventeenth century felt that it was precisely the existence of the family and the strength of family feelings which rendered it unpractical and so required its abandonment.[21] Perhaps Plato's judgement was sounder than Sir Thomas More's or Winstanley's here.

The battle between Michael and the Dragon is one internal to each human being. Yet during the rule of the Serpent (stage two) there is a fourfold visible power on earth 'which must be shaken to pieces': 'the imaginary teaching power', by which is meant a university-trained, professional ministry; 'the imaginary Kingly power', by which here at least he meant any government upholding the existing social order and economic system; 'the imaginary Judicature, called the Law of Justice'; and 'buying and selling of the Earth, with the fruits of the Earth'. These correspond to the four beasts in the *Book of Daniel* (thereby ringing the changes on the beasts in *Revelations*): the lion with eagle's wings is kingly power; the one like a bear is 'the power of the selfish laws'; the third one, 'spotty like a leopard', is 'the thieving art of buying and selling'; the fourth and the worst of all is 'the Imaginary Clergy Power', which has really bred the other three; the 'little horn' coming out of it is 'the Ecclesiastical power', that is any church establishment. Any university-educated and 'hired' ministry is but another aspect or by-product of this fourth and worst beast. These monsters and the rule of the Serpent will be destroyed by Christ, the righteous spirit within the individual soul, when pure Reason will again rule as king. But the Fall was not a single temporal event in the Garden of Eden 6,000 years ago; like the forthcoming restoration will be, it was a process within all and every one of us. We are all under either innocency (perhaps

[21] W. Bradford, *History of Plimouth plantation,* ed. W.T. Davis (Original Narratives of American History, 1908; reprinted 1964), 146-7. There was of course an imbalance of sexes at New Plymouth as in all the early American colonies, for which the remedy would have been polyandry rather than polygamy; communal cultivation seems to have been given up after only one or two years, so the disruptive effects of family interests must have acted very speedily. Like Winstanley, Bradford writes 'community' where we would use 'communism'.

this is still true of young children), or the curse, or grace (the few who have achieved regeneration, sometimes also called the saints). Private property, buying and selling, and the like, are simply one aspect of life under the curse or bondage. Then, suddenly, he seems to re-establish the link between theology and politics: 'this is the battell, that is fought between the two powers, which is propriety on the one hand, called the Devill or covetousnesse, or [? and] community on the other hand, called Christ, or universall love.'[22] But, whatever may be true elsewhere in Winstanley's writings, the primacy of the spiritual over the temporal (such as institutional changes) in the process of restoration or regeneration is here beyond dispute. Whether this was due to his awareness that the Digger experiment had failed, and he felt that there was a need to restate fundamental principles, remains open to argument.[23]

VII

Winstanley's last published work raises somewhat different issues. *The Law of Freedom in a Platform: Or, True Magistracy Restored* was dedicated to Oliver Cromwell in November 1651, just after the battle of Worcester (the final military defeat of the royalists), and its publication was dated by Thomason to February 1652. Winstanley says that it is based on notes largely composed two years before, but then set aside, first during the last phase of the Digger period and then because he had learnt of Hugh Peter's preparation of his reform tract, *Good Work for a Good Magistrate* (acquired by Thomason in June 1651). Although it comprises the most detailed description of what the new social and political order should be like, it is scrappily put together, stylistically less effective, and with more internal inconsistencies than are

[22] *Fire in the Bush,* ch. 7 (*Works*, 493; Hill, 268).

[23] Although I do not agree with his overall argument about Winstanley's use of typology, I am grateful to T.W. Hayes, *Winstanley the Digger: A Literary Analysis of Radical Ideas in the English Revolution* (Cambridge, Mass., 1979), ch. 5, for having stimulated me to reconsider my own, I now think rather naïve, remarks about *Fire in the Bush* in *P. and P.* 40 (1968), 6-7.

found in Winstanley's most powerful pieces of writing. *The Law of Freedom* is said by some commentators to mark a double transition in his thought: from a primarily religious to a primarily secular and material emphasis, and from a belief in social change brought about by the spontaneous action of individuals and small groups to a belief in the use of state power to effect social and hence moral changes.[24]

The first of these theses is easier to rebut than the second. It is clear that, while institutional reform and reorganization are his main preoccupation in *The Law of Freedom*, 'kingly power' is still equated with the curse or inward bondage, and 'commonwealths power' with mankind restored to a state of grace. In the prefatory letter to Cromwell, who had succeeded Fairfax as Commander-in-chief of the Army in the previous year, not long after the end of the digging, an Old Testament parable is used to illustrate the immediate burdens and grievances by which English society is currently beset and which the Lord General is asked to take in hand straight away.[25] It is here that we find the often-quoted passage: 'And indeed the main Work of Reformation lies in this, to reform the Clergy, Lawyers, and Law; for all the Complaints of the Land are wrapped up within them three, not in the Person of a King.'[26] Likewise, as if to stress his moderation, Winstanley denies that he wants to establish a society without any titles of honour or distinctions of rank, and in doing so he incidentally rebuts the charge of anti-intellectualism which we might otherwise be tempted to bring against him:

As a man goes through Offices, he rises to Titles of Honor, till he comes to the highest Nobility, to be a faithful Commonwealths man in a Parliament House. Likewise he who finds out any secret in Nature, shall have a Title of Honor given him, though he be a young man. But no

[24] For the latter view, see especially Davis, 'Winstanley and the Restoration of True Magistracy'.

[25] Jonah 4: 5-11, tells the story of the gourd which grew up overnight to shelter Jonah while he was sitting outside Nineveh, to see whether or not God would destroy that city. But the gourd was attacked by a worm, and destroyed as suddenly as it had grown up; as a result Jonah got sunstroke. God then said to Jonah that he had taken pity on Nineveh, just as he forces Jonah to admit that he was sorry for the gourd.

[26] 'To his Excellency Oliver Cromwell, General of the Commonwealth's Army' (*Works*, 505; Hill, 280).

man shall have any Title of Honor till he win it by industry, or come to it by age, or Office-bearing. Every man that is above sixty years of age shall have respect as a man of Honor by all others that are younger, as is shewed hereafter.[27]

Once again he emphasizes that the individual family and household are to be maintained, and that the private sector is to be allowed to continue for an interim period: 'for others . . . let them stay in the way of buying and selling . . . till they be willing.'[28]

There is certainly far more about law and order and the mechanisms of coercion in this tract than in any of his others. And his alleged shift from a belief that human nature itself could and would change spontaneously to an acceptance that social change through state action was the way in which to bring about moral regeneration is what one recent authority means by Winstanley having changed from advocating 'a perfect moral commonwealth' to a 'Utopia'. By the former is meant an ideal society whose character is made possible by a fundamental change in human nature having preceded the creation of a new social order; by the latter one where institutional changes come first and impose a different pattern of behaviour on people whose individual natures remain unchanged.[29] The passage most often quoted in support of this apparent inversion of priorities comes near the beginning of the main text:

I speak now in relation between the Oppressor and the oppressed; the inward bondages I meddle not with in this place, though I am assured that if it be rightly searched into, the inward bondages of the minde, as covetousness, pride, hypocrisie, envy, sorrow, fears, desperation, and madness, are all occasioned by the outward bondage, that one sort of people lay upon another.[30]

And a good deal later in the pamphlet we find the same point being made again in only slightly different words: 'Now this

---

[27] Ibid. (*Works*, 512; Hill, 288).

[28] Ibid. (*Works*, 513; Hill, 290).

[29] J.C. Davis, *Utopia and the Ideal Society. A study of English Utopian Writing 1576–1700* (Cambridge, 1981), especially the introduction, ch. 1, and the conclusion. Despite Dr Davis's learning and eloquence, I do not agree that writers about ideal societies can all be classified in this way; some of them seem to embrace a mixture of his categories (which also include 'millennium', 'arcadia', and 'cockaygne'). [30] Ch. 1 (*Works*, 520; Hill, 296).

same free practice [i.e. of community] will kill covetousness, pride, and oppression.'[31] In far greater detail than before he denies the charges that his system will encourage idleness, sexual promiscuity, or anarchy. Indeed what has recently been called 'true magistracy restored', from the subtitle of *The Law of Freedom*,[32] seems to involve all too much regulation and discipline in order to gain these objectives. And those of us who have lived through the twentieth century may well find him alarmingly naïve in his apparent belief that government action can force people to behave well, can indeed make them good, when the most that it can be expected to do is to limit the amount of harm that they would otherwise do to each other.

So it is very tempting to say that the Digger movement represented an attempt — heroic but doomed to failure — to attain the ideal society through spontaneous popular action, and that its collapse pushed Winstanley back on to a belief in coercive authority instead. But it is not quite as simple as that. He himself tells us in the prefatory letter to Cromwell that a draft, or the notes on which his tract was based, had been written during the period of Digger activity; and it was largely through the apparatus of the coercive state — troops, lawyers, the rights of private landowners, and the consequent employment of both legal action and physical force — that the Diggers were defeated. It therefore seems fair to say that Winstanley was entirely realistic in seeing that a new kind of government and a radically different system of law were prerequisites for the new society which he wished so ardently to see brought into being, but that he was unrealistic if, and in so far as, he believed that such institutional changes would themselves effect a moral revolution within individuals. His conception of 'Commonwealths Government', which he says 'depends not upon the Will of any particular man, or men; for it is seated in the spirit of mankinde',[33] seems all too reminiscent, or rather anticipatory, of Rousseau's 'General Will', and the idea of an infallible Party in the thought of Lenin and his successors. Perhaps more fairly, it can also be likened to a

[31] Ch. 5 (*Works*, 584; Hill, 371).
[32] Davis, 'Winstanley and the Restoration of True Magistracy'.
[33] *Law of Freedom*, ch. 2 (*Works*, 534; Hill, 312).

covenant or contract, made by the members of a 'gathered church' or even a whole community. This heightened sense of unity and conviction of divine purpose can be found in the Mayflower Pilgrims on their way to New Plymouth in 1620, or indeed with the first Christians as they are portrayed in the early chapters of the *Acts of the Apostles.*

Winstanley argues that 'the roots' of law and government are twofold: common preservation and self-preservation, which must inevitably and permanently conflict with each other. Once more his only citations of other authors are biblical. It is a sobering thought that he must have been completing this work and preparing it for submission to Cromwell and then for publication in the very year when Thomas Hobbes's masterpiece of political theory was first published. Winstanley's conviction that 'true magistracy' and tyranny had always been totally distinct seems strange, on the evidence of the Old Testament alone, even without invoking the arguments of *Leviathan.*

What sort of government was it to be on which so much faith was set? His criteria for appointment to public office include tests of moral and political fitness and age (he was himself by this time into his forties); as safeguards against the corrupting effects of power, he prescribed frequent popular elections, by all males over twenty who had not forfeited their own freedoms, and rotation in office, these also being Leveller requirements. As one would expect, much of the work of these elected 'Overseers' was to do with regulating exchange (though not apparently with primary agricultural production), with trades, with training of the young, and with public instruction more generally. By trades he included what we would call manufacture or industry, as well as crafts and skills. We may not all agree whether it was a sign of realism or reaction that the death penalty, specifically banned in *The New Law* (of January 1649) and in *An Appeale to all Englishmen* (of March 1650), was now reintroduced. It was to be reserved for repeated and obdurate offenders and was otherwise limited to rape, murder, and counter-revolution. Attempts to overthrow 'Commonwealths Government' and to reintroduce private ownership, buying and selling, and any machinations towards these ends were to be punished with death. Commerce, as we understand it, indeed as it was practised in Winstanley's time, and most particularly the use of money, were to be strictly limited to state trading with other nations. Here, as elsewhere in his writings, he obviously hoped that the other nations of the world would follow England's example without too long delay, in getting rid of kingly power, and even these narrowly drawn provisos would then be unnecessary. Wars too would come to an end when kingly power had been overthrown everywhere.

By contrast his provisions for education seem altogether more sensible and constructive. This involved what we should call training in civics and current affairs, with much emphasis on science and technology. This part of the work certainly refutes any notion that he wanted a static society whose economy was merely based on subsistence agriculture.[34] Closely linked to education was public instruction and inculcation of the right convictions in young and old alike. His strictly ideological interpretation of the origins and character of religion, as it was professed and practised by the clergy and others under kingly bondage, is worthy of being set beside that of Hobbes in chapter 12 of the *Leviathan*. And his utter disillusionment with the government of the Commonwealth as it actually was in the early 1650s is well summed up in the section headed 'An Army may be Murtherers and unlawful'.[35] Much of the education and training envisaged seems to be aimed at preventing 'idleness and Machivilian cheats'. The nearest that Winstanley comes to explaining how the economy will operate is to be found in his sections on the two kinds of storehouses, how these were to be supplied and drawn upon. The stern provisions against idleness seem to imply exchange based on units of work or productivity: 'for as other men partakes of their labours, it is reason they should partake of other mens.' And, over and above the emphasis on age and experience, a measure of specialization seems to be permitted, since some will have more aptitude to manage storehouses than others.[36]

[34] *Law of Freedom*, the latter part of ch. 4 and part of ch. 5 (*Works*, 562-71, 576-80; Hill, 345-56, 361-6).
[35] Ibid. (*Works*, 574; Hill, 359).
[36] Ibid. ch. 5 (*Works*, 581-4; Hill, 367-71).

Finally Winstanley tried to sum up his programme or 'platform', as he prefers to call it, as the means to the society he wants. Under the heading 'What may be those particular Laws, or such a method of Laws, whereby a Commonwealth may be governed', there follow sixty-two brief statements recapitulating the whole argument.[37] At one point earlier in the pamphlet, this 'Platform of Government', or 'Model' as he also terms it, is offered as desirable, even if buying and selling (and so private ownership of land) still continue; it is not quite clear but presumably this can only apply to the constitutional and other administrative arrangements for office-holders, Parliament, and Army set out in chapter 4.[38] It is difficult to give Winstanley's thought a greater consistency than it had if this work, the Digger pamphlets (or anyway some of them), and *Fire in the Bush* were all being composed concurrently and not consecutively. If historians of thought are correct in their belief that *The Law of Freedom* is his most important work, it is also his most disappointing.

How much connection was there between Winstanley's ideas and those of the Levellers? The Diggers actually called themselves 'the True Levellers'; but it does not necessarily follow from this alone that the more radical of the Levellers were somehow nearer to Winstanley in their convictions than they were to Lilburne himself, which seems to be the argument developed in part of Christopher Hill's *The World Turned Upside Down*.[39] A few Leveller publications do call for the restoration of wrongly enclosed commons, but there is no suggestion of abolishing private ownership of land and practising communal cultivation.[40] The Levellers found it necessary to disavow 'the levelling of men's estates and making all things common', before Winstanley had come out in favour of 'community' and 'the earth as a common treasury'.[41]

---

[37] At the end of ch. 6 (*Works*, 591-600; Hill, 379-89).

[38] Ibid. ch. 5 (*Works*, 581; Hill, 367).

[39] Especially ch. 7.

[40] 'Certain Articles for the good of the Commonwealth' at the end of Overton's *Appeale from the Degenerate Representative Body . . . to . . . The free People . . . of England* (July 1647), in Aylmer (ed.), *The Levellers in the English Revolution* (1975), 87; *The Humble Petition of divers wel affected Persons* (Sept. 1648), in Aylmer (ed.), *Levellers*, 135-6.

[41] *The Humble Petition*, in Aylmer (ed.), *Levellers*, 136.

One of their later pamphlets, probably drafted by Walwyn, leaves the door open for communism if it can be established by universal consent, as against its being imposed by Parliament, even by a reformed, more democratic Parliament.[42] And the idea of a link or overlap between the more radical Levellers and the Diggers is strengthened by the three Buckinghamshire pamphlets of 1648-9. These seem to emphasize economic grievances, especially against lords of manors, more than most Leveller writings, and to anticipate some of Winstanley's and the Diggers' ideas.[43] In the third of them, which was acquired by Thomason on 10 May 1649, there is both an appeal on behalf of the Leveller leaders then under arrest in the Tower of London and what may be a reference to the Diggers: 'We . . . likewise will further and help the said poor to manure, dig, etc., the said Commons, and to fell those woods growing thereon to help them to a stock.'[44] So the Buckinghamshire group may well have had links with both Diggers and Levellers. On the other hand, there is nothing in these pamphlets — still less in the works of Overton or Walwyn — like the ideas most characteristic of Winstanley: the nature of the Fall or curse, and the way in which it is to be overcome. The differences are not just in style and idiom but in fundamental matters of content. The nearest approach to Winstanley's ideas is found in the anonymous *Tyranipocrit* of August 1649. H.N. Brailsford and O. Lutaud have argued that its author was in fact William Walwyn. It is certainly a remarkable work which attacks both the theology of predestination and the imperialism of Europeans exercised over other races and which advocates the relative equalization of incomes. But even here we do not find open support for common ownership.[45]

[42] *A Manifestation* (Apr. 1649), in Aylmer (ed.), *Levellers,* 153-4.
[43] *Light Shining in Buckingham-shire* (Dec. 1648); *More Light Shining in Buckingham-shire* (Mar. 1649); *A Declaration of the Wel-affected in the County of Buckinghamshire* (May 1649), in *Works,* 609-47.
[44] Works, 646-7.
[45] The complete text has never been reprinted. For part of it see G. Orwell and R. Reynolds (eds.), *British Pamphleteers,* i (1948), 81-112. The pamphlet is written around the familiar sixteenth-seventeenth-century theme that the white devil of hypocrisy is worse than the black devil of tyranny.

VIII

Soon after the end of the Digger experiment, Winstanley moved to Hertfordshire with some of his companions. He took up work, as a kind of overseer and rent collector for an eccentric aristocratic prophetess, Lady Eleanor Douglas. She appears to have accused him of falsifying his accounts, and in reply he wrote a long — and characteristic — letter denouncing her and denying these charges. This episode may seem no more than a sad and silly quarrel between two religious enthusiasts, but we find even here echoes of the style and imagery used in his major writings: 'Surely', he writes, 'you have lost the Breeches which is indeed true Reason, the strength of A man. And you must wear the long coat's tail, till you know yourself.' It may well have been this which gave the ex-Ranter, Laurence Clarkson or Claxton the opportunity to denigrate Winstanley as a backslider, who had taken to tithe-gathering after using the digging as a form of self-advertisement.[46] As with the criticism of those modern historians who think that it was only symbolic, the Diggers' twelve months on the Surrey commons seem a prolonged form of masochism by way of self-advertisement.

The appeal to Cromwell in Winstanley's last published work does not appear to have borne fruit. It is unlikely that the ex-Digger leader was the Mr Winstanley who was consulted by Major-General Skippon on behalf of the Protector's Council in February 1654. This arose from a ban on the import of cotton wool and fustian and the consequent complaints of the Lancashire fustian weavers. This Mr Winstanley is more likely to have been James, a fairly prominent merchant-tailor and brother-in-law of Christopher Love, the Presbyterian minister who was executed in 1651 for having engaged in a royalist conspiracy against the republic.[47] How-

[46] See P.H. Hardacre, 'Gerrard Winstanley in 1650', *Huntington Library Quarterly*, xxii (1959); Hill, 31-2, for the reference to Clarkson's *The Lost Sheep Found* (1660), 27; T. Spencer, 'The History of an Unfortunate Lady', *Harvard Studies and Notes in Philology and Literature*, xx (1938), for the best account of Lady Eleanor's career, the Winstanley episode excepted.

[47] See *CSPD, 1653-4*, 385, 396; *1654*, 73-4. For other references to James Winstanley, see ibid. *1651*, 368; *1652-3*, 228; *1655-6*, 427; *1659-60*, 224.

ever, since our Winstanley was at one time a dealer in fustians (as we know from the first of his two lawsuits, that in 1660), it cannot be completely ruled out. Printed sources for Lancashire show how common the name was, though I have not myself come across another Gerrard, apart from the Digger's son by his second wife.[48]

Winstanley was twice married. It was his first marriage, in 1640, to Susan King, daughter of a London surgeon, which established his connection with the county of Surrey, and almost certainly explains why he went there after his business failure in 1643. His father-in-law actually made over his property in Cobham to Winstanley and his wife in 1657, but he revoked this in his will of 1664, by which time Susan Winstanley was dead. There seem to have been no children by this marriage. Around 1664–5 Winstanley married again. It was probably as a result of his first wife's death and his remarriage that he returned to live in London. By his second wife, Elizabeth Stanley, he had two sons, who outlived him but died in their teens. It was through his second wife's mother's family, called Turner, that Winstanley became embroiled in his capacity as a trustee in the second lawsuit of which we have record, versus the ex-merchant and Herefordshire landowner, Ferdinando Gorges, which was still in progress at the time of his death.[49]

Nor does it seem to be of great consequence how and when Winstanley returned to private business on his own account, or how successful he was at it. That he may latterly have become a corn chandler is no more shocking, and does no more to invalidate his principles, than the fact that Engels was a factory manager in nineteenth-century Manchester. On the other hand, the exact circumstances of his becoming a Quaker would be of interest, because this may be said to represent the final phase of his intellectual and spiritual quest for truth and understanding. Although Dr Reay, the

[48] For example, J. Bankes and E. Kerridge (eds.), *The Early Records of the Bankes family at Winstanley* (Chetham Soc., Remains, 3rd series, xxi, 1973); J. Corry, *The History of Lancashire* (1825), ii. 717–18.

[49] The main authorities for Winstanley's later life are R.T. Vann, in *Journal of the History of Ideas*, xxvi (1965) and J. Alsop in *P. and P.* 82 (1979), the latter being particularly well researched. I dissent only from his conclusion.

co-editor of this volume, has discovered evidence of a possible contact between Winstanley and the early Friends in 1654, it has generally been supposed that he could not already have been a Quaker when he was the plaintiff in a chancery law suit in 1660, because of the Friends' disapproval of litigation and their hostility to the existing legal system.

IX

We must now consider the wider question of why his ideas made so little impact in his own time and immediately after. Although the Diggers caused temporary (and probably needless) alarm among the rulers of the infant Commonwealth in 1649, they never seriously looked like becoming the spearhead of a mass movement. Was this because Winstanley's ideas — embodying the themes of both *Paradise Lost* and *Paradise Regained* within densely packed prose pamphlets — were simply too difficult, or too disturbing for those of his contemporaries who might have responded to his call? Or was it rather the case that — hard as was the lot of many copyholders, cottagers, and landless labourers in mid-seventeenth-century England — the way of life which the Diggers offered was even worse? This certainly is a legitimate reaction to the excellent film *Winstanley* made by K. Brownlow and A. Mollo in 1972. It need not surprise us so much why more people did not want to brave the elements on St George's Hill and Cobham common, as well as braving the neighbouring landowners and their various allies. What is surprising, in view of the probable decline in living standards for many in the previous century or so, and the hard times of 1647-9, is that there were no English *Jacqueries*, nothing remotely comparable to 1381, or even 1536-7 and 1549, and that after 1641-2 there were no anti-enclosure riots on the scale of 1607 (when the Diggers first got, or took their name) or of 1629-31. Although the Diggers were mentioned in a parliamentary debate in 1656, the record of their activities seems to have virtually disappeared from the historical record for over three hundred years. Despite the evidence for the relative popularity of some at least of his pamphlets,

Winstanley's following was so small and his impact so limited that, as was suggested at the beginning of this chapter, his radicalism was not that of a mass movement. Why then has he had so wide an appeal since his rediscovery in the 1890s? Left-wing sentimentalism and a preference for a kind of communism which is 'safe' because it is pacific and patently unrealistic would no doubt be one answer, if a cynical one. Failing that, we are left with what is — at its best — his marvellously vigorous and evocative prose, his passionately sincere concern for the underdog, and his consuming vision of a better world. In the last resort it can only be said that for some people, the present writer included, who remain unmoved, or relatively so by the communism of Plato, More, and Marx, there is a disturbing force and even relevance in Winstanley's vision. He is supremely successful, not in persuading us that either the Englishmen of his own time or those of today should adopt his remedies, but rather in holding a mirror up to us in which we can see all too clearly the vices and defects of both mid-seventeenth- and late-twentieth-century society. An uncompromisingly idealistic revolutionary can perhaps do no more than this; but because perfection is not of this world, we should never discard the imperative to improvement.

5 Seekers and Ranters

J. F. McGregor

I

Historians of popular religion during the English Revolution have largely inherited the problems of the revolutionaries themselves in attempting to reduce to intelligible order the confusing mass of speculation and controversy which followed the collapse of the coercive power of the established church. The religious debates of the 1640s were principally concerned with the true model of church government and it was therefore relatively easy to categorize such denominations as Presbyterian, Independent, and Baptist according to their expression of the congregational principle. But the disparate range of enthusiastic doctrines, not obviously tied to any model of ecclesiastical discipline, created and continues to pose considerable problems of interpretation. Enthusiasm may be defined as the immediate guidance of the Holy Spirit superseding any worldly or scriptural authority. It was intrinsically individualist, anarchic, and generally incompatible with the common discipline of church or sect. Contemporaries, however, were prone to assume that a doctrine required a sect to propagate it. So this mass of enthusiastic sentiment was collected by hostile observers from printed tracts and disputes with individual enthusiasts and reduced to a system of heretical sects said to be sprouting like weeds in the chaotic climate of the civil wars. Some were resurrections of early Christian heterodoxy, displays of the erudition of Puritan divines: Pelagians, Manicheans, and Marcionites infested mid-seventeenth-century England. Others characterized individual causes. John Milton's tracts on divorce were assumed to be the tenets of the Divorcers: Richard Overton's mortalist writings pointed to a sect called Soul-Sleepers.[1]

[1] E. Pagitt, *Heresiography* (1662), 231-4.

Those expressions of enthusiasm for which there appeared
to be some evidence of sectarian organization acquired more
mundane denominations: Quakers, Seekers, and Ranters.
Quaker enthusiasm, the doctrine of the indwelling light, can
be identified from its inception with an informal, evangelical
movement. After the Restoration George Fox adapted that
enthusiasm to accommodate a particularly effective model
of congregational order. His success, however, was unique.
There is little objective evidence that either Seekers or
Ranters formed coherent movements or that they existed in
any considerable numbers. An examination of the source
and context of the types of surviving evidence for the two
sects suggests that they are largely artificial products of the
Puritan heresiographers' methodology; convenient categories
in which to dispose of some of the bewildering variety of
enthusiastic speculation.

II

The essential doctrine of the Seekers, as defined by contemporaries and largely accepted by historians, reflects the
millenarian anticipation of the revolutionary age.[2] Fundamental to the Puritan ideal of establishing godly rule in a
godly society was the necessity to restore the church to its
primitive model. It was not, however, sufficient for the
Puritan churches to constitute themselves according to
Pauline precepts. They had also to identify themselves with
the true saints, the visible church established by the apostles
which had survived the centuries of apostasy and persecution.
Legitimacy came from continuity. The Puritan divines found
their continuity in the tradition of ordination; the separatists
in a heretical tradition which had sustained the faith through
a millennium of popery. The Seeker position was more his-
torically realistic. The true church was defunct, all ordinances
and rituals invalid. The sign of the visible church of Christ
was its possession of the grace given to the apostles and
demonstrated through miracles. Since none of the Puritan

---

[2] Ibid. 233; *A Relation of Severall Heresies* (1646), 15; J. Saltmarsh, *Groanes
for Liberty* (1646), 23; R. Baxter, *A Key for Catholics* (1659), 331–4.

churches claimed such charismatic gifts the Seeker could only withdraw from them and patiently await a new divine dispensation. The Seeker was therefore a defector from the Puritan churches; more importantly he or she was an opponent of all their claims to be the true church. How the Seekers were to organize themselves in this period of millenarian expectation, whether they anticipated a new set of apostles or believed the charismatic spirit of the everlasting gospel would fire the hearts of all believers, these were questions to which commentators were prepared to draw their own conclusions according to their perspectives and prejudices. For there survive no Seeker confessions of faith, no unambiguous statements of the Seeker position as a guide to religious life.[3] It is therefore more prudent to approach the Seekers as the personification of a point of religious debate than as a movement, let alone a sect, professing a particular doctrine.

It is possible to trace the origins of the Seeker position to the debates about the validity of the ordinances inherited from the apostate national church which had been in progress among the London separatist congregations from the mid-1630s. Over the following decade many of the saints rejected infant baptism and gathered in Baptist churches practising the immersion of believers. In 1642 the Independent separatist Praisegod Barbon objected to adult baptism by immersion on the grounds that its practitioners had no 'special and particular warrant from heaven, and a Commission, as John the Baptist had'. Such warrant would not come until the last days which, he reminded the Baptists, they believed to be imminent.[4] Taken out of context, Barbon is expressing the essential Seeker doctrine. Subsequent descriptions of the Seekers frequently refer to their awaiting a commission 'such as John the Baptist had'. But Barbon was no Seeker. He was defending the retention of such ordinances as infant baptism as matters of relative indifference against an innovation, believers' baptism, without

[3] J. Jackson's *A Sober Word to a Serious People* (1650) is usually cited as the classic Seeker manifesto. Jackson, however, sympathized rather than identified with the Seekers.
[4] P. Barbon, *A Discourse tending to prove the Baptisme* (1642), 6-7.

apostolic commission, which was threatening the unity of the separatist saints. There is some evidence that Barbon's plea for unity was counter-productive in that it encouraged a Seeker attitude, a disillusionment with all external worship since none could be guaranteed to be the true sign of a visible church. Such evidence, however, comes largely from the more doctrinaire parties to the separatist debate who were convinced of the sole validity of their version of scriptural ordinances. It is likely that the Seeker emerged as a polemical image designed to warn of the inherent dangers of a wider sentiment represented by Barbon that ordinances were not the substance of the true church. Many Independents doubted whether either form of baptism had scriptural warrant. Some refused to have their children baptized without, as far as we know, succumbing to Seeker doctrine.[5] Whatever defections there were from the separatists' ranks in the early 1640s were more likely to have been the result of disenchantment with their domestic squabbles about the validity of various forms of worship rather than a significant movement of enthusiastic disillusionment with formal worship as such.

By the time the Seekers acquired public notoriety, with the appearance of Thomas Edwards's *Gangraena* in 1646, the conventional definition was well established. *Gangraena* contains frequent anecdotal references to a sect of Seekers. Edwards's principal literary evidence is the tract, no longer extant, by the future Ranter Laurence Clarkson, *The Pilgrimage of Grace, by church cast out, in Christ found, seeking truth* (1646). The passages cited are a confused muddle of Baptist and Seeker doctrines: 'the Saints as pilgrims do wander as in a Temple of smoak, not able to finde Religion, and therefore should not plant it by gathering or building a pretended supposed house, but should wait for the coming of the Spirit, as the Apostles did.'[6] While he was against the use of church ordinances, Clarkson claimed that any person could baptize, but the act, in apostolic manner, had to be accompanied by miracles. In the process of transition

---

[5] M. Tolmie, *The Triumph of the Saints* (Cambridge, 1977), 53–5.

[6] *Gangraena,* i. 28–9. Clarkson later described himself as having been a Seeker in 1646: *The Lost Sheep Found* (1660), 19–20.

from Baptist to enthusiast, Clarkson most closely approximates to the model of a Seeker. Whatever the limitations of his information, Edwards was not slow to bestow the denomination of Seeker on various religious radicals and his attributions have generally survived. Three of the more notable of these Seekers defended themselves against the heresiographers' charges: John Saltmarsh, the Army chaplain; William Walwyn, the Leveller; and William Erbery who was known as the champion of the Seekers. Erbery acknowledged no exclusive doctrinal label although he was accused of more than one heresy. He believed that Christians could 'sit still, in submission and silence, waiting for the Lord to come and reveal himself to them' but his most obvious expressions of resigned waiting were inspired by the defeat of the radical cause in 1653. In the 1640s he was anticipating the imminence of a spiritual millennium, the full revelation of divine glory in the hearts of believers.[7] Saltmarsh described the Seekers in conventional terms as those who 'wait onely in prayer and conference, pretending to no certain determination of things, nor any infallible consequences or interpretations of scripture'. But this he rejected as a 'desert wilderness condition' because the fullness of Christ 'is already in the Saints' and 'all growth, improvement, or reformation that is to be, is onely the revelation or appearance of this'.[8] 'That now in these times there is no such ministry as the Apostles were' seemed to Walwyn self-evident:

yet am I not thereby of the opinion that we may not make use of those things they have left unto us in the scriptures of the mind and will of God. . . . I carry with me in all places a touch-stone that tryeth all things, and labours to hold nothing but what upon plain grounds appeareth good and usefull . . . there are plain usefull doctrines sufficient to give peace to my mind: direction and comfort to my life.[9]

Whether interpreted as right reason, conscience, or spiritual illumination, Walwyn, Saltmarsh, and Erbery promoted the self-sufficiency of personal grace. They did not consider themselves in that state of spiritual limbo and vulnerable

[7] *WTUD* (1972 edn.) 155, 157–8.
[8] J. Saltmarsh, *Sparkles of Glory* (1647), 292, 294, 296.
[9] W. Walwyn, *A Whisper in the eare of Mr. Thomas Edwards* (1646), 6.

quietism conventionally attributed to the Seekers. But the Puritan churches, established on the literal word of Scripture, could not appreciate the distinction.

Each of our alleged Seekers saw some truth in all religious forms. Erbery taught the need to avoid 'one particular manifestation of God' and 'the humane mixtures, adhering thereto' but to see the 'several portions of the same truth, manifesting themselves in the professions other Saints'.[10] Saltmarsh thought 'differences of judgement, and divisions' were 'Gods secreet or engine for discovery, as well as truth, as errour'.[11] Walwyn accepted that he had been accused, on good grounds, of many heresies: 'nor do I take upon me peremptorily to determine what is truth, and what is error, amongst any of them: all have a possibility of error: I judge all Conscienscious.'[12] This personal Christianity, grounded in the principle that there was an element of truth in all religious forms, with its logical requirement of liberty of conscience and worship, presented itself quite differently to the Puritan churches as the typical Seeker position that there was no absolute divine truth, no true visible church, no confidence of sainthood. It was necessarily a doctrine of disillusionment and despair, leading to scepticism and libertinism. 'He that is not a stark Atheist or Infidel', wrote Richard Baxter, 'but believes that he has a soule to save or lose, must needs know the necessity of seeking his salvation in some religion or another.' Baxter identified six 'subdivisions or sects' of Seekers, ranging from those confused by the conflicting claims of rival churches to those who claimed to have 'over-grown the Scripture, Ministry and Ordinances'.[13] Impatience or bewilderment with sectarian bickering, resigned attendance on a new apostolic ministry or addiction to the self-sufficiency of the spirit or private conscience, were equally aspects of the essential Seeker mentality which rejected the secure discipline of church order for, to turn Saltmarsh's phrase against him, 'a desert wildernesse condition'.

[10] *The Testimony of William Erbery* (1658), sig. A3.
[11] J. Saltmarsh, *Dawnings of Light* (1645), 58.
[12] Quoted by A.L. Morton, *The World of the Ranters* (1970), 162.
[13] Baxter, *Key for Catholics*, 331–4.

Erbery, Saltmarsh, and Walwyn are representative of many radicals during the Revolution who refused to accept the exclusive claims of any church or sect. Some were less inhibited in using Seeker principles to defend their position. By arguing that no ministry or conversion was valid without the signs of the apostolic spirit, Clement Writer, a Worcestershire clothier, challenged the various churches to prove their monopoly of the true faith. Edwards reported in 1646 that Writer 'fell to be a Seeker, and is now an anti-Scripturist, a Questionist and Sceptick, and I fear an Atheist'. Those more circumspect than Writer could more safely be accommodated as Seekers: Roger Williams, Richard Coppin, John Webster, William Dell, Giles Randall, and John Milton. Even Oliver Cromwell has been tentatively allotted to the sect for his response to the information that his daughter Elizabeth had adopted Seeker doctrine, probably under the influence of William Erbery.

She sees her own vanity and carnal mind, bewailing it; she seeks after (as I hope also) that which will satisfy. And thus to be a seeker is to be of the best sect next to a finder; and such an one shall every faithful humble seeker be at the end. Happy seeker, happy finder.[14]

The Seeker position was reduced by Cromwell to some very conventional Puritan thoughts on the search for spiritual comfort. In general those described as Seekers shared a common inability to find that comfort in allegiance to a particular church and to some degree a millenarian belief that an age of greater religious understanding was at hand. Otherwise they are characterized by doctrinal diversity. They therefore present problems to historians attempting to impose an analytical structure on the ideas and attitudes of those who rejected organized religion during the Revolution. Baxter's eclectic definition of the Seeker has become a useful portmanteau term to accommodate those who cannot be consigned to some more convenient denominational category. It must be questioned, however, whether a definition constructed by champions of church order, with its implications of spiritual infirmity and moral vulnerability, is an appropriate

---

[14] *Gangraena*, i. 82; *The Writings and Speeches of Oliver Cromwell*, ed. W.C. Abott (Cambridge, Mass., 1937-47), i. 416. For Writer and others who have been described as Seekers, see *WTUD* 153-4.

description of the ideals of such as Milton and Walwyn.

The term has not been applied simply to the notable and the literate. It has, perhaps with more justification, come to describe the indeterminate number of individuals who withdrew from the national church and the Puritan congregations during the revolutionary decades. There is incidental evidence of informal groups of Seekers, occasionally attracted to some charismatic prophet,[15] but rarely much information about their doctrines. The historical convention is that George Fox fashioned the Quaker movement from bands of Seekers, particularly those in north-west England.[16] But most of our evidence for these groups, Friends' spiritual autobiographies and testimonials, was written two or three decades after the events described. (Quaker evangelists reported notably few sightings of Seekers in the 1650s.) These sources follow a conventional pattern, describing a period of fruitless seeking after true religion before a final submission to the light within. They use such phrases as 'a seeking man . . . a true Seeker and Inquirer after the best things'. The first Quaker recruits are generally described in such terms as 'a people that was then seeking after ye Lord'.[17] But it is obviously injudicious to draw doctrinal conclusions from the retrospective accounts of spiritual states. Margaret Fell, Fox's wife, was a Seeker for twenty years while continuing to attend the national church. Thomas Taylor is described as a 'seeking man' while he was apparently the minister of a separatist meeting, albeit one which had abandoned most church ordinances. Other future Quakers drifted into religious groups which had some of the characteristics attributed to the Seekers, although they are closer to the Quaker model. The enthusiasts met in silent meetings, with fasting and prayer, waiting upon the Lord.[18] The Seeker connection is a

---

[15] H. Ellis, *Pseudochristus* (1650), 61-2.

[16] W.C. Braithwaite, *The Beginnings of Quakerism* (Cambridge, 1961 edn.), 26-7. A more recent writer has preferred the term 'separatist': H. Barbour, *The Quakers in Puritan England* (New Haven, 1964), 31.

[17] T. Camm and C. Marshall, *The Memory of the Righteous Revived* (1689), prefatory testimonials (no pagination); T. Taylor, *Truth's Innocency* (1697), sigs. B2, C1; *FPT* 55, 56, 106, 243, 244.

[18] J. Tomkins, *Piety Promoted* (1703); iii. 199; C. Marshall, *Sions Travellers Comforted* (1704), sig. D3ᵛ; *FPT* 18, 52, 124, 235.

convenient explanation of the antecedents and birth of
Quakerism. But the existence of a Seeker movement cannot
be established on the fragile base of the early Quakers'
accounts of their spiritual insecurity before the arrival of
George Fox. These are judgements of hindsight; professions
of faith in the Quaker light.

There was no sect of Seekers in revolutionary England.
There were, however, alienated individuals in plenty for
whom we have no better general category than the heresiographers' definition of the Seeker as a lost, wandering soul,
finding no solace in the discipline of church or sect, anticipating wondrous events in the last days, vulnerable to the
charisma of a crackpot messiah or the solipsism of the divine
inner light. It was a description of their religious attitudes
which few enthusiasts would accept, except in retrospect.
Whether applied to the spiritual state of future Quakers or
to the religious principles of Erbery, Saltmarsh, or Walwyn,
the term requires sufficient qualification to deprive it of
much of its meaning and utility.

III

The problems of interpreting the evidence for Seekers and
Ranters have their similarities. There do, however, survive a
handful of Ranter professions of faith which appeared in
1650.[19] Their authors were not spokesmen for a sect or
movement but prophets of certain universal truths which
they had come to comprehend through personal revelation.
Their tracts differ in style and purpose but present a reasonably consistent set of doctrines. The Ranter prophets were
mystical antinomians: mystical in their claim to have become
one with God; antinomian in denying the reality of sin to the
believer. The spiritual man's freedom from the carnal world
extended to a moral indifference to his behaviour since all
human acts were inspired by God. 'A man as man hath no

---

[19] J. Bauthumley, *The Light and Dark Sides of God*; L. Clarkson, *A Single
Eye*; A. Coppe, *A Fiery Flying Roll*; the anonymous *A Justification of the Mad
Crew*; J. Salmon, *Heights in Depths* (1651), an ambiguous recantation of his lost
Ranter tract, *Divinity Anatomized* (1650).

more power or freedom of will to do evill than he hath to do good', wrote Jacob Bauthumley. Sin, according to Laurence Clarkson, 'hath its conception only in the imagination'.[20] Bauthumley and Joseph Salmon, both soldiers, leaned towards mystical introspection, possibly in reaction to the apparent failure of the radical cause. The spiritual man was indifferent to the material world: possessed by the divine principle, he could not be defiled by any act of the flesh. Bauthumley wrote 'not to countenance any unseemly act or evill in any man'. But Clarkson and Abiezer Coppe, both experienced itinerant preachers, actively demonstrated their belief that 'till acted that so called sin, thou art not delivered from the power of sin'.[21] Clarkson's proclivity was for adultery; Coppe resolved a common Puritan obsession with swearing by public indulgence in mildly blasphemous, ecstatic rants. His gestures characterized the new sect and, with Clarkson's, were the foundation of a popular image of adultery, fornication, drunkenness, and blasphemy justified by religious inspiration. Throughout 1650 the catchpenny news-books were filled with merry tales of Ranter orgies. There were reports of bawdy songs to the tunes of psalms, blasphemous parodies of the eucharist at a dinner of beef and ale before the inevitable couplings when the Ranters exercised their liberty with their fellow creatures.[22]

This fictional detail can disguise the immediate impact of Ranter doctrine on radical Puritanism. John Bunyan remembered in his autobiography the interest which the Ranters' ideas aroused among his peers.[23] Their tracts appear to have had wide circulation both among Baptist congregations and in the Army. Oliver Cromwell conducted a purge of Ranter and similar doctrines, as well as the abominable practices they were supposed to promote, from the ranks of the New Model Army.[24] This interest appears to have been ephemeral;

[20] Bauthumley, *Light and Dark Sides*, 37; Clarkson, *A Single Eye*, 8.
[21] Bauthumley, *Light and Dark Sides*, 39; Clarkson, *A Single Eye*, 14.
[22] *The Ranters Religion* (1650), 8; *The Routing of the Ranters* (1650), 6; *Strange newes from Newgate and the Old-Baily* (1651), 2–3.
[23] J. Bunyan, *Grace Abounding to the Chief of Sinners*, in *Works*, ed. G. Offor (1864), i. 11.
[24] *The Best and Most Perfect Intelligencer*, 1 (1–8 Aug. 1650), 8; *Perfect Diurnall*, 28 (17–24 June 1650), 318–19; *Impartial Scout*, 53 (21–28 June 1650),

no doubt discouraged by the authorities' penal legislation
and exemplary treatment of the Ranter propagandists. There
were no printed tracts after 1650 nor is there any concrete
evidence for an organized Ranter movement apart from the
transient camp followers of Clarkson and the Wiltshire
Ranter Thomas Webb.[25] Yet a popular image of Ranterism
remained as expressions of extreme heterodoxy compatible
with the prophets' doctrines: God as the author of sin; Hell
a figment of the imagination; the Devil a scarecrow; Scripture
at best the writings of other spiritual men useful only to the
uninspired, at worst a pack of lies. Whatever the prevalence
of such sentiment there is no doubt that the Ranters'
notorious reputation was nourished for its polemical utility
in the religious controversies of the Revolution. Puritan
divines blamed Ranterism on the Baptists who in turn identified it with Seekers and Familists.[26] All were to agree that
the Ranters were honest Quakers who did not disguise their
religious anarchy with a veneer of moral righteousness.[27] In
response the Quakers presented the Ranters as the logical
extreme of Calvinist predestination.[28] Royalist propagandists
employed them as satirical material for their theme of a
world turned upside down by the Revolution.[29] Ranters also
demonstrated the decadence of youth and the susceptibility
of 'silly women laden with sins'. Richard Baxter counted
Ranterism among the symptoms of melancholia.[30]

Even with due regard for the polemical nature of many of
our sources, it is difficult to assess the influence of Ranter

219; B. Whitelock, *Memorials of the English Affairs* (1682), 20 June 1650;
HMC, Leyborne-Popham MSS. (1899), 78; C.H. Firth, *Cromwell's Army* (1962),
288-9, 400.

[25] E. Stokes, *The Wiltshire Rant* (1652).
[26] R. Baxter, *The Quakers Catechism* (1655), sig. B1; *Heart-Bleedings for
Professors Abominations* (1650), 12-15.
[27] Pagitt, *Heresiography*, 259; R. Baxter, *Reliquiae Baxterianae* (1696), i.
77; T. Collier, *A Looking-Glasse for the Quakers* (1657), 7.
[28] J. Pitman and J. Batt, *Truth Vindicated* (1658), 23; R. Barclay, *An
Apology for the True Christian Divinity* (1678), 163-6.
[29] *Mercurius Democritus*, 32 (10-17 Nov. 1652), 254; 66 (27 July-3 Aug.
1653), 521-5; *Mercurius Fumigosus*, 68 (5-12 Sept. 1655), 534-6.
[30] R. Abbot, *The Young Mans Warning-piece* (1657), epistle dedicatory;
The Ranters Creed (1651), sig. A; W.M. Lamont, *Richard Baxter and the Millennium* (1979), 40.

doctrine on the religious radicals of the 1650s. One source of information is the prosecutions under the act of August 1650 'against several Atheistical, Blasphemous and Execrable Opinions'.[31] The so-called Blasphemy Act was at least occasioned by the activities of the Ranter prophets and presented a reasonably accurate and dispassionate summary of their doctrines. It condemned the justification through divine inspiration of a variety of offences, from drunkenness and swearing to sodomy and murder; the denial of the reality of sin, Heaven, and Hell. The Act was, however, more than a simple proscription of Ranter doctrine. It was represented in the preamble as one of a series of parliamentary measures towards 'the suppression of Prophaneness, Wickedness, Superstition and Formality', following closely on legislation against adultery and common swearing. The penalty for the first offence, six months in prison or a house of correction, suggests that the Act was as much an instrument of moral reformation as an attempt to extirpate false doctrine. Offenders were subject to much the same treatment as vagrants, beggars, bawds, pilferers, and night-walkers. The Ranter was regarded less as a heretic than as a social deviant. Nevertheless the Blasphemy Act served by default as the legal definition of heresy during the Interregnum, superseding the Presbyterian legislation of 1648, the 'Draconick Ordinance', which too comprehensively proscribed radical Puritan doctrine. The interpretation of the bench is therefore as important for the study of Ranterism as the intentions of the legislators. Magistrates were required to proceed against any who maintained 'him or her self, or any meer Creature, to be very God, or to be Infinite or Almighty, or in Honor, Excellency, Majesty and Power to be equal, and the same with the true God, or that the true God, or the Eternal Majesty dwells in the Creature and no where else'. This definition was flexible enough to accommodate not only Ranterism but a variety of enthusiastic sentiment; both the indwelling light of the Quakers and other claims to a particular monopoly of divine power. The activities of the Ranter leaders coincided with an epidemic of prophets and messiahs, also influenced by the

---

[31] *Acts and Ordinances of the Interregnum 1642-1660*, ed. C.H. Firth and R.S. Rait (1911), ii. 409-12.

momentous events of 1649. The career of the Hampshire pseudo-Christ, William Franklin, was published in May 1650 and probably influenced the framing of the Blasphemy Act.[32] More notorious was John Robins, a small farmer who had settled in London, who claimed that he was God the Father incarnate and that his wife was carrying the new Christ. He was regarded as a Ranter and, like the Ranter leaders, was imprisoned until he recanted.[33] Robins was replaced by other prophets from his London circle, men with more modest aspirations. Thomas Tany, a highly eccentric enthusiast, changed his name to Thereau John, announcing in April 1650 that he was ordained to lead the Jews to Zion. He has been described as a Ranter, more frequently by historians than by his contemporaries.[34] Two other acquaintances of Robins, John Reeve and Lodowick Muggleton, claimed to be the witnesses spoken of in Revelation to whom God had given his final commission. Although imprisoned under the Blasphemy Act, they founded a sect, the Muggletonians, which lingered on until recently in England.[35] From 1649 there emerged in London an interconnected group of religious eccentrics, fanatics, and lunatics whose confused enthusiasm contemporaries found difficult to distinguish from the Ranters. All, however, could be accommodated within the flexible provisions of the Blasphemy Act.

Victims of the Blasphemy Act were accused of a variety of religious and irreligious sentiments. One Harrison was convicted at Chester for asserting 'desperate blasphemous things — as that the soul within a man was God, and that there was neither heaven nor hell but in a man's own self, and some other things very gross'.[36] William Bond, a weaver, was indicted at the Wiltshire Quarter Sessions because he

publicly professed and affirmed that there was no God or power ruling above the planets, no Christ but the sun that shines upon us, that the

[32] Ellis, *Pseudochristus, passim.*

[33] J. Taylor, *Ranters of Both Sexes . . . taken and imprisoned* (1651); *The Ranters Creed* (1651).   [34] For Robins and Tany see *DNB*; *WTUD*.

[35] See C. Hill, B. Reay, and W. Lamont, *The World of the Muggletonians* (1983).

[36] *The Autobiography of Henry Newcome,* ed. R. Parkinson (Chetham Soc., xxvi, 1852), 37.

twelve patriarchs were the twelve houses, that if Scriptures were a
making again Tom Lampire of Melksham would make as good Scripture
as the Bible, that there was neither heaven nor hell but in a man's own
conscience, for if he had a good fortune and did live well in the world
that was heaven, and if he lived poor and miserable that was hell and
death itself, for then he would die like a cow or horse.

Bond combined rustic materialism, at least superficially
similar to Ranterism, with, in the words of Keith Thomas,
'astrology run wild'. His fellow weaver, Thomas Hibbord,
was in trouble for claiming that he would trade all religions
for a jug of beer.[37] The Quaker Francis Ellington was indicted for the sentiments: 'confounded be thee and thy
God, and I trample thee and thy God under my feet'; and
Henry Walker as a gross and revolting blasphemer for writing
to Anne Rose from the East Indies that he had rather be
in bed with her than in paradise with Jesus Christ.[38] The
zealous Puritan magistrate could accommodate radical
enthusiasm, not necessarily Ranterish, incoherent popular
atheism, simple blasphemy, and the crude courtship of
a homesick traveller within the flexible provisions of the
Act. No doubt he made no such fine distinctions: popular
enthusiasm, irreligion, and immorality were all threats to
social order.

A more fertile source for the prevalence of Ranter sentiment is the early literature of the radical sects, the Baptists
and Quakers. The uniquely comprehensive records of the
Fenstanton General Baptist church chronicle between 1651
and 1654 the regular expulsion of members for extreme
enthusiastic opinions, often of the type attributed to Seekers
and Ranters. Most believed that they were inspired by God in
all their actions and that the Scripture was a dead letter. The
opinions of the wife of William Austin who 'looked upon the
scriptures as nothing', trampling them, and faith, under her
feet, who was 'wrapt up in God', 'had lieve be with the devil
as with God himself' and did not care for 'he that died upon

---

[37] *HMC, Various Collections*, i. 132-3; *RDM* (1971 edn.) 385.
[38] *Quarter Sessions Records of the County of Northampton* (Northants.
Rec. Soc., i, 1924), 136; *Middlesex County Records*, iii (Middlesex County Rec.
Soc., 1888), 215-16.

the cross at Jerusalem', are exceptional in their vehemence.[39]
Most opinions from this source reflect the unsophisticated
religious understanding of transient, probably semi-literate,
sect members rather than conscious commitment to Ranter
doctrine. They were justifications for 'forsaking the assembly
of the saints' extracted from them, in their own houses, by
visiting elders subjecting the backsliders to an intimidating
process of admonition, exhortation, and interrogation. The
constant demands to justify themselves from Scripture may
be sufficient to explain some of the extreme, Ranterish
responses. One group refused to come to the congregation to
defend their opinions because the elders would only 'multiply
many scriptures'.[40] It is significant that such cases ceased
immediately with the arrival of Quaker evangelists who made
considerable inroads into the congregation.

After 1655 the blunt, articulate confidence of Quakerism
replaced the crude incoherence, Ranterish in its expression
and implications, as the manner in which Fenstanton's fringe
enthusiasts rejected the authority of sect and Scripture. While
the evidence does not support the general assumption that
the Quakers absorbed many Ranters, contemporary opponents of the new movement thought them simply Ranters
with, in Bunyan's words, 'an outward legal holiness'.[41] In
their concern to refute this common opinion George Fox and
his followers did not define Ranterism with any great pre-
cision. They condemned it as a consequence of the Puritan
belief in justification without sanctification in contrast with
their own pursuit of perfection through the inner light. So
George Fox could describe an orthodox Puritan minister as a
'Ranter in his mind' and radicals who dabbled in the doctrine
of free grace as 'Civil Ranters'. Others were 'partlie of a
Ranting straine' and 'gotten into a notion of Ranterism'.[42]
Like the Muggletonians, the early Quakers encountered the
odd advocate of Ranter doctrine. In general, however,

---

[39] *Records of the Churches of Christ gathered at Fenstanton, Warboys and
Hexham 1644-1720*, ed. E.B. Underhill (1854), 89-90.
[40] Ibid. 8. See *WTUD* 183-4.   [41] Bunyan, *Works*, ii. 182.
[42] *The Journal of George Fox*, ed. J.L. Nickalls (1952), 113; FHL, Swarthmore MSS, i. 134; iii. 50; *The Christian Progress of George Whithead* (1725),
27.

Ranterism was a particularly diffuse element of the anti-christian ungodliness which confronted those who fought the Lamb's War. To Fox it was 'wantonness and drunkenness, and cursed speaking, sporting yourselves in the daytime, following oathes and swearing', indulgence in tobacco and ale as well as singing, dancing, and whistling, particularly while the Quakers were preaching.[43] Invariably the Ranters were described as rude, swinish, and filthy, as indeed was much of the popular opposition which the Quakers encountered. The rustic preachers found London populated with 'rude savage apprentices and young people and Ranters'.[44] Rudeness and Ranterism were practically synonymous; convenient explanations of the abuse, ridicule, and general excitement so often inspired by their dramatic evangelism. The evidence of Quaker sources after 1660, journals and spiritual autobiographies, is less passionate and polemical than the early itinerants' accounts of their contacts with Ranterism but no more objective. In the revolts and schisms which plagued Restoration Quakerism, George Fox and his supporters condemned as Ranters the supporters of the primitive charismatic spirit who opposed the growth of congregational discipline in the movement. The Society of Friends first developed its sense of the past, the desire to document its origins, by way of demonstrating that the dissidents' scruples were simply the principles of the old Ranters. Our sources for the Ranters from the Restoration period, including Fox's own journal, must be judged in the light of this use of Ranterism as a weapon in the movement's domestic disputes.[45]

A gentleman sympathetic to the Quakers was reported by Fox as claiming that 'if God had not raised up this principle of light and life, the nation would have been overspreade with rantisme'.[46] Richard Baxter was of the opinion that 'they were so few and of short continuance that I never saw one of them'. He thought their 'horrid villanies' soon

---

[43] G. Fox and J. Nayler, *A Word from The Lord* (1654), 13; *Journal of George Fox,* ed. Nickalls, 79.

[44] *Letters of Early Friends,* ed. A.R. Barclay (1841), 13.

[45] See my 'Ranterism and the development of early Quakerism', *Journal of Religious History,* ix (1977).

[46] *Journal of George Fox,* ed. Nickalls, 90.

extinguished them.[47] Baxter's assessment is particularly credible since he regarded enthusiasm in general as a Jesuit conspiracy and was unlikely to minimize the strength of its most asocial manifestation. He expressed his opinion in the course of some anecdotal reminiscences about Abiezer Coppe whom he had known as a successful Baptist preacher before the latter's conversion to Ranterism. It may be that Baxter was reluctant to apply a theological label to every scurrilous religious opinion which he encountered. Many of his conservative contemporaries were more convinced that the subversive attitudes of the unlettered and ungodly multitude could find their expression in the doctrines of enthusiasm. Only recently have historians developed a superficially similar interest in the social implications of popular religion and irreligion, particularly since the publication of Christopher Hill's *The World Turned Upside Down* in 1972. Seekers and Ranters are well represented in its pages; the Ranters in particular embodying a plebeian tradition which rejected the fundamental doctrines and institutions of orthodox Christianity. Ranterism articulated the ideology of a counterculture; the society of masterless men and women: the vagrants, itinerants, cottagers, and urban immigrants. Hill catalogues the similarities between expressions of Revolution enthusiasm and popular irreligion as well as the radical social implications of many of the prevailing heresies.[48]

The nature of the evidence for this heretical enthusiasm requires that any assessment of the motives of its adherents must be largely conjectural. Village atheism may have been made articulate by the impact of radical ideas during the Revolution: it may always have been so articulate but silenced by censorship. The rustic materialist may have been influenced by Ranter doctrine: it is more likely that popular irreligion was conceived in Ranter terms by those suspicious, zealous Puritans who observed it. The religious enthusiasts who were attributed with Ranterish opinions may have been spokesmen for a radical popular culture but there are other,

---

[47] *Reliquiae Baxterianae*, i. 77.
[48] See below, ch. 8; *WTUD passim*; Morton, *World of the Ranters*, 70–114.

more immediate, explanations for their sentiments. Much of
it was an inevitable effect of radical preaching, of antinomian
freedom from the moral law, and of the mystical perfectionist
ideal that the spiritual creature could become one with God.
Ranter prophets such as Abiezer Coppe preached an ideology
of liberation from the intolerable guilt and anxiety which
Puritan election could produce. Seeker, Quaker, and Muggletonian doctrines could serve the same purpose. Enthusiasm
was a refuge from both the emotional tyranny of Calvinism
and the collective tyranny of the congregation. The so-called
Seekers and Ranters of the Fenstanton records employed the
rhetoric of enthusiasm to justify the rejection of the rigorous
demands of sect membership. It is even more likely that the
most basic expressions of enthusiasm were no more than
popular attempts to reduce complex and subtle doctrines to
simple terms. Much, however, may have been provoked by
disillusionment with the incessant religious controversies of
the age and the strident claims of competing churches to be
the one true faith. The appeal of enthusiastic sentiment may
have been its obvious, immediate utility, in a variety of
situations, rather than the more profound moral and social
implications drawn out by both heresiographers and
historians.[49]

Perhaps the most confident use which can be made of the
evidence for Seekers and Ranters is in illustrating the mentality of the religious parties which condemned them. Traditional doctrinal definitions were obviously inadequate in
dealing with the chaotic mass of religious speculation during
the 1640s and 1650s. 'Seeker' and 'Ranter' were more

---

[49] 'Heaven was when you were happy in this world, Hell was when you were
miserable, and that was all': quoted by E. Le Roy Ladurie, *Montaillou* (1980 edn.)
320; see also pp. 197, 260–1, 263, 289. A fourteenth-century Pyrenean Cathar
proceeded to develop these sentiments to a degree of indelicacy never attributed
to the Ranters by their most mischievous or imaginative critics. Ladurie's description of the tension between mountain heresy and the orthodoxy of the
plains has obvious parallels with Hill's identification in *WTUD* of radical enthusiasm with the masterless men of heath, forest, and fen. Ladurie does, however,
offer another explanation of such 'Ranterish' sentiment: 'The atmosphere of
mental contestation created by the goodmen [the Cathar priests] undermined
the Catholic monopoly and opened the way to the emergence of pre-existing folk-
lore elements, pre-Christian, non-Christian or anti-Christian' (ibid. 322). There is
some similarity to the situation in Revolutionary England.

functional terms which seemed to represent what conservatives feared would be the subversive consequences of religious freedom. The Seeker in the 1640s epitomized the rejection of the church discipline which was fundamental to the Puritan reform programme. The Ranter in the 1650s characterized the social and moral anarchy which could result from ignorant minds dabbling in the heady doctrines of enthusiasm and, more generally, from the breakdown of traditional authority during the civil wars. The terms were also useful instruments of propaganda to belabour those radical Puritans who supported liberty of conscience and worship. So effective, indeed, were these polemical labels that they were adopted by the sects whose principles they were intended to disparage. The church order of the Baptists, as well as the Presbyterians, was threatened by Seeker individualism. The Quakers had as much reason as the Baptists to fear that their followers might succumb to the extreme antinomianism which had come to be associated with the name of the Ranters. Seekers and Ranters there may have been, but never so many as in the imaginations of those hostile observers on whose evidence we must generally rely. They had, however, significance beyond their numbers in their ability to instil the fear of anarchy in the minds of those, whether Anglican, Presbyterian, Baptist, or Quaker, who sought stability in the flux of revolution.

6 Quakerism and Society

B. Reay

I

In 1652 George Fox and fellow itinerant preachers moved through the rural areas of northern England linking together groups of separatists. This was the beginning of the Quaker movement. These early 'converts' were for the most part ordinary men and women who had spurned the wishes of their betters and who had already rejected much of the ideology and organization of orthodox Puritanism. Many were engaged in some form of agricultural work (either as yeomen or husbandmen). Several, it seems, had in the 1640s been in conflict with landlords over their opposition to excessive rents and manorial services; others had been refusing to pay tithes. From the start the Quaker movement was a movement of political and social as well as religious protest.[1]

Quakerism, then, began in the North. But it was not until 1654 and 1655, with the movement of Quaker preachers southwards, that the movement really made its impact. It was now a national problem rather than a regional nuisance. The prediction of Jeremiah 1:14 had finally proved true: 'That out of THE NORTH AN EVILL SHALL BREAK FORTH UPON ALL THE INHABITANTS OF THE LAND .'[2]

Indeed the Quakers' success was impressive. Within a decade there were certainly from 35,000 to 40,000 Quakers (men, women, and children), perhaps as many as 60,000. They were as numerous as Catholics, more numerous than Fifth Monarchists and Baptists. As Hugh Barbour has suggested, it must at times have seemed as if the whole of England

---

[1] B.G. Blackwood, 'Agrarian Unrest and the Early Lancashire Quakers', *JFHS* li (1965), 72-6; B. Reay, 'Quaker Opposition to Tithes 1652-1660', *P. and P.* 86 (1980), 100, 103-4.

[2] W. Prynne, *The Quakers Unmasked* (1655), 36.

would turn Quaker.[3] Not one county escaped the effects of Quaker proselytizing. Nor did Quakers concentrate on towns and cities; in fact, in contrast with all the stereotypes of early nonconformity as an essentially *urban* affair, the indications are that (although Bristol and London were important Quaker strongholds) Quakerism was predominantly a rural movement. The Quakers, Bernard Capp has reminded us, demonstrated that sectarianism could flourish in the villages.[4] They were the most successful as well as the most radical of the Revolution sects.

Not surprisingly there is no shortage of studies of the early Quakers: from the materialist approach of Eduard Bernstein to Geoffrey Nuttall's concern with the spiritual.[5] Yet it would still be true to say that we have no short survey of early Quaker thought and behaviour, no short synthesis which takes into account recent work on the movement. Nor, as far as I am aware, is there any study which deals with what could be described as the other side of the coin of Quakerism: the image of the early movement, how Quakers were perceived by contemporaries, their actual impact on seventeenth-century politics and society. This essay is an attempt to redress the situation.

II

What sort of people became Quakers? What do we know about their religious and political backgrounds, about the sect's socio-economic composition?

As far as the better-known Quakers are concerned (the 'ministers' and pamphlet writers) the influence of Puritanism is indisputable. Many, like Isaac Penington, had become 'exceedingly entangled' about Calvin's theory of predestination, 'having drunk in that doctrine, according as it was then held forth by the strictest of those that were termed Puritans'. They were thoroughly imbued with the Puritan

---

[3] H. Barbour, *The Quakers in Puritan England* (New Haven, 1964), 182.
[4] B.S. Capp, *The Fifth Monarchy Men* (1972), 79.
[5] E. Bernstein, *Cromwell and Communism* (1963 edn.); G.F. Nuttall, *Studies in Christian Enthusiasm* (Wallingford, 1948).

sense of sin; they despaired of their salvation. George Fox
spent his pre-Quaker days sitting in hollow trees, and tobacco,
psalm-singing, and blood-letting were suggested to him as
potential cures for his despair. Before he became a Quaker
George Rofe was 'smot by the hand of the Lord into many
fears of what should become of me hereafter, and have often
wept exceedingly in secret and in my bed, so that I have
wetted much clothes with teares'.[6] We could go on. Quakerism
was to some extent a reaction to this psychological *malaise*.

Many Quakers began as Presbyterians and then, influenced
by radical Puritan doctrine, Familist ideas, and the translated
works of continental mystics, progressed to sectarianism.
Some were what were called Seekers (those who taught that
people should 'sit still, in submission and silence, waiting for
the Lord to come and reveal himself to them'). When Quakers
entered an area they sometimes carried lists of advanced
separatists residing in that area, those who were most likely
to be receptive to the Quaker message.[7] Again and again they
converted sectaries, sometimes whole meetings: many
Baptists, Seekers, some Ranters and Fifth Monarchists. There
is also some evidence that in Cambridgeshire (and perhaps in
Essex) 'spiritual seeking and unrest was extremely widespread . . . and that the Quaker position was reached, or
nearly reached, *before* the arrival of the Quakers'.[8]

We now know quite a bit about the social origins of the
early Quakers. Although there was regional variation in the
movement's social composition, it seems that it mainly drew
its membership from what were known as the middle sort of
people: wholesale and retail traders, artisans, yeomen,
husbandmen. Those, with the exceptions of Quaker women
and husbandmen, from the more literate, or rather less
illiterate, sections of the population.[9] Few belonged to the

---

[6] R.T. Vann, *The Social Development of English Quakerism* (Cambridge,
Mass., 1969), 22; G. Rofe, *The Righteousnes of God to Man* (1656), 14-15;
Journal of George Fox, ed. J. Nickalls (Cambridge, 1952), 4-9.

[7] Vann, *Social Development*, 10-11.

[8] M. Spufford, *Contrasting Communities* (Cambridge, 1974), 283. For Essex,
see the hints in A. Macfarlane, *The Family Life of Ralph Josselin* (Cambridge,
1970), 26; *The Diary of Ralph Josselin 1616-1683*, ed. A. Macfarlane (1976),
271, 348.

[9] D. Cressy, *Literacy and the Social Order* (Cambridge, 1980), ch. 6.

gentry élite, few to the *labouring* poor. Hearth-tax returns enable a socio-economic profile of the early Quakers in comparison with the general population, and here the evidence is that (again with regional variation) although there were substantial numbers of the poorer sort in the movement most belonged to the relatively comfortable middle section of the community and were slightly wealthier than the population at large.[10]

What else can we say about the early Quakers? As we noted above, several northern Quakers had been involved in anti-tithe activity in their pre-Quaker days. The same was true of other parts of the country: for example, Somerset, Kent, Essex, Suffolk. Many Quakers had a history of active resistance to tithes. Unlike the Levellers, the Quakers responded to agrarian grievances; indeed during the Revolution they were among the most unrelenting opposers of tithes.[11]

Then there were radical political connections. A number of Quakers had been county committee men and sequestrators.[12] The New Model Army was, we shall see, an important source of Quaker recruitment. A few had been in the Navy. John Ward, the vicar of Stratford-upon-Avon (and others), thought that 'Several Levellers setled into Quakers'. Francis Harris and other contemporaries claimed that many Quakers had been Diggers as well as Levellers.[13] Leveller and Digger ideas do crop up in Quaker literature (a comparison between this chapter and the chapter by Brian Manning should make that clear) and we know that the Digger leader Gerrard Winstanley and the Leveller leader John Lilburne became Quakers.[14] But there is no evidence of any real influx.

Finally a sizeable number of women joined the Quaker movement. The sect did not offer them equality but certainly more independence than that offered by society. Quaker

[10] B. Reay, 'The Social Origins of Early Quakerism', *Journal of Interdisciplinary History*, xi (1980).

[11] Reay, 'Quaker Opposition to Tithes', *passim*.

[12] e.g. D. Underdown, *Somerset in the Civil War and Interregnum* (1973), 186.

[13] *Diary of the Rev. John Ward,* ed. C. Severn (1839), 141; F. Harris, *Some Queries* (1655), 23.

[14] J. Alsop, 'Gerrard Winstanley's Later Life', *P. and P.* 82 (1979). The Quaker Christopher Cheesman was also a former Leveller (see Manning, p. 71 above).

women preached, proselytized, wrote and printed tracts, participated in church government (though in separate meetings and mainly in the area of welfare), and assumed a militant role in the sect's various campaigns. Of well over 300 Quakers in trouble for disrupting ministers during the period 1654 to 1659, 34 per cent were women; of the fifty-nine Quaker ministers who arrived in America during the period 1656 to 1663, 45 per cent were women. Gone was the old precept: 'Let your women learn in silence, with all subjection.'[15]

III

The Quakers of the Interregnum were not preoccupied with theology; it was only later, in the 1670s, that they set out their religious doctrine in any systematic form. Before that, in the words of Christopher Hill, they usually defined their beliefs 'defensively, by negatives'.[16]

Quakers rejected predestinarian doctrine and proclaimed the possibility of salvation for all. 'God woulde have all men to bee saved Marke all men.' Calvin's theory of predestination, they argued, would have God 'the most Cruel of all Beings'. They urged men and women to turn to the light, Christ, spirit within (they used the terms interchangeably). We 'call All men to look to the Light within their own consciences', wrote the Quaker Samuel Fisher; 'by the leadings of that Light, if they will, they may come to God, and work out their Salvation'.[17]

There was a strong sense of unity with God. Not all Quakers were as outspoken as Thomas Holme who declared that he was 'above St. Peter & equall wth god', but most would have agreed with Fox when he said that 'He that

---

[15] Vann, *Social Development*, 81-2; K. Thomas, 'Women and the Civil War Sects', in T. Aston (ed.), *Crisis in Europe* (1970), 324-6; M.M. Dunn, 'Saints and Sisters', *American Quarterly*, xxx (1980), 595-601. The figures for disruption of ministers are my own calculations from GBS i, ii.

[16] *WTUD* (1972 edn.) 190.

[17] *The Journal of George Fox*, ed. N. Penney (NY, 1973), ii. 149; W. P[enn]., *The New Witnesses Proved Old Hereticks* (1672), 27, 33; S. Fisher, *Rusticus Ad Academicos* (1660), sig. B3.

sanctifieth, and they that are sanctified, are of one, and the Saints are all one in the Father and the Son.' Quaker schismatics were said to have forsaken 'the devine sap & vertue of Crist Jeesus'.[18]

The notion of the light within — an extension of the Puritan emphasis on the Holy Spirit[19] — is central to Quaker religious ideology. They were spiritual millenarians. 'The coming of Christ in the flesh . . . was one coming . . . and his appearance in Spirit to save his people from sin; is another coming', wrote George Whitehead in 1660. Christ had come in Quakers and would come in others; social and political change would accompany this inward millennium.[20]

Like other radicals, the Quakers thought that the spirit was above the Scriptures. It was the uneducated man's and woman's way of rejecting the hegemony of a learned élite. The emphasis varied. Barbara Siddall said that the Bible was 'not the word of God but onely a dead letter'; Katherine Crook, 'Shee had Knowne ye Lord if Shee had never seene nor read ye Scriptures.' Other Quakers would have been shocked by such talk, but again few would have argued with Fox's claim that it was 'not the letter, nor the writing of the Scripture, but the ingrafted Word is able to save your soules'.[21] Indeed Samuel Fisher was to subject the Bible to close critical analysis. The effect, according to Christopher Hill, was to 'demote the Bible from its central position in the protestant scheme of things, to make it a book like any other'.[22]

The sect rejected conventional ideas about the Trinity: the doctrine of three distinguishable identities. 'God and the

[18] Cheshire RO, QJF 82/4/39; G. Fox *et al., Saul's Errand to Damascus* (1654), 10-11; *JFHS* xiv (1919), 144.

[19] See G.F. Nuttall, *The Holy Spirit in Puritan Faith and Experience* (Oxford, 1946).

[20] See T.L. Underwood, 'Early Quaker Eschatology', in P. Toon (ed.), *Puritans, the Millennium and the Future of Israel* (1970), 98.

[21] PRO, Assi 44/6; FHL, Swarthmore MS iv. 52; G.F[ox]., *A Declaration of the Difference* (1656), 12. George Keith, who led a schism in Pennsylvania in the 1690s, was to complain that large numbers of Quakers slighted the Bible: J. Butler, ' "Gospel Order Improved": The Keithian Schism and the Exercise of Quaker Ministerial Authority in Pennsylvania', *William and Mary Quarterly*, xxxi (1974), 434.

[22] *WTUD* 214.

Spirit hath no Person, nor cannot truly be distinguished into Persons.'[23] Francis Howgil, one of the better-known Quakers, disregarded notions of 'God at a distance'. As far as Christ was concerned, T.L. Underwood has explained, 'the outward physical work of Christ in the past was of little consequence without an inward, spiritual experience of Christ by men in the present'.[24] The implication was that the historic role of Christ was of little more import than the role of any leading Quaker.

Quaker eschatology was equally unorthodox. The tendency was to internalize, with the emphasis once again upon the present. They did not actually deny that there would be a Final Judgement and resurrection, but the stress was on the resurrection and judgement within each Quaker. 'The great judgment is already begun (this we know, who have tasted of it).'[25] There was a tendency to talk of Heaven and Hell as internal states. Heaven was in the hearts of God's people: Hell was to be found in the conscience of every malefactor. Nathaniel Smith claimed that he was attracted to Quakerism because of its belief that 'the Kingdom of Heaven was in Man'.[26]

IV

People are not always aware that the early Quakers were essentially an ecstatic movement, that like the Shakers their name derives from their behaviour — that is, trembling and shaking. Quaking was an outward manifestation of the inward workings of the power of God. In London in 1654 when Quakers first visited the city, women cried while Richard Hubberthorne preached and Edward Burrough trembled; 'almost all ye Roome was Shaken', Richard Farnworth reported of another early meeting, this time in Yorkshire.[27]

[23] Edward Burrough, quoted in Barbour, *Quakers*, 145.
[24] F. Howgil, *The Inheritance of Jacob* (1656), [21]; Underwood, 'Early Quaker Eschatology', 96.
[25] Isaac Penington, quoted in Underwood, 'Early Quaker Eschatology', 102.
[26] Barbour, *Quakers*, 187; N. Smith, *The Quakers Spiritual Court* [1668], 1.
[27] FHL, William Caton MS iii. 143–4; Swarthmore MS iv. 83.

Quaker perfectionism (the doctrine that believers could become free from sin), their belief in the potential powers of the light within, could lead to bizarre behaviour. The spirit within 'moved' the one-time Quaker John Toldervy to put his hand in a pan of boiling water, to burn his leg by the fire, and to thrust a needle into his thumbs (to the bone).[28]

Toldervy's test of endurance was unusual and he was on the fringes of the movement. Yet better-known Quakers did find it necessary to demonstrate divine approval. Christ had fasted: so could the Quakers. James Nayler, Fox, and many others fasted for seven, twelve, and even twenty days. Richard Hubberthorne was so weak after a fast 'people thought hee was dead'. James Parnell did die (in Colchester gaol) after taking nothing but water for ten days.[29]

Some claimed the ability to heal and work miracles. As Farnworth wrote, God manifested his power in 'his servants' so that they could 'lay hands on the sick, and recover them, as the Apostles did'.[30] There are traces too of the Hermetic tradition, a belief that man has fallen out with the creation but that in a state of perfection (of restoration) unity can once more be achieved and nature's secrets revealed.[31] A few Quaker women claimed that they had experienced painless childbirth.[32] Fox kept a record of his cures, some 150 in all: smallpox, scrofula (the King's Evil), dumbness, ague, toothache, the stone, convulsions, scabs, headache, ulcers, gout, blindness, paralysis, a broken neck. Few claimed the successes of Fox. Francis Howgil failed in his attempt to cure a lame boy: 'the boy stode up but . . . he fayled and sat downe agayne.'[33] One or two were even more ambitious and attempted to raise the dead. A Worcester Quaker dug up the corpse of a Quaker apprentice and 'commanded him in the

[28] J. Toldervy, *The Foot out of the Snare* (1656), 35-7.
[29] G.F. Nuttall, *James Nayler: a Fresh Approach* (1954), 9; K.L. Carroll, 'Quaker Attitudes towards Signs and Wonders', *JFHS* liv (1977), 74-6.
[30] R. F[arnworth]., *Antichrists Man of War* (1655), 62.
[31] G.F. Nuttall, 'Unity with the creation: George Fox and the Hermetic Philosophy', *Friends' Quarterly*, i (1942).
[32] *George Fox's 'Book of Miracles'*, ed. H.J. Cadbury (NY, 1973), 22-3; FHL, Swarthmore MS iii. 158.
[33] *George Fox's 'Book of Miracles'*, *passim*; *RDM* (1973 edn.) 149; FHL, A.R. Barclay MS 21.

name of the living God, to arise and walk'. It was said that
Quakers travelled to Colchester to see the resurrection of their
co-religionist James Parnell after his death in prison in 1656.[34]

V

The success of Quakerism, Christopher Hill has reminded us,
witnessed to the continued existence of the radicalism of the
1640s.[35] Perhaps Winstanley had this in mind in 1654 when
he told the Quaker Edward Burrough that the Quakers were
carrying on the work of the Diggers.[36]

Certainly the Quakers inherited the anticlericalism of the
Revolution radicals. The clergy were more concerned with
their bellies than with their parishioners' souls. When a priest
dies, Fox wrote, his colleagues scramble for his benefice;
'they are like a company of crowes when a rotten sheepe is
deade they all gather togeather to plucke out his puddinges'.[37]
Through the system of tithes, priests were maintained in
'idleness' by the 'labours of poor people'. The church owed
its wealth to the labour of others. 'From whence I pray were
these [riches] squeezed', Thomas Ellwood asked, 'was it not
from the people?'[38] Quakers called for the disestablishment
of the state church and the abolition of tithes. Men and
women should hire their own ministers or else ministers
should labour to support themselves. The Quakers wanted
a movement away from the university-bred, privileged clergy
towards a ministry of simple men and women 'who spoke
plaine words, and reached to the consciences of men of the
meanest capacity'.[39] During the Revolution, the Quakers
became a pressure group campaigning for the overthrow of

[34] *George Fox's 'Book of Miracles'*, 14-15; *Diary of Ralph Josselin*, 367.
[35] *WTUD* 193.
[36] 'Wilstandley [i.e. Gerrard Winstanley] sayes he beleeves we are sent to perfect that worke which fell in their [i.e. the Diggers'] handes hee hath bene with
us': FHL, William Caton MS iii. 147.
[37] Reay, 'Quaker Opposition to Tithes', 107; *Journal of George Fox*, ed.
Penney, i. 195.
[38] E. Burrough, *A Just and Lawful Tryal* (1660), 5; T. Ellwood, *The Foundation of Tythes Shaken* (1678), 446.
[39] F. H[owgil]., *The Great Case of Tythes* (1665), 55.

tithes: bombarding those in power with anti-tithe propaganda, organizing petitions, supporting parliamentary candidates who were likely to be sympathetic to their cause, and, above all, refusing to pay tithes and inciting others to resist.[40]

But Quaker social comment was not limited to criticism of the church and ministry. Some Quakers spoke out bravely against the nobility and gentry, claiming that they either owed their position to the Norman Conquest when their ancestors 'killed an English man, and took his possession', or they had founded their families on 'fraud, deceit, and oppression'. The 'Clargey & ye gentry, hath ye land betwixt them', wrote Elizabeth Hooton. Edward Billing approved of the sentiments of those who had said that it 'would never be a good World so long as there was a Lord in England'; 'for the whole rabble of Duke, Marquesse, Lord, Knight Gentleman by patents; I find no room . . . in Scripture'.[41]

The law (the 'badge of the conquerour' according to Billing) also kept 'the poore people in bondage'. For the poor 'the remedy is frequently worse then the desease' when it came to using the law. Like property, protection of the law was the prerogative of a few — 'the rich bears with the rich, and the poor have been trodden underfoot'.[42] Instead of 'covering the naked, and feeding the hungry, you set out Laws to punish them', Benjamin Nicholson complained in a pamphlet aimed at the magistrates of England. Quakers advocated the removal of lawyers, trial by jury, Anglicization and codification of the law ('let all be drawn up in a little short Volumn, and all the rest burnt').[43]

We can get some idea of the sort of society the Quakers would have envisaged. There would have been some redistribution of wealth. Quakerism, Fox explained, was opposed to those who 'have long cumbered the ground'; 'such

---

[40] See my 'Quaker Opposition to Tithes', *passim*.

[41] E. B[illing]., *A Word of Reproof* (1659), 10, 73, 77-8; J. Parnell, *The Trumpet of the Lord* (1655), 1; FHL, MS Portfolio iii. 5.

[42] Billing, *Word of Reproof*, 20; FHL, MS Portfolio iii. 5; E. B[illing?]., *A Declaration of the Present Sufferings* (1659), 27-8; G.F[ox and P.M.]., *An Instruction to Judges & Lawyers* (n.d.), 27-8.

[43] B. Nicholson, *A Blast from the Lord* (1653), 10; G. F[ox]., *To the Parliament . . . Fifty nine Particulars* (1659), 4-5; E. B[illing]., *A Mite of Affection* (1659), 2-3, 5; G. Fox, *Several Papers Given Forth* (1660), 32-3.

are harlotted from the truth, and such gets the earth under their hands, Commons, Wastes and Forrest, and Fels, and Mores, and Mountaines, and lets it lye wast, and calls themselves Lords of it, and keeps it from the people, when so many are ready to starve and begg'. 'You wallow your selves in the earths treasure like swine in the mire', Nicholson told the gentry, 'and never consider that the earth is the Lords . . . and that he hath given it to the sons of men in general, and not to a few lofty ones which Lord it over their brethren.'[44] In 1659 Fox suggested that old monastic properties and glebes should be given to the poor, that 'great houses', churches, even Whitehall, should be converted into almshouses. Benjamin Furly was to suggest that a form of income tax could finance hospitals, free-schools, and alms-houses.[45] Those who 'are taught of Christ' must make themselves 'equall with them of the lower sort'.[46] This statement reveals more than it intends. The Quakers were not communists: they probably had in mind a nation of small producers, with some limitations on the accumulation of wealth.

Quaker political allegiances were relatively uncomplicated. The civil wars, according to Fox the younger, had been fought between (on one side) those 'accounted the wisest, richest, noblest and stoutest men' who 'did glory in their Wisdome, Riches, Nobility . . . and vaunted themselves over them that were made of the same Blood', and (on the other side) the 'contemptible Instruments, (as to outward appearance) as in Tradesmen, Plough-men, Servants, and the like, with some others'. The Quakers left no doubt that they were against 'the tyrannicall Kings and bloody Bishops'.[47] The Revolution had gone smoothly with the execution of the King, destruction of episcopacy, and abolition of the House of Lords. But it had halted midway with, Joseph Fuce seems to suggest, the defeat of the Levellers at the end of the 1640s.[48] Cromwell had been God's instrument, and despite some

---

[44] G. F[ox]., *A Declaration Against all Profession and Professors* (1655), 12; Nicholson, *A blast,* 10.

[45] Fox, *Fifty nine Particulars,* 8; M. Cranston, *John Locke* (1957), 281.

[46] FHL, A.R. Barclay MS 167.

[47] G. Fox the younger, *A Noble Salutation* (1660), 5; *The Lambs Defence Against Lyes* (1656), 21.   [48] J. Fuce, *A Visitation* (1659), 2.

complaints Quakers served in the Protector's commission of the peace and in the Army and Navy until they were purged. Though far from satisfied with the Protectorate, the Quakers would do nothing to bring it down if it meant the return of the Royalists.

Yet Quakerism is devoid of any coherent and identifiable political philosophy. Their attachment to parliamentary democracy varied, as did that of many of the radicals at this time. Some Quakers were willing to use the parliamentary system.[49] When in 1659 republican agitation in the Army did annual parliaments and rationalization of the electoral system.[49] When in 1659 republican agitation in the army did bring down the Cromwellian regime, Quakers declared their willingness to serve the republican cause, with some, it seems, taking up positions in the militia and Army. But there was also a tendency in 1659 to support intervention against Parliament if it looked like furthering radicalism. According to Francis Howgil it was no crime to remove parliaments when they 'will not hearken to the cry of their Masters [the People]'.[50] George Fox the younger condemned the parliamentary system as the agency of the propertied and suggested instead a benevolent dictatorship, acting on behalf of the people.[51]

The Quakers of the 1650s were not consistent pacifists. True, some do seem to have reached the pacifist position before 1660.[52] But most were either concerned with stressing the peaceful nature of the movement rather than the sect's opposition to the use of force under any circumstances (the distinction is important); or they were making statements approaching that of Edward Burrough, who told those in power in 1659 that if they would 'establish Righteousnesse' they were assured of Quaker support: 'Oh then we should rejoyce, and our lives would not bee Deare to lay downe.'[53]

[49] Billing, *Mite of Affection, passim.*

[50] Quoted in A. Cole, 'The Quakers and the English Revolution', in Aston (ed.), *Crisis in Europe*, 352.

[51] G. Fox the younger, *A Few Plain Words* (1659), 1-3.

[52] For example: *The Resurrection of John Lilburne* (1656), 10; J. Harwood, *To All People* (1663), 4; J. Price, *The Mystery and Method of his Majesty's Happy Restauration* (1680), 31.

[53] B. Reay, 'The Quakers and 1659: two newly discovered broadsides by Edward Burrough', *JFHS* liv (1977), 110.

It is not until 1661 that we get, in Hill's words, the first 'official declaration of absolute pacifism in all circumstances'.[54] Before that time it is impossible to talk, as it is later, of the Quakers as a predominantly pacifist group. Self-preservation after the restoration of the monarchy in 1660, disillusionment with the effectiveness of political action, encouraged them to project their pacifism backwards. 'Pacifism was not a characteristic of the early Quakers: it was forced upon them by the hostility of the outside world.'[55]

VI

So much for Quaker ideology and activity; but what of the movement's actual impact? Obviously the arrival of the Quakers in the 1650s brought mixed reactions. Yet if we had to weigh support against hostility, the scales would tip in favour of hostility and fear. The Quaker threat — it was seen as a threat — had to be faced at all levels of political power: in the Army, in the borough and county communities, and in London.

Quaker successes in the Army were perhaps predictable, for the New Model Army was an acknowledged breeding-ground for radical ideas. Garrison commanders were not always sympathetic, but Quakers got a lot of support from officers and the rank and file. Quaker letters and journals mention progress during the 1650s in garrisons in York, Bristol, Holy Island and Berwick-upon-Tweed (Northumberland), Lancaster, Carlisle, Chester, Kent, Northamptonshire, Norfolk, London, Shrewsbury.[56]

The Quakers were most successful in the garrison towns of Ireland and Scotland — and it is in these places that we know most about their activity, mainly because of the reactions of

[54] *WTUD* 194.

[55] A. Cole, 'The Quakers and Politics, 1652–1660' (Univ. of Cambridge Ph.D. thesis, 1955), 284; Cole, 'Quakers and the English Revolution', 346.

[56] FHL, Swarthmore MS i. 373; R. Farmer, *Sathan Inthron'd* (1657), 56; G. Whitehead, *The Christian Progress of that Ancient Servant* (1725), 125; *Journal of George Fox*, ed. Penney, i. 52, 110, 114–15, 181, 183, 189; Swarthmore MS i. 179; iii. 80, 151; iv. 69, 141, 170.

certain officers. The peak of Quaker activity in Ireland was in 1655 and 1656; and the sect enjoyed some influential support.[57] Colonel Nicholas Kempson (brother-in-law of the better-known Edmund Ludlow) encouraged Quaker settlement in Cavan, 'promising he would build a meeting-house and do great Matters to promote Truth'. The governor of Cork, Robert Phayre, later to become a Muggletonian, was reported as saying that 'more is done by the Quakers than all the priests in the country have done in a hundred years'. The governor of Kinsale, Richard Hodden, kept a Quaker to preach to his troops and even hinted to Henry Cromwell (Lord Deputy of Ireland) that he should encourage Quaker settlement.[58] We know of meetings and conversions, mainly of soldiers, in Cork, Kinsale, Youghal, Cashell, Limerick, Bandon, Londonderry, Belturbet, Cavan, Dublin, Galway, Wexford, New Ross, Mountmellick, and Kilkenny.[59]

A similar kind of success was reported in Scotland in 1657, again with support in high places. The order books of General George Monck, the commander of the regiments in Scotland, provide clues to Quaker penetration, for Monck was to purge Quakers from his army. Though not numerous — about forty Quaker soldiers were purged — Quaker converts were widespread. Three of his five regiments of horse were affected; five of his eleven foot regiments; and his regiment of dragoons. If Monck had not acted the indications are that his forces would have become riddled with Quakers.[60]

Both Henry Cromwell (in Ireland) and George Monck (in Scotland) moved against what they perceived to be Quaker subversion of their regiments. Occasionally, it is true, military protection of Quakerism had brought conflict with the civilian population or even clashes between fellow soldiers.[61]

[57] For Ireland, see K.L. Carroll, 'Quakerism and the Cromwellian Army in Ireland', *JFHS* liv (1978).

[58] *A Journal of . . . William Edmundson* (1715), 28-9; FHL, A.R. Barclay MS 61; BL, Lansdowne MS 821, fo. 68.

[59] See B. Reay, 'Early Quaker Activity and Reactions to it, 1652-1664' (Univ. of Oxford D. Phil. thesis, 1979), 59-62.

[60] Worcester College Library (Oxford), Clarke MS 48: 2, 13, 27 Mar.; 9, 15, 18, 20, 25, 29 May; 6, 16, 26, 27, 31 Oct.; 2, 20, 21, 23 Nov. 1657.

[61] See, for example: W. Stockdale *et al., The Doctrines and Principles of the Priests of Scotland* (1659), 5; *Thurloe,* iv. 672, 757; *Mercurius Politicus,* 307 (24 Apr.-1 May 1656), 6940.

Yet it was probably fear of ideological contamination rather
than a few sporadic outbursts of disorder which convinced
Monck and Cromwell to act. The Quaker soldier's refusal of
the customary compliments due to a superior, and the
Quaker officer's deeming of such compliments to be unnecessary, were certainly not conducive to military discipline.
'Our most considerable enemy nowe in our view are the
quakers', Henry Cromwell wrote in 1656, 'I thinke their
principles and practises are not verry consistent with civil
government, much less with the discipline of an army.'
Quaker insubordination reminded one of Monck's commanders of 'that factious temper of the army about the tyme
the levellers appeared at the first'; 'the levellinge principle
lyes at the bottome'.[62] Monck agreed. 'Truly I thinke they
will prove a very dangerous people, should they increase in
your army', he wrote in a letter to Oliver Cromwell, 'and
be neither fitt to command nor obey, but ready to make a
distraction in the army, and a mutiny uppon every slight
occasion.'[63] So the ranks of the Irish and Scottish regiments
were purged; Quaker officers were cashiered.

VII

There was great variation in the gentry's response to Quaker
penetration of the provinces. Influential radical support
could stave off persecution and encourage Quaker growth.
John Herring, who represented Herefordshire in the short-
lived Barebone's Parliament of 1653, and Henry Smith,
former member for Leicestershire in the Rump Parliament of
1649-53 and a radical republican associate of the Levellers,
both allowed Quakers to meet in their homes.[64] In Bristol in
1654, where in the words of Alan Cole 'the bulk of the
Radical party were among the earliest converts to the new
religion' (garrison commanders, a former MP, the wife of an
assize judge, a high-ranking government bureaucrat), the
common council was eager to rid the city of Quakerism but

---

[62] *Thurloe*, iv. 508; vi. 168.   [63] Ibid. vi. 136.
[64] FHL, Luke Howard MS 7; 'Swarthmore MS Letters of John Audland',
ed. C. Horle (typescript, FHL, 1975), no. 18.

felt inhibited by the sect's influential allies. Colonel Adrian
Scrope, in charge of the army in Bristol, had said that 'if the
Magistrates did put them [the Quakers] in prison one day, he
would put them out the next'.[65] There is evidence of similar
influences in Lancashire and Cheshire, mainly because of the
presence — in the Lancashire Quarter Sessions and the Cheshire
Assizes — of Thomas Fell (his wife was later to marry George
Fox) and the regicide John Bradshaw. In 1655, when Cheshire
justices were attempting to crush Quakerism, Fell and Bradshaw were ordering the release of Quakers from prison. They
were to do the same again in 1656.[66]

But examples such as those above (and there are one or
two others) were the exception rather than the rule. In Newcastle the corporation, clergy, and Merchant Adventurers'
Company all banded together to deal with the Quaker
menace. Meetings were barred from the town and forced
across the river to Gateshead; the employment of Quaker
apprentices was prohibited.[67] When Quaker itinerants arrived
in Norwich in 1654 they were promptly escorted back out of
town.[68] In Chester, during the 1650s, a succession of mayors
ensured, often quite brutally, that Quaker progress in this
city would be limited.[69] Much the same happened in Plymouth,[70] Maidstone,[71] and Arundel,[72] to give a few more
examples.

My general impression, then, is that there was little reluct-
ance to act against the Quakers. In fact in mid-1656 there
was a concerted drive in several counties to limit the expansion

[65] Cole, 'Quakers and the English Revolution', 342; R. Farmer, *The Impostor
Dethron'd* (1658), 43.
[66] PRO, Chester 24/131/2, 4; PRO, Chester 21/4, fo. 326; J.S. Morrill,
Cheshire 1630-1660 (Oxford, 1974), 231.
[67] R. Howell, *Newcastle-upon-Tyne and the Puritan Revolution* (Oxford,
1967), 258-61.
[68] Norfolk RO, Norwich QS Minute Book 1654-70, 1 Jan. 1654/5.
[69] For example: F. H[owgil]. *et al.*, *Caines Bloudy Race* (1657); Chester
City RO, MF 75/11, 32, 66, 71; 76/42; 77(2)/55-7; Chester City RO, ML 3/375.
[70] A.D. Selleck, 'Plymouth Friends', *The Devonshire Association*, xcviii
(1966), 292.
[71] M.V. Jones, 'The Political History of the Parliamentary Boroughs of Kent,
1642-1662' (Univ. of London Ph.D. thesis, 1967), 473-5.
[72] East Sussex RO, SOF 5/1, pp. 7-8, 12-13, 24-5.

of the movement. The Essex Quarter Sessions ordered the suppression of 'all unlawfull tumultous Assemblyes' and the arrest of all members of the sect found 'within this County wandring and haunteing from place to place'. Similar directions were issued by the courts in Devon and Cornwall, where watches were set up on highways and bridges 'for the preventing of this great contagion, that infects almost every corner of this Nation'. In Devon 'psons of estate' with 'sufficient weapons' were engaged to apprehend those 'styled by ye name of Quakers disaffected to ye psent govmt', and over a score of itinerants were netted in a matter of weeks. Wiltshire and Somerset justices were urged by their grand juries to do something about 'the increase of persons known by the name of Quakers'.[73] Clearly Oliver Cromwell's policy of toleration was only what the local communities would make of it.

Quakers appeared before the quarter sessions and assizes for a variety of offences. A few were prosecuted under the Blasphemy Act of 1650.[74] Many were in trouble for disturbing ministers and disrupting church services, offences punishable either by an act instituted in the reign of Mary (1 Mar. St. 2 c. 3) or by the provisions contained in Cromwell's proclamation of 1655 which was specifically aimed at Quakers.[75] Several justices used the Vagrancy Act (39 Eliz. c. 4), before its revision in 1657, bending the spirit if not the letter of the law in an effort to contain Quakerism. North Country men and women were whipped out of southern towns.[76] Magistrates

[73] *Essex Quarter Sessions Order Book, 1652–1661,* ed. D.H. Allen (Chelmsford, 1974), 88; Cornwall RO, DD/SF 285/64; A.H.A. Hamilton, *Quarter Sessions from Queen Elizabeth to Queen Anne* (1878), 164–5; [G. Bishop], *The West Answering to the North* (1657), 69–70, 76–8, 107; Devon RO, QS Order Book 1652-61, July 1656; Wiltshire RO, QS Great Rolls, Trinity 1656; *Somerset Assize Orders 1640–1659,* ed. J.S. Cockburn (Somerset Rec. Soc., lxxi, 1971), 46–7.

[74] *Quarter Sessions Records of the County of Northampton,* ed. J. Wake (Northants Rec. Soc., i, 1924), 155, 186; A. Audland *et al., The Saints Testimony* (1655), 2–3, 4, 8, 24.

[75] For disturbances of ministers (1654–9), see GBS i, ii (listing over 350 instances, more than 300 of which were taken to the courts). For Cromwell's proclamation: *A Proclamation Prohibiting the Disturbing of Ministers* (1654).

[76] For example: R. Hubberthorne, *The Immediate Call* (1654); [J. Stubbs and W. Caton], *A True Declaration of the bloody Proceedings of the Men in Maidstone* (1655); East Sussex RO, QO/EW3, fo. 27ᵛ.

proved both flexible and imaginative in their interpretation
and use of the law. In Plymouth in 1655 the Quakers Miles
Halhead and Thomas Salthouse were prosecuted under
Cromwell's proclamation against the provoking of duels.[77]
There is evidence too that the oath of abjuration, intended
for Catholics, was employed against Quakers in Oxford and
Devon.[78]

VIII

It is quite clear that there was growing discontent in the
provinces, dissatisfaction with a central government which
permitted groups like the Quakers to flourish. There were
rumblings about official encouragement of radical sectarianism.[79] In 1656 a single event, the Nayler episode,
revealed these fears and tensions.

In October 1656 the Quaker James Nayler entered Bristol
on a donkey as a sign of the Second Coming of Christ. ('Thy
name is no more to be called James but Jesus' wrote one of
his devoted followers.) Nayler and his companions (mostly
women) were promptly arrested and sent to London where
Nayler was examined by a parliamentary committee. The
adulation continued during his detention. One follower
repeated her claim that she had been dead for two days and
that Nayler had resurrected her; others continued to kneel
before him.[80]

The reaction of MPs was intense. The outburst revealed
real concern at the dramatic increase in Quaker numbers.
'These vipers are crept into the bowels of your Commonwealth, and the government too', explained one member;
'They grow numerous, and swarm all the nation over; every
county, every parish.' Nayler was a leading Quaker, some
said *the* leading Quaker, so it was an ideal opportunity to
demonstrate the effectiveness of savage punishment as a

---

[77] M. Halhead and T. Salthouse, *The Wounds of an Enemie* (1656), 62.
[78] GBS i. 344; Devon RO, QS Order Book 1652–61, Oct. 1657; Bodleian
Library (Oxford), MS Top. Oxon. F. 47, fo. 18ᵛ·
[79] See *Diary of Ralph Josselin*, 348, 367.
[80] *A True Narrative of the Examination, Tryall . . . of James Nayler* (1657).

deterrent. 'Cut off this fellow, and you will destroy the
sect', Dennis Bond argued. Richard Cromwell told the
diarist Thomas Burton that he was convinced Nayler 'must
die', and there were Mosaically inspired suggestions of
stoning. Others were less certain of the political wisdom of
providing the movement with a martyr, though they agreed
on the need for 'some endeavour to suppress the growth of
them in general'. In the end the death penalty was defeated
(narrowly: by 96 to 82) and a more 'lenient' punishment
settled upon. Nayler was to be branded, bored through the
tongue, whipped, and pilloried. He was then to be confined,
indefinitely, without outside contact and at hard labour.[81]

IX

Stiffer legislation came with the aftermath of the Nayler
affair, partly because of pressure from the provincial gentry,
partly because Cromwell was the good constable. In mid-
1657, with the Quakers in mind, Parliament extended the old
Elizabethan Vagrancy Act. The new version gave justices or
officers of corporations *carte blanche* to move against 'all and
every idle, loose and dissolute person and persons . . . found
. . . vagrant and wandring from his or their usual place of
living or abode, and shall not have such good and sufficient
cause or business for such his or their travelling'. It was this
question of definition, 'these *terminis generalibus*', which
worried some MPs. 'If you leave it in the power of justices
to judge who shall be wanderers, for ought I know I myself
may be whipped.' But the critic, Major Audley, did not balk
at the statute's use against Quakers: 'I could freely give my
consent that they should be whipped.' Originally proposed
stipulations of distance, allowing wandering of up to ten
miles, were rejected by the House. Stipulations of wealth
were not even discussed. All depended upon the vagaries of
local justices; they had a weapon to restrict movement not

---

[81] *Diary of Thomas Burton,* ed. J. Towill Rutt (1828), i. 25, 96-8, 126; *The
Devil turned Quaker* (1656), sig. A7; *Journals of the House of Commons,* vii. 468.

only from county to county and parish to parish, but within the parishes.[82]

Parliament also passed (in June 1657) an act for better observance of the Lord's Day. The Act provided for a maximum fine of five pounds or six months' hard labour for disruption of ministers. Attendance at church became compulsory once again — at church or other 'meeting-place of Christians', but the latter had to conform to a new definition of 'Christian' which excluded Quakers. Quakers could now be prosecuted for not attending church. The half-a-crown fine seems small but it was roughly equivalent to the weekly wage of a labourer. Quakers could also be fined ten shillings for travelling on the sabbath.[83]

Justices made use of their increased repertoire. The law against vagrants was made only for Quakers, an Ipswich JP told the Quaker George Whitehead; and it was used against the sect in Suffolk, Somerset, Devon, Wiltshire, and Dorset. Sometimes the offenders were taken only a matter of three or four miles away from their homes. They were often men of substance, merchants or tradesmen combining economic and spiritual business. It would be tedious to relate examples, but the case of John Evans, a wealthy Englishcombe yeoman taken at Plymouth in November 1658 and whipped back to his Somerset home, was not untypical.[84] The Lord's Day Act had some impact as well. A few Quakers were presented for not attending church — in Cornwall, Suffolk, Essex, and Northamptonshire.[85] Justices in Gloucestershire, Devon, Essex, Suffolk, and Yorkshire prosecuted other members of the sect for profanation of the Lord's Day (usually by travelling on the sabbath).[86] Some felt that the political climate permitted a tougher line. Thus in Devon in 1658 the Court of Quarter Sessions ordered that Quaker itinerants be apprehended and their books burned.[87]

---

[82] *Acts and Ordinances of the Interregnum 1642-1660,* ed. C.H. Firth and R.S. Rait (1911), ii. 1098; *Diary of Thomas Burton,* i. 21-3; ii. 112-13.

[83] *Acts and Ordinances,* ii. 1162-70.

[84] Whitehead, *Christian Progress,* 133; GBS i. 340, 341, 356-7; ii. Wilts, 3-4; Somerset RO, DD/SFR 8/1, pt. 1, fo. 31.

[85] GBS i. 151; ii. Suffolk, 14; Essex RO, Q/SR 375/18; *Quarter Sessions Records of the County of Northampton,* 173.

[86] *Extracts from State Papers,* ed. N. Penney (1913), 33, 47, 59; BL Add.

X

Why were the governing classes so worried by the inroads of Quakerism? Edward Butler, MP for Poole, explained his fears. Quaker 'principles and practices are diametrically opposite both to magistracy and ministry; such principles as will level the foundation of all government into a bog of confusion'.[88] Many others shared his alarm. There was, quite simply, fear of social anarchy.

It was an age in which people were convinced of the power of ideology — a conviction only reinforced by the events of the 1640s and 1650s. Religion was the 'foundation of government'. It is 'hardly to be doubted', wrote Charles Davenant in 1698, many years after the period with which we are concerned, 'but that if the common people are once induced to lay aside religion, they will quickly cast off all fear of their rulers'.[89] Presbyterian and Anglican alike stressed the political and social necessity of their brands of orthodoxy. 'If there was not a Minister in every Parish, you would quickly find cause to encrease the number of Constables.' It is the duty of all good Christians to be meek, gentle, humble, patient, obedient to superiors'; and it is 'the duty of all good Pastors to exhort their people to the practise of these and the rest of the fruits or graces of the Spirit.'[90]

Early modern England was a society 'classed by subordination', and the patriarchal doctrines of the state were imbibed, quite literally, from the cradle onwards. Children, servants, and apprentices who understood their status in the household needed little political sophistication to grasp that the same applied to their place in the state.[91] As the New

MS 38856/74; GBS i. 413, 414, 422; ii. Suffolk, 10; Yorks, 15, 16.

[87] Devon RO, QS Order Book 1652-61, July, Oct. 1658, Jan. 1658/9.
[88] *Diary of Thomas Burton*, i. 137.
[89] Quoted by B. Easlea, *Witch Hunting, Magic and the New Philosophy* (Brighton, 1980), 221.
[90] R. South, *Ecclesiastical Policy* (Oxford, 1660), 7; R. Sherlock, *The Quakers Wilde Questions* (1656), 217-18.
[91] See L. Stone, *The Family, Sex and Marriage in England 1500-1800* (1977), ch. 5; G.J. Schochet, 'Patriarchalism, Politics and Mass Attitudes in Stuart England', *Historical Journal*, xii (1969), 420-1.

England catechism put it, by honouring thy father and
mother the fifth commandment had in mind all superiors
'whether in family, school, church and commonwealth'.[92]
Status and rank were reflected in manners, speech, and dress.[93]

But the Quakers rejected the hegemony of the élite. They
questioned the primacy of the Scriptures, rejected the need
for an established church or ministry, and challenged the
rigid hierarchical structure of society. When they talked to
superiors Quakers used the egalitarian (possibly northern[94])
'thee' and 'thou' instead of 'you', thus breaching the social
etiquette of discourse. They refused to recognize titles, to
bow or to doff hat. In their own dress (plain dress) they
threatened the conventions of social distinction.[95] They
even permitted their women to preach (a 'monstrous' practice, 'condemned as against nature').[96]

'Such as now introduce Thou and Thee will (if they can)',
Thomas Fuller warned in 1655, 'expel Mine and Thine,
dissolving all property into confusion.'[97] 'My Lord, the
whole world is governed by superiority and distance in
relations, and when that's taken away, unavoydably anarchy
is ushered in.'[98] The gentry and ministers were alarmed by
the sect's effect upon the common people. The Quakers were
involved in an intransigent and property-threatening campaign against tithes. They stirred up the people against lawful
authority and tempted the lower orders with dangerous
doctrines. 'O how did this take with the vulgar sort', wrote
Lord Saye and Sele shortly before the Restoration, 'when
they thought they should enjoy that liberty, as to be under
no rule, no reverence to be given either to Magistrate or
Minister, Parent or Master . . . and this was it that made it
so easily embraced, and so suddenly spread it about the
Kingdom.'[99]

[92] Stone, *Family, Sex and Marriage,* 152.
[93] See P. Stubbes, *The Anatomie of Abuses* (1583), no pagination.
[94] Barbour, *Quakers,* 164.
[95] J. Parnell, *A Shield of the Truth* (1655), 26–7; Barbour, *Quakers,* 163–8.
[96] J. Miller, *Antichrist in Man* (1655), 27.
[97] Quoted in *WTUD* 198–9.
[98] *Scotland and the Protectorate,* ed. C. Firth (Scottish Hist. Soc., xxxi,
1899), 362–3.
[99] [W. Fiennes], *Folly and Madnesse Made Manifest* (1659), 4.

XI

During the Interregnum, then, there was, for one reason or another, considerable hostility towards Quakers. We have seen that this tension helped to intensify dissatisfaction with the Cromwellian regime, forcing a more conservative religious settlement. In Kent, for instance, the Quaker issue was splitting the radicals and giving a boost to 'the re-emergence of political moderation'.[100] All this had happened by 1658. But it was in 1659 that the real impact of anti-Quaker feeling was felt.

I have dealt elsewhere (in some detail) with the events of 1659; but it is worth repeating — if somewhat baldly — some of my arguments, for the year was important for both the Quakers and the Revolution. In fact in 1659, as part of a more general fear of sectaries, hostility towards Quakerism led many to look to the monarchy as the only salvation from social and religious anarchy. In other words, hostility towards Quakers *contributed* to the restoration of the Stuarts.[101]

1659 was a year of uncertainty and confusion. Agitation in the regiments brought down Cromwellian rule. The Rump Parliament was restored, replaced by the Committee of Safety, then re-restored. Royalists and Presbyterians planned and attempted a series of risings. The Army split. And then in 1660 the King returned. The uncertainty, the panic of that year, had led many to look to the King, as Ralph Josselin put it, 'out of love to themselves not him'.[102] Fear of Quakers was an important ingredient.

The Quakers certainly looked with hope to the events of that year, and, more than at any other stage in their development, moved towards 'a militant revolutionary position'. They demanded the restoration of all members of the sect purged from office because of their beliefs. They sent to London lists of Quakers eligible to sit as JPs. Burrough assured

---

[100] P. Clark, *English Provincial Society . . . Kent, 1500–1640* (Hassocks, 1977), 394, 396.
[101] B. Reay, 'The Quakers, 1659, and the Restoration of the Monarchy', *History*, lxiii (1978).
[102] *Diary of Ralph Josselin*, 457–8.

Parliament and Army of Quaker support provided they carried out the right reforms. Quakers served in the militia, the Army, and probably in the volunteer regiments raised to crush the Presbyterian-Royalist risings.[103]

People were alarmed at the increased activity of the movement. George Fox reported that it was being preached that 'Quakers would kill', 'the Quakers would rise'. Ministers were warning their congregations that England was about to become another Münster.[104] When a member of the Norfolk gentry was asked to explain his cache of weapons, he said it was 'to secure himselfe agaynst Quakers & Annibaptists who he feared would ryse to Cutt His throat, & if they did soe he was resolved to cutt theire throats First if he could'.[105] It was feared that God was abandoning England. There was talk of a 'second Deluge of Antichristianisme over the Protestant Churches'.[106] And so by the beginning of 1660 Presbyterians 'began openly to desire the king; not for good will to him, but only for destruction to all the fanatics'.[107] Charles II returned at the end of May.

The advent of Quakerism, then, had political repercussions. But the Quaker impact had been somewhat negative. Its main effect was to stimulate political conservatism, to provoke and to some extent vindicate Presbyterianism, and to provide a shot in the arm to the reaction which in 1659-60 ended in the restoration of Charles II.

[103] Cole, 'Quakers and Politics', 277; Reay, 'Quakers, 1659, and the Restoration', 195, 202-3.
[104] Fox, *Several Papers,* 43; R. South, *Interest Deposed* (Oxford, 1660), 19.
[105] Bodleian Library, MS Clarendon 64, fos. 190-190ᵛ.
[106] J.S., *The Jesuite Discovered* (1659), 11-12; R. Baxter, *A Key for Catholicks* (1659), 328-30.
[107] L. Hutchinson, *Memoirs of the Life of Colonel Hutchinson* (1968 edn.), 317.

7 The Fifth Monarchists and Popular Millenarianism

Bernard Capp

Until quite recently popular millenarianism meant a caricature of the Fifth Monarchy movement: brain-sick and blood-thirsty fanatics who aimed to rule as tyrants in the name of King Jesus. They aroused fear and revulsion among contemporaries, and were understandably dismissed with scorn or ignored by later generations. The surge of religious fundamentalism in modern Iran is a reminder, however, that the passions which produced the Fifth Monarchists are by no means extinct. Once again, though in very different circumstances, the collapse of an oppresive regime contemptuous of traditional religious values has been followed by a fiercely idealistic movement seeking to purify and purge the nation.

Millenarianism may be defined broadly as belief in an imminent kingdom of heaven on earth to be established with supernatural help; its inspiration sprang from the biblical prophecies, especially in Revelation. Fifth Monarchism was in fact only one of many forms which such hopes could take. In the turbulent years of civil war and revolution it was easy to be swept along by the fiery rhetoric of prophecy, and in varying ways the creed also influenced the Baptists, Congregationalists, Ranters, Diggers, and Quakers. It was indeed the sense of exhilaration, of triumphant expectation, which was at the heart of popular millenarianism, not a set of precise doctrinal beliefs. As the landmarks of the old order were thrown down one by one — bishops, the House of Lords, monarchy, Parliament itself — many people were led to believe that these must be the upheavals foretold in Scripture to herald the world's end or its transformation. This sense of living in the shadow of the Apocalypse produced strong and confused emotions which help to explain the extravagant language and behaviour of the time. Euphoria mingled with fear, doubt, and disillusion as the situation changed, and changed again. Forever on the threshold, the godly never entered the promised land, and the confident hopes of the 1640s turned to feelings of defiant bitterness and betrayal in the later 1650s. Those who looked further ahead to the millennium itself cherished a vision of England remoulded in the biblical pattern. That pattern was sufficiently vague and flexible, however, to sustain a wide variety of hopes; New Jerusalem might be an ordered moral commonwealth, a Geneva writ large, but it could also stand for social revolution or a simple, arcadian world of peace and plenty. The cheap tracts, newspapers, and almanacs which popularized millennial ideas brought still greater diversity by incorporating astrological predictions and other prophetic material, from the Roman sibyls to Merlin and Mother Shipton. In some popular writings there was little distinction between the millennium and the golden age, or between Antichrist and the Norman Yoke.

Though millenarianism was certainly popular, it cannot be seen as part of a distinct, self-contained 'popular culture'. Millennial hopes were by no means confined to the lower classes or the radical sects and influenced many prominent politicians, intellectuals, and clergymen. From the Reformation onwards, many contemporaries had interpreted current events in the light of biblical prophecies of the latter days. Professor William Lamont demonstrated some years ago how apocalyptic hopes indeed formed part of the mainstream of English thought in the Elizabethan and early Stuart period. By the sword of the monarch and the zeal of the preacher Rome would be thrown down and a godly commonwealth would arise in England.[1] From 1640 many moderate parliamentarians believed passionately that the Long Parliament would take over the duty long ignored by the Stuarts

---

[1] W. Lamont, *Godly Rule* (1969). For general surveys, see also P. Christianson, *Reformers and Babylon: English Apocalyptic Visions from the Reformation to the Eve of the Civil War* (Toronto, 1977); C. Hill, *Antichrist in Seventeenth-Century England* (Oxford, 1971); B.S. Capp, 'The Political Dimension of Apocalyptic Thought' in C.A. Patrides and J. Wittreich (eds.), *The Apocalypse in English Renaissance Thought and Literature* (forthcoming, 1984).

and at last erect the New Jerusalem through a godly, ordered reformation of church, state, and society. In the excitable mood of the time the apocalyptic dream made a greater impact on the lower classes than ever before and, more important, began to take new forms which used the language of the common people and reflected their particular hopes and fears.

Early in Elizabeth's reign John Foxe the martyrologist had set out a version of church history in which, down the centuries, the small band of true Christians struggled against the might of antichristian Catholicism. The Reformation had exposed the papal Antichrist, paving the way for its fall and Christ's return to Judgement. Most Elizabethan Protestants accepted a framework of ideas along these lines. The obvious fact that England was the major Protestant state and so the natural protector of the reformed cause led patriots to believe that their nation had a special role in God's providential scheme. Traces of this idea are evident in Foxe's works and especially in the writings of his contemporary, John Aylmer, and the idea of England as the 'elect nation' became widespread after the defeat of the Armada in 1588. This success and the gains of Calvinism on the continent undermined the established view that the world's end was imminent. Biblical scholars began to stress instead the overthrow of antichristian Rome by the godly, leading to a period of 'latter-day glory' before the Last Judgement. At the very end of Elizabeth's reign Thomas Brightman developed this idea further, arguing that the thousand years' reign of the saints (Rev. 20) belonged not to the distant past but to an age of increasing glory calculated from the first glimmerings of the Reformation. Some continental theologians were pursuing a similar course, and the 1620s saw the appearance of major works by Johannes Alsted in Germany and Joseph Mede in England placing a perfect millennial world firmly in the future.[2]

After 1603 James I became the focus for hopes that the English monarchy would lead the struggle against Rome. As a young man he had published evidence identifying the papacy

[2] J.H. Alsted, *Diatribe de mille annis Apocalypticis* (Frankfurt, 1627); J. Mede, *Clavis Apocalyptica* (Cambridge, 1627).

as Antichrist, but his policies as King provided little encouragement and he flatly refused to intervene in the Thirty Years War in defence of the Protestant cause. Many contemporary Englishmen (unlike most historians) saw the European war as a religious conflict. In 1619 Archbishop Abbot of Canterbury hoped that the new Protestant king of Bohemia, Frederick, would drive Catholicism from Germany and lead a crusade against Rome.[3] Within a few months however, Frederick had been driven out by the Habsburg armies, and it was Protestantism which suddenly appeared to be facing extinction. James had married his daughter to Frederick and many were deeply shocked by his indifference to family ties and to his duty to foreign Protestants in danger. English observers rested their hopes first on Frederick himself and then on the victorious Swedish king, Gustavus Adolphus, who drove back the Catholic tide till his death in 1632. With James and then Charles I standing coldly aside, it was hard to sustain faith in England's apocalyptic role. Charles moreover promoted the Laudian, 'popish' wing of the Church, married a Catholic bride, and allowed Catholicism to flourish at court. Many Puritans in despair emigrated to New England and God himself, it was suggested, was ready to abandon England for America. Puritans remaining in England came to believe that the cosmic struggle was being waged at home as well as in Germany. Traditional Puritan willingness to accept the established church was strained by Laudian policies and repression, and Laud's critics and victims began to regard his church as the tool of antichristian Rome. The policies of king and primate alienated the nation at large and when the regime collapsed in 1640 it was isolated and almost universally distrusted.

The national mood when the Long Parliament assembled late in 1640 was of confident hope that a new age of harmony and reform was dawning. But within a few months it became clear that the euphoria was misplaced. Deep political divisions made peaceful change impossible, and the nation drifted into civil war. For some the optimism vanished for ever. But

[3] S.L. Adams, 'Foreign Policy and the Parliaments of 1621 and 1624', in K. Sharpe (ed.), *Faction and Parliament* (Oxford, 1978), 146-7.

among Parliament's more committed supporters there emerged
a fierce conviction that the war was a part of the great
struggle between the forces of Christ and Antichrist. The
dangers and suffering must be endured, they argued, for if
England was indeed God's chosen instrument 'was it not
necessary that the nation itself be first purged?'[4] Eventual
victory was sure, and then would begin the latter-day glory.
Preachers before Parliament advanced such ideas with great
force, echoed by lesser clergymen throughout the country,
and the MPs appear to have welcomed this assessment of
their role as God's agents.

Yet even before the end of the civil war the mood of
apocalyptic ebullience was faltering, as moderate Puritans
grew reticent or even denounced the millenarian creed.[5] Part
of the explanation lies in the rise of the New Model Army,
and Cromwell's prominent place within it. The New Model
was by no means an army of saints, but Cromwell's toleration
of heretical and subversive ideas among his troops aroused
deep fears. This shadow darkened the moderates' vision of a
latter-day glory, and the Army's revolt in 1647 confirmed
their worst fears. Instead of an age of purity and peace, the
civil war seemed to have brought heresy, chaos, and confusion. Propaganda tracts with such dramatic titles as
Englands Alarm to War against the Beast (1643) had been
only too successful in spreading the idea that the war was
an apocalyptic crusade. In the hands of soldiers and artisans
the future age of glory took forms horrific to the propertied
and educated classes. In 1645 a collector of current heresies
warned that millenarians were numerous and highly
'dangerous to all estates. 1. For to promote the kingdom of
Christ, they teach that all the ungodly must be killed. 2. That
the wicked have no property in their estates'.[6] Moderate
divines were shocked to hear Presbyterianism labelled as the
Beast of Revelation, and backed away from apocalyptic
dreams. At the same time, the events of the late 1640s
brought radicals to a new pitch of excitement. The purge of

[4] C. Syms, *The Swords Apology* (1644), 10.
[5] For the themes of this paragraph, see Tai Liu, *Discord in Zion* (The Hague, 1973).
[6] E. Pagitt, *Heresiography* (2nd edn., 1645), 126.

Parliament in December 1648 led rapidly to the execution of
the King, 'the sickle of divine justice cutting him down';
and, it was claimed, the accession of King Jesus 'took place,
as soon as the fatal blow was given'.[7] The Army, during its
invasion of Scotland in 1650, denounced the Stuarts as one
of the horns of the Beast and called on the Scots to help set
up Christ's kingdom. When the rout of the Scottish army at
Worcester in 1651 brought peace at last, the time seemed
ripe to put Christ on his English throne. In anticipation 'the
lawyers quaked, the formal clergy were down in the mouth,
the malignant trembled, the loose nobility and gentry looked
pale'.[8] But most Rump MPs were in fact moderate men, un-
easy about the King's death and anxious to hold back the
revolution. Moreover many of the Independent and Baptist
churches, while sharing millenarian hopes, were willing to
settle for liberty of worship and were opposed to further upheavals. As the cautious conservatism of the Rump Parliament
became clear, radicals felt themselves thwarted at the very
threshold of the New Jerusalem.

It was in this atmosphere that the Fifth Monarchy movement emerged, taking its name from Daniel's vision of an
everlasting kingdom to follow the four great world monar-
chies.[9] The Fifth Monarchists were resolved that Christ's
cause should not go by default through the betrayal of the
Rump and Cromwell's ambivalence. The movement was a
pressure group rather than a new denomination or party.
Its supporters came from a variety of Congregationalist and
Baptist churches, and included Calvinists and free-willers,
soldiers and civilians, in a loose and sometimes acrimonious
alliance. Led by fiery London preachers, its first aim was
to undermine the Rump and replace it with a church-parlia-
ment drawn from the gathered congregations and modelled
on the ancient Jewish Sanhedrin. With such a programme the
group's prospects would appear slim, but it was able to
capitalize on the Rump's massive unpopularity and had important allies in the Army command, notably Cromwell's

---

[7] *The Cause of God* (1659), 3; J. Spittlehouse, *The First Addresses* (1653), 23.
[8] *The Cause of God*, 3.
[9] For two studies of this movement, see B.S. Capp, *The Fifth Monarchy Men*
(1972); Tai Liu, *Discord in Zion*.

close associate Major-General Harrison. In April 1653 Cromwell was at last brought to stage a military coup, and dissolved
the Rump. Many sectarians now hailed him as a second Moses
leading his people from bondage, and a millenarian Baptist
urged that he be given absolute power as God's lieutenant on
earth.[10] Instead Cromwell chose to summon an assembly of
men nominated directly for their religious and moral virtues,
bypassing the traditional electorate. The new body, known
as Barebone's Parliament, was the nearest millenarianism
came to capturing the revolution and in many ways the high-
water mark of radicalism.[11] In his inaugural speech Cromwell
drew heavily on Daniel and Revelation, and called for
sweeping reforms. With a dozen Fifth Monarchists (including
Harrison) and many other radicals in his audience he found
a ready response, but the Parliament ended in embittered
failure. Cromwell's zeal resembled the Fifth Monarchists'
only in rhetoric, not substance, and within the House there
were deep divisions on almost every issue. Attempts to throw
down tithes and the legal system aroused fears for property
and order. Disillusion grew quickly on all sides, and in
December Cromwell readily accepted the Assembly's con-
trived resignation. Henceforth he ruled directly as Protector,
the champion of order and stability.

From this point onwards the Fifth Monarchists were in
unwavering opposition, refusing to accept the new regime
and asserting their right to take up arms against it. They
were naturally condemned as irresponsible anarchists spoiling
for blood and confusion, but most of the violence was
merely verbal and there were no major uprisings. Their
leaders were former Army officers, sometimes from a gentry
background, and university-trained ministers; though they
denounced the government in sweeping terms, they shared a
deep horror of anarchy with the rest of the landed and
educated classes. Their duty was to testify against Cromwell's
antichristian power and prophesy its doom, but not to take
up arms until God gave an unmistakable signal. Colonel
Nathaniel Rich for example was a staunch Fifth Monarchist

[10] J. Spittlehouse, *A Warning-piece Discharged* (1653), 7, 10.
[11] For a full study of Barebone's Parliament see Austin Woolrych, *Commonwealth to Protectorate* (Oxford, 1982).

but he was also the kinsman of the Earl of Warwick, later married the daughter of another peer, and had shown his deep concern for private property at the Putney Debates. Cromwell, though frequently irritated by the vicious language of Fifth Monarchist leaders, felt safe enough to be lenient. They knew, as he probably realized, that a hasty civilian rising against his large and professional army could end only in pointless slaughter.

The Fifth Monarchists posed a greater threat to Cromwell however than might at first appear. They were able to mount a concerted propaganda campaign in 1654 to coincide with the tense meeting of the first Protectorate Parliament. Knowing that the regime rested solely on military power, they reprinted a number of old Army declarations to convince the soldiers that the government was betraying the promises and principles of the 1640s. They also made direct attempts to subvert units of the Army and Navy. Cromwell outmanœuvred these efforts, but his repeated purges of the Army showed that it was by no means solidly behind him and that the dangers were real. In addition Fifth Monarchist leaders negotiated secretly with other disaffected groups, Commonwealthsmen, Baptists, and former Levellers, seeking to create a broad opposition alliance. Moreover not all Fifth Monarchists followed their leaders in confining violence to words, and in 1657 a group meeting in Swan Alley, Coleman Street, did attempt an uprising. Its leader, Thomas Venner, was a cooper, his lieutenants included a button-seller and cow-keeper, and his followers were obscure artisans and labourers. The plot was crushed but Venner survived to lead a second, bloodier rising against the restored Charles II in 1661. Another artisan preacher, also executed for alleged treason in 1661, was barely literate and having been forced to give up his trade selling coal was only just able to support himself as a weaver. The desperate Fifth Monarchism of such men was very different from the creed of a Colonel Rich. Their millennial dreams were sharpened by poverty and they had no social position at stake to restrain them. There was also a further threat to Cromwell, more difficult to counter: assassination. Killing the Protector might not guarantee the Fifth Monarchy, but it would almost certainly bring down the regime. At a fiery meeting in Swan Alley in 1656 a preacher argued that Cromwell was the true murderer and that killing God's enemies was a worthy deed. The notorious tract *Killing No Murder* was fathered on a Fifth Monarchist who allegedly denied responsibility but praised its arguments.[12] Cromwell survived several assassination attempts and was deeply concerned at the danger.

The Fifth Monarchists sketched at least the outlines of the future millennial regime. If King Jesus ruled through human instruments, as seemed likely, government would be in the hands of an assembly chosen by the sectarian churches. 'Mere natural and worldly men', it was agreed, could have no political rights.[13] The programme called for sweeping ecclesiastical changes: there would be no national church, no parochial system, no tithes. Suggestions for law reform produced even more outrage. Many radicals denounced the legal system with justifiable bitterness: it was slow, expensive, and centralized, its language archaic and its penalties both ferocious and ineffective. Gaoling debtors for trivial sums, for example, ruined the victim without helping the creditor, and this area of the law was of direct relevance to the artisans and small tradesmen who bulked large in the radical groups. The Fifth Monarchists, like many, demanded cheap, local justice with a clear and concise legal code. Their distinctive proposal was to base this new code on the Mosaic laws of the Old Testament. In some respects these were surprisingly humanitarian — no imprisonment for debt, no death penalty for theft. But on moral and religious offences the Mosaic laws were Draconian, imposing death for adultery, blasphemy, and profanation of the sabbath. Drawing most of their programme from Scripture, the Fifth Monarchists could see nothing anachronistic in this proposal. How could 'the dim light of nature'[14] (frail human reason) ever surpass the wisdom of God? It is tempting to join contemporaries in ridiculing the idea but we need to remember that it grew out of a long-standing Puritan tradition, which

---

[12] C.H. Firth, *The Last Years of the Protectorate, 1656–1658* (1909), i. 1229.
[13] *Certain Quaeres* (1649), in A.S.P. Woodhouse (ed.), *Puritanism and Liberty* (1974 edn.), 246.
[14] Ibid.

had led eventually to the Rump's Act of 1650 making adultery a capital offence.

Fifth Monarchism indeed shared many of the moral objectives of the earlier Puritans. This may help to explain its ideology but presents problems in trying to understand its popular appeal, for the Puritans had won their support mostly from the upper and middle classes. The size of the Fifth Monarchy movement is uncertain. The highest contemporary guess, at 40,000, was probably too large and even if correct represents less than 1 per cent of the population. 'The world turned upside down' was a striking alarmist phrase, but in fact the traditional social hierarchy survived almost unscathed and most of the poor continued to acquiesce, whether through conviction, fear, or apathy. None the less the Fifth Monarchists did become a considerable force in London, East Anglia, and even Wales (probably through the influence of Vavasor Powell and other preachers and General Harrison's sweeping powers in Wales in the early 1650s). There were groups in places as far apart as Dartmouth, Liverpool, Oxford, and Hull, and a rudimentary national organization developed in the later 1650s. Overall the rise of the Fifth Monarchists owed less to evangelism than to the political drama of the 1640s which first created a millenarian tide and then, with the 'apostasy' of the Rump and Cromwell, diverted it into a movement of protest against the great betrayal. The theme of betrayal was central to the Fifth Monarchists. Vavasor Powell's attack on Cromwell after the fall of Barebone's Parliament as 'the dissemblingest perjured villain in the world'[15] was typical of much which was to follow. Bitter personal attacks could appeal to all radicals dismayed at the collapse of their hopes, and with the demise of the Levellers the Fifth Monarchists were for a time the only significant radical group. Their leading preachers, Feake, Simpson, and Rogers, possessed at least some of Lilburne's flair for publicity and self-dramatization. The preachers also stirred up the forces of popular anti-Catholicism, the most deep-rooted prejudice of the seventeenth century. A former member of Barebone's Parliament told a large congregation

---

[15] *Thurloe*, i. 641.

that Cromwell as Protector would 'protect you in slavery and popery'. Feake declared that 'This power and monarchy are one and the same; and this army doth as really support popery, and all the relics of it, as ever King Charles and the archbishop of Canterbury . . . did.' The same theme was conspicuous in Venner's rebel manifesto of 1661 which attacked the popish king, lords, and bishops recently restored. 'The Devil and the Pope hath at this day a great design upon England', readers learned, for papists were planning a general massacre to 'suck out our very heart blood' and destroy English Protestantism for ever.[16] Much Fifth Monarchist propaganda thus appealed to feelings of betrayal, hatred, and fear, and preachers often laid more stress on the bloody day of vengeance than on the millennial age. They quoted with relish the biblical image of binding kings with chains and nobles with fetters of iron (Psalm 149), and repeated Isaiah's promise that kings and queens would bow down and lick up the dust at the feet of the godly (Isa. 49:23).

The Fifth Monarchy now arising would be a world transformed. Nobility by birth would disappear as a 'fancy for children and fools'[17] giving way to a new aristocracy of the godly. Some anticipated a similar economic reversal. Venner's rebels planned to seize and share out the possessions of all who opposed them — doubtless the whole of the landed classes. Moderate spokesmen were anxious to protect private property and suspicious of the 'rabble', but most contemporaries shared Cromwell's firm belief that the Fifth Monarchists aimed to overturn the whole social and economic order. In some areas Fifth Monarchist thought was much closer to the main reforming currents of the period, and was certainly influenced by them. John Rogers denounced the Norman as well as the Babylonian Yoke, and attacks on lawyers, clergy, and monopolists were common to all the radical groups.[18] Venner's manifestos, like Leveller tracts, called for annual elections, while Rogers even demanded that Army officers should be re-elected each year. A critic

[16] Ibid. ii. 128; v. 756; *A Door of Hope* (1661), 6.
[17] J. Rogers, *Ohel* (1653), 22.
[18] J. Rogers, *Sagrir . . . and Alarum for New Laws, and the Peoples Liberties from the Norman and Babylonian Yokes* (1653), sig. A2, pp. 39, 47, 110, 125.

accused Vavasor Powell of being inconsistent or insincere on
the grounds that, in Powell's *A Word for God* (1655), 'you
strangely jumble together heterogeneous matter of the Kingdom of Christ, the privileges of Parliaments, the liberty of
the subjects'.[19] Though Powell was indeed hoping to build
a broad alliance against Cromwell, his paper was not merely
a cynical device, as was alleged. New Jerusalem symbolized a
holy society but also one freed from tyranny, exploitation,
and suffering. Even the dictatorship of the saints has to be
set alongside the Fifth Monarchists' confident expectation of
a massive conversion when Christ set up his kingdom. 'Natural
men' too, they promised, 'will be at rest also and much satisfied.'[20] These promises were vague, but probably much of
millenarianism's positive appeal lay in the simple vision of an
age of prosperity, health, and rest (a theme discussed below),
rather than in detailed proposals for specific reforms. Contemporaries were not surprised that after years of hardship
and upheaval there should be a ready response to promises
of 'times of refreshing — a golden age — at hand'.[21]

This casual reference to the Age of Gold, a classical myth, is
a reminder that the Bible was not the only inspiration for
idealized visions of the future. Many of the prophecies circulating in the 1640s sprang from non-biblical sources, of
which astrology was by far the most important. It was
generally accepted in medieval Europe that the stars were
God's instruments and contained a key to the future, and the
traditional link between astrology and the Apocalypse survived the Reformation little changed. Heated speculation on
the conjuction of Saturn and Jupiter in 1583 produced
assertions that the Last Judgement was at hand. A total
eclipse of the sun predicted for 29 March 1652, 'Black
Monday', aroused still more excitement. Many pamphleteers
announced the end of the world, while others, including
William Lilly, the most famous astrologer of the day, prophesied upheavals leading to a final, millennial age. There are

[19] *Animadversions upon a Letter and Paper* (1656), 71.
[20] *Certain Quaeres,* in Woodhouse (ed.), *Puritanism and Liberty,* 242.
[21] R. Vaughan, *The Protectorate of Oliver Cromwell* (1839), i. 156.

stories of the rich loading their coaches and fleeing from London, and of the poor laying in supplies of uncontaminated drinking water and sealing their windows.[22]

The German theologian Johannes Alsted had drawn heavily on astrological data in his millenarian treatise, first published in England in 1643. Scholars such as John Napier and Thomas Brightman had confined themselves to the scriptural text, but the hacks who popularized their works in the 1640s observed no such restraint. Even Brightman's collected works, published in 1644, contained an appendix drawing on Nostradamus and other assorted prophets. A series of *Bloody Almanacks* publicized Napier's claim that Judgement Day was at hand and added an endorsement by a leading astrologer, John Booker. Distinctions between biblical and non-biblical prophecy became blurred, and even the Fifth Monarchist John Rogers was willing to use the prophecies of Nostradamus.

Astrological pamphlets played an important part in spreading apocalyptic ideas. The print runs for almanacs expanded rapidly, and Lilly's series was allegedly selling 30,000 copies a year on the eve of the Restoration, many of them to husbandmen and artisans who would buy few if any other books. Some compilers claimed that the chaos of the age proved that the end was nigh; others expected a short period of glorious peace to come before the Last Judgement. Still others, notably Lilly and Nicholas Culpeper, prophesied the millennium. Lilly condemned the Fifth Monarchists but matched their relish in predicting the downfall of tithes, lawyers, priests, and landlords. Using both biblical and astrological data, Culpeper prophesied with great assurance that Rome would fall in August 1655 and that the government of England would 'come into the hands of the people', inaugurating the millennial age.[23] His premature death in 1654 was perhaps fortunate. Many of these predictions were pirated in chap-books and newspapers, spreading millennial ideas still more widely. Though there was never a

[22] See B. Capp, *Astrology and the Popular Press* (1979), ch. 5, pt. iv., for astrology and the apocalypse.
[23] N. Culpeper, *Catastrophe Magnatum* (1652), 72.

Fifth Monarchist newspaper, the Baptist editor Daniel Border published millenarian and astrological material in his *Faithful Scout*, and during the years 1649–53 many newspapers gave prominence to millenarian petitions and declarations.

There was a further important tradition merging with the mainstream of apocalyptic thought: the ancient prophecies ascribed to Merlin, the sibyls, and many others.[24] Merlin's predictions can be traced back for centuries but many were spurious, and the writings of Mother Shipton were conveniently 'discovered' and published only in the early 1640s. Most of these prophecies were not obviously apocalyptic. Often based on animal symbolism, they spoke mysteriously of eagles and dragons, of the White King and the Dreadful Dead Man. Their cryptic messages could be made to support almost any cause, and hints of desolation, war, and peace fitted easily into current preoccupations with Judgement Day or the millennium. William Lilly collected secular prophecies of all kinds and combined them indiscriminately with biblical and astrological material. In the early 1650s the diary of Ralph Josselin, a cautious Puritan minister in Essex, shows the author speculating excitedly about the White King and *Pullus Aquile* (the eagle's chick) as well as the prophecies of Daniel and Revlation.[25] The distinctions were largely blurred in popular chap-books, such as *Five Strange and Wonderfull Prophecies* (1642) where the Puritan Thomas Brightman became simply another ancient prophet set without explanation alongside the Jesuit Ignatius Loyola, Merlin, Mother Shipton, and one Otwell Bins. At this level the reading public seems to have ignored the distinctions between Protestant, Catholic, and pagan, and the inevitable discrepancies. Cheap works of this kind were immensely popular, especially in the early 1640s. Perhaps, as Keith Thomas has suggested, they helped to make the traumatic experiences of those years emotionally acceptable, by showing how the upheavals had been long foreseen, were somehow inevitable, and played a significant part in the world's destiny.[26] There was a long-standing popular taste for sensational material with a super-

---

[24] *RDM* (1971 edn.) ch. 13.
[25] *The Diary of Ralph Josselin 1616–1683*, ed. A. Macfarlane (1976), 255, 338, and see p. 327 (Grebner's prophecy).   [26] *RDM* 423.

natural element, and ancient prophecies were almost certain to find a ready market when presented as inspired warnings of the current crisis. Monstrous births and apparitions in the sky, explained as portents of divine anger, were also a traditional subject of ballads and chap-books. A short tract of 1641 provides a good example of how apocalyptic ideas could be grafted on to such prodigy stories. It told, with much circumstantial detail, of the recent death of a sixteen-year-old Nottinghamshire girl, daughter of a husbandman. Shortly before the funeral she returned suddenly to life, declaring that God had sent her back to earth as his messenger for five days. In this role she attacked the vanity of modern fashions, predicted wars and disasters, and prophesied a final age of peace before the world's approaching end. After taking communion from the local vicar and denouncing the Roman Whore she died again peacefully at the appointed time, surrounded by family and friends.[27] Chap-book accounts of events abroad could be still more bizarre. Another brief pamphlet of 1641 reported an infant born in Malta and believed to be the Messiah. Local misfortunes persuaded the islanders that it must instead be Antichrist but when they went to investigate the child flew off into the sky.[28] Twenty years later stories were circulating that two hundred aged men, each a thousand years old, had arrived in Aleppo and were prophesying wars and desolation leading to the Last Judgement.[29] Such accounts tell us much of the mental climate in which popular millenarian movements could flourish.

Crude though they are, these tracts suggest that even at the humblest level readers were looking for a wider significance in the upheavals shaking the land. The same approach led many preachers and pamphleteers to declare with renewed confidence that England was indeed the elect nation; God was using 'our nation as a theatre to act a precedent of what he intends to do in all the nations under the cope of heaven'.[30] It was natural to set events at home in the context of the

---

[27] *The Wonderfull works of God. Declared by a strange Prophecie of a Maid* (1641).
[28] *New News, and Strange News from Babylon* (1641).
[29] *A true Discovery of a Bloody Plot* (1661), 3.
[30] Spittlehouse, *First Addresses*, 5.

Thirty Years War, and to hope that Antichrist's fall in England
would have repercussions abroad. The struggle would go on
till popery was thrown down everywhere. 'The sword is not
sheathed', wrote an almanac-maker after the civil wars; 'other
nations must drink of this cup: the vial of wrath is pouring
out.'[31] Many radicals pressed for an apocalyptic crusade by
the New Model, seeing it as God's instrument in pouring out
the vial. The Fifth Monarchists were naturally to the fore.
'The blade of that sword (whose handle is held in England)
will reach to the very gates of Rome ere long', John Rogers
declared, adding a rousing call to the Army: 'To the other
side of the water, away sirs! and help your brethren beyond
seas.'[32] By making peace with the Dutch in 1654 Cromwell
appeared to be renouncing an apocalyptic foreign policy, but
the Fifth Monarchists refused to give up hope. Even in the
desperate rising of 1661, after the restoration of the Stuarts,
Venner and his rebels saw their cause as 'much more than a
national quarrel'. The plight of the godly in England, they
explained, paralleled 'the ruin and destruction of the Protestant cause and reformed interest both in France, Savoy,
Bohemia, Poland etc.'. After rooting out popery from England
they would therefore 'go on to France, Spain, Germany and
Rome, to destroy the Beast and Whore'.[33]

The apocalyptic crusade had a secular equivalent, the
desire for England to help other nations throw down tyranny
and establish freedom.[34] The two ideas were closely related
and often merged. The English associated European monarchy
with popery and persecution, and as early as 1642 a millenarian writer had proclaimed that Christ's return would
liberate the world from the 'tyranny and oppression of
kings'. John Rogers called on the New Model to rescue
Frenchmen from the 'iron yoke of tyranny', and many
radicals declared God's vengeance against all kings. Even the
cautious Ralph Josselin noted in his diary in 1650 that
monarchy was part of the Beast's power and that the English
were to be instrumental in its universal ruin.[35] The major

[31] John Booker, quoted in Capp, *Astrology*, 80.
[32] Rogers, *Sagrir*, sigs. A2, B2.   [33] *Door of Hope*, 3, 7.
[34] C. Hill, *Puritanism and Revolution* (1962 edn.), ch. 4.
[35] J. Archer, *The Personall Reigne of Christ upon Earth* (1642), 53; Rogers,
Sagrir, 14; *Diary of Ralph Josselin*, 233, 220.

astrological writers agreed that the downfall of all kings was at hand. Culpeper prophesied this as the effect of the 'Black Monday' eclipse, and observed with satisfaction that 'Monarchy begins to stink in the nostrils of the commonalty'.[36]

The dream of a European crusade grew out of the circumstances of the 1640s, but it also aroused echoes of a more distant apocalyptic tradition: the messianic conqueror of the last days. For centuries prophecies had circulated of a second Charlemagne, a great emperor who would impose peace and unity, and prepare the way for Christ's return.[37] Though medieval England was little affected by this speculation, the Tudor period saw the growth of a theory of Protestant imperialism. Elizabeth especially was hailed as a new Constantine, bringing peace, truth, and stability. From the late sixteenth century biblical commentators stressed the central role of godly princes, in particular the English king, in throwing down Antichrist by armed force. James I's elder son, Prince Henry, was eager to lead an army against Rome and a contemporary scholar ventured to apply the Charlemagne prophecies to him and other members of the Stuart royal family. Royal inertia during the Thirty Years War undermined such hopes but from 1640 interest revived in an English conqueror. In the euphoria of 1640-1 it seemed possible that Parliament might persuade Charles to follow the true path of Protestant imperialism. A Puritan veteran of the continental wars, one John Spencer, saw the calling of Parliament as an opportunity for Charles to send an army to restore his sister and family to the Palatinate and then join German Protestants in attacking Rome.[38] In the obscure jumble of *Five Strange and Wonderfull Prophecies* Charles himself appeared as hero, steering his country through the crisis to an age of unity and destined to destroy Rome and rule over new lands. Another 'ancient' prophecy, published in 1642, linked the English King with a great European emperor. Together they would establish an age of peace, and the King of England would add France to his dominions and

---

[36] N. Culpeper, *An Ephemeris for ... 1653* (1653) sig. D7.
[37] M. Reeves, *Prophecy in the Later Middle Ages* (Oxford, 1969), pt. 3.
[38] J. Spencer, *A Discourse of divers Petitions of High Concernment* (1641), 7, 8.

open a path to Jerusalem. It soon became impossible, however, to ignore the gulf dividing Charles from the parliamentary cause. Increasingly it was great noblemen with Puritan leanings, such as the Earls of Essex, Warwick, and Pembroke, who were urged to take on the mantle of apocalyptic conqueror. Doggerel verses published as early as 1641 implored Essex to rout the Irish rebels and then join the Elector Palatine in driving the Habsburgs from Germany:

> Fight you the battles of King Charlemagne,
> You shall speed well in Ireland, France and Spain,

and in time fulfil the vow of Queen Elizabeth's Essex to 'pull the popedom down'.[39] Even earlier the eccentric prophetess Lady Eleanor Davies had told the King to beware the year 1642, adding an ominous anagram: 'R. Essex. ESSE REX.'[40] Essex never became king but he did become Parliament's commander-in-chief. An Army chaplain hailed him as the 'General, and Champion of Jesus Christ to fight the last and great battle with Antichrist', while some soldiers had heard that Essex was John the Baptist preparing the way for King Jesus.[41] Essex showed no appetite for any such role and the mantle passed instead to other generals, notably Cromwell. Marvell's famous ode presented Cromwell as the conqueror and liberator of Europe, a vision which certainly appealed to Oliver. In 1653 Cromwell appeared to many as a new Moses liberating the people from the Rump's bondage; John Rogers declared that the tyranny of William the Conqueror and his successors had been overthrown at last by 'our General Oliver the Conqueror'. Rogers urged a European crusade, citing a medley of prophecies to prove that the Pope's fall was at hand, and told Cromwell of another old prediction that 'a C shall sound within the walls of Rome'.[42] Ralph Josselin, the Essex diarist, also believed – for a time – that Cromwell had a major role in the overthrow of Antichrist.

[39] J. Crag, *A Prophecy concerning the Earle of Essex* (1641), sig. A2^{v}.
[40] E. Audeley (later Davies), *Amend, Amend; Gods Kingdome is at Hand* (1643), sig. A2 (first published Amsterdam, 1633).
[41] T. Palmer, *The Saints Support* (1644), sig. A2; Hill, *Puritanism and Revolution*, 326.
[42] Rogers, *Sagrir*, sigs. A2, B2, p. 89.

And only a few months before Cromwell's death a rash Welsh compiler published prophecies of the fall of kings, Pope, and Turks, claiming that the Protector was the man destined to destroy them.[43]

Though Charles I's defeat in the civil war discouraged apocalyptic dreams centred on the monarchy, such ideas proved surprisingly resilient. As late as 1648 a well-known Puritan preacher, William Sedgwick, argued that England's millennial future depended on a lasting agreement with the King, for God 'saith openly . . . I'll reign over you in and by King Charles'.[44] Shortly after the King's execution some more committed royalists seized on a suggestion that the Prince of Wales might be the Charles, son of Charles, who was predicted to arise as the new Charlemagne. Several pamphlets in 1649-50 proclaimed the glorious future reign of Charles II on the basis of this prophecy, in a version by the German scholar Paul Grebner. The parliamentarian expert, William Lilly, hastened to explain that Grebner's 'true' meaning was the ruin of monarchy in England for ever.[45] During the course of the 1650s several royalist eccentrics predicted that Prince Charles would return as king through the surprising help of Oliver Cromwell. The best known, Arise Evans, pressed Cromwell repeatedly to restore the Prince who he claimed was destined to reign in the millennium and lead the Jews back to Jerusalem.[46] Cromwell responded with friendly amusement and also gave a personal audience to another royalist prophet, Walter Gostelo. The younger son of an Oxfordshire gentleman, Gostelo began his prophetic career in Ireland where he had connections with the Boyle family. After a series of visions he revealed that Cromwell must restore Charles II, leading to a Stuart world monarchy, the fall of Rome, conversion of the Jews and, more marvellous still, the conversion of the Irish Catholics to Anglicanism. Another vision showed that Charles was to marry Lady

[43] *Diary of Ralph Josselin*, 225, 231-2 (but later Cromwell appeared in a darker guise, perhaps as the little horn of the Beast: see pp. 330, 336, 357, 404, 416); T. Pugh, *British and Outlandish Prophecies* (1658).
[44] W. Sedgwick, *The Leaves of the Tree of Life* (1648), 71.
[45] W. Lilly, *Monarchy or No Monarchy* (1651).
[46] C. Hill, 'Arise Evans', in his *Change and Continuity in Seventeenth-Century England* (1974).

Elizabeth Boyle, daughter of the Earl of Cork, and Gostelo
wrote to inform the Prince of his future bride. The Boyles
gave hospitality for several months but took fright when
Gostelo began to spread his treasonable ideas in public.[47] A
third visionary, John Sanders, was once a prosperous iron-
monger but now working as a humble nailer in Harborne,
near Birmingham. He too predicted that Charles would
return with Cromwell as a loyal subordinate; the new king
would re-establish the Anglican Church and crush the radical
sects. Sanders behaved in the exotic style of an Old Testament prophet but his economic ideas belonged firmly to the
present age. In a broadsheet proclaiming the royalist Fifth
Monarchy he went on to urge fellow nailers to form an
association to fight for better prices from the ironmongers
who employed them, and called for a strike if negotiations
failed.[48] All three prophets were called mad by contemporaries
and it is not clear if any of them won support. The idea of
Cromwell's regime paving the way for a monarchy was by
no means absurd, of course, though it was on Cromwell
himself that Lord Broghill (a Boyle) and other courtiers
later pressed a crown. Sanders's populist royalism was very
unlikely to find official favour, but the appearance of a
royalist, radical, episcopalian millenarian is a dramatic
warning against imposing rigid categories on the mid-century
flux of ideas. On the eve of the Restoration an almanac-
maker hailed Charles as a mighty conqueror who would
destroy the Pope and establish a world empire, and throughout the 1660s a host of writers gave a heroic, apocalyptic role
to the new King.[49]

The civil wars also threw up a considerable number of
obscure men and women claiming a messianic role for themselves. A line of such deluded pretenders stretched back to
the Reformation; the most notorious of them, William
Hacket, had proclaimed in London in 1591 that he was the
Messiah returned to rule over New Jerusalem. In many of

[47] W. Gostelo, *Charles Stuart and Oliver Cromwell United* (1655).

[48] J. Sanders, *An Iron Rod for the Naylors* (1655) and *An Iron Rod put into
the Lord Protectors Hand* (1655).

[49] On the Restoration cult of Charles, see M. McKeon, *Politics and Poetry in
Restoration England* (1975).

these cases the authorities responded leniently but Hacket boldly declared that Elizabeth was deposed and, even more fatally, attracted a large crowd of followers. Though he was promptly executed there were many successors. In 1636 for example two Colchester weavers asserted that they were the Two Witnesses of Revelation II, claiming that if put to death they would rise again and reign as king and priest for ever. When they died in prison in 1642 a number of disciples clung to the belief that they had indeed returned to life. In 1650 the case of a Hampshire rope-maker, William Franklin, aroused still more notoriety. Franklin claimed to be the Messiah, though he abandoned this when put on trial, and like most of the claimants he appears to have been unbalanced. The significance of these messiahs lies in the degree of interest and sometimes support they attracted. Franklin allegedly had several hundred followers, and even allowing for the idly curious it seems that they included people of apparent good sense and some education, as Lord Chief Justice Rolle noted with concern at his trial. In a period of intense religious expectation, the coming of a new prophet or even the Messiah could seem plausible. Even Cromwell and his officers, we should remember, listened with sympathy to a succession of obscure and self-appointed messengers from God who repeatedly interrupted their meetings. The officers were not deceived by popular messiahs but they were certainly ready to look for the commands of God in the mouths of the humble.[50]

When millenarian writers looked beyond the days of 'overturning' to the New Jerusalem itself, they cherished a very different vision: an age of peace, harmony, and joy. Revelation itself, after prophecies of war and desolation, ended with a world made new in which 'there shall be no more death, neither sorrow nor crying, neither shall there be any more pain'. The Old Testament provided vivid images of swords beaten into ploughshares, and of the lion lying down with the lamb. Other traditions may have contributed to popular conceptions of the millennial age, for example the

[50] *RDM* 132-7; R. Bauckham, *Tudor Apocalypse* (Appleford, 1978), ch. 10; H. Ellis, *Pseudochristus* (1650).

Arcadian dream of harmonious peace in a bountiful environment and the earthy, sensual peasant paradise known as the Land of Cockaygne.[51] Another vision, of a third and last 'Age of the Spirit', derived from the medieval Italian Abbot Joachim and was certainly widespread among English millenarians.[52] It appeared too in the almanacs of William Lilly who in the 1650s and later prophesied an age of unity, peace, spiritual harmony, and enlightenment. Joachimist influence was most dramatic in the Ranter movement, where the idea that the enlightened were liberated from the constraints of dark, formal religion developed into a rejection of all traditional morality.

The biblical vision of harmony and peace closely paralleled the Arcadian myth and had a powerful appeal after years of war and confusion. The image of the lion and lamb recurred often. John Fenwick, a Newcastle merchant and former Puritan refugee, explained that men of a 'wolvish, ravening, lionish, raging' spirit would be transformed by Christ's rule.[53] Mary Cary, a Fifth Monarchist, thought that Christ would also literally change the nature of ferocious beasts so that the lion would eat straw like the ox. The whole of nature would change. Instead of hostile and unpredictable, the environment would be idyllic and benevolent. John Bunyan promised a world always green and beautiful, enjoying perpetual sunshine and summer. John Fenwick promised 'sweet and refreshing walks in fair and pleasant vallies and green pastures, by the still and limpid waters'. The curses of age, disease, and premature death would be taken away. John Archer, whose millennial treatise went through several editions in 1642-3, promised that the godly and their children would live in health and happiness to the age of a hundred, with no violent or untimely death and no infant mortality. Mary Cary repeated these assurances, while some authors went still further and declared that the godly would be immortal.[54]

[51] For a recent, brief discussion of both, see J.C. Davis, *Utopia and the Ideal Society* (Cambridge, 1981), ch. 1. [52] Reeves, *Prophecy*.
[53] [J. Fenwick], *Zions Joy in her King* (1643), 121.
[54] J. Bunyan, *Works* (1862), iii. 459; Fenwick, *Zions Joy*, 120; M. Cary, *The Little Horns Doom* (1651), 289, 294; Archer, *Pesonall Reigne*, 30-1.

In the millennial world the godly would enjoy 'abundance of outward glory' instead of their present obscurity. Fifth Monarchists frequently spoke of poor saints becoming a new aristocracy in the kingdom of Christ. George Foster, an idiosyncratic Ranter, told the godly: 'you shall be as so many kings and princes that shall reign here on earth, every one of you no less than a king.' Foster may have echoed many popular millennial dreams with his simple promise that 'sons and daughters of Sion shall have of the best, they shall eat and drink of the best, and wear of the best'.[55] Though Mary Cary thought this new élite would be in a 'high and heavenly frame' above worldly vanities, she too emphasized that the saints would enjoy 'rich apparel'.[56] An age of boundless prosperity and plenty was a recurring theme in millennial writings from Brightman to Fifth Monarchist pamphlets and popular chap-books, and even writers who laid most stress on spiritual blessings added guarantees of worldly wealth. Creature comforts would be readily provided. Houses would be solid and comfortable, food and drink abundant. John Fenwick had biblical texts to document the point: the saints 'shall be brought to a land of corn and wine, Joel 2.19. Corn shall make the young men merry, and new wine the maids, Zech. 9.17.'[57] John Bunyan promised that the Lord would 'make unto his people a feast of fat things, a feast of wine on the lees, of fat things full of marrow'.[58] Bunyan too had a text (Isa. 25:6) but it is easy to see how New Jerusalem and the Land of Cockaygne could merge. In the millennium, as in Cockaygne, the grinding toil of the labourer would cease. The Nottinghamshire maid who returned from the dead in 1641 announced 'the day of rest coming to rejoice us, our charge shall be taken away, and our travail shall have an end'.[59] Some writers claimed that work would cease altogether. Mary Cary thought that men would still 'follow several employments as now they do; but doubtless in a more regular and comfortable way'. In particular

---

[55] G. Foster, *The Pouring Forth of the Seventh and Last Viall* (1650), 9, 31. On Foster, see *WTUD* (1975 edn.) 223-4.

[56] Cary, *Little Horns Doom*, 270.   [57] Fenwick, *Zions Joy*, 120.

[58] Bunyan, *Works*, iii. 444.

[59] *The Wonderfull works of God*, sig. A3ᵛ.

'some shall not labour and toil day and night . . . to maintain others that live viciously, in idleness, drunkenness, and other evil practices'. The saints would 'comfortably enjoy the work of their own hands'.[60] This perhaps was the nub of the popular vision. A world with no work at all was almost inconceivable except as an idle dream; but work freed from the burdens of rent, taxes, tithes, excise, and manorial dues was an image of earthly paradise with instant appeal. A critic complained that millenarian preachers attracted the ignorant with promises that debts and rent would cease.[61] The Fifth Monarchists taught further that the citizens of New Jerusalem would face no unfair competition. Venner's manifesto in 1661 called for a ban on the export of fuller's earth (used in dyeing cloth) to protect English workers from Dutch competition. John Sanders, the royalist prophet, sought a closed shop and better prices for the Birmingham nailers. Such demands suggest a conception of the millennium rooted in contemporary life, far from the other-worldliness of the biblical New Jerusalem. The Fifth Monarchists' zeal for the Dutch War of 1652-4 sprang in part from hostility to the enemy as a trade rival. General Harrison allegedly preached that victory would bring control of the seas and enormous wealth: 'the Dutch must be destroyed; and we shall have an heaven on earth.'[62] Trade and industry would flourish in the millennium. There were of course short cuts to wealth: Venner's artisan rebels planned to seize the goods of their opponents, and the Ranters taught that in the age now dawning there would be no more private property. Even millenarians who supported private property might feel differently about the goods of popish foreigners. John Fenwick described in crude but vigorous lines how Christ would give his army rich plunder in the crusade against Rome:

> Crowns, sceptres, jewels, earrings,
> Gold, rich robes and costly things
> Thou gavest thy soldiers to the spoil,

---

[60] Cary, *Little Horns Doom*, 307-8, 310.
[61] T. Hall, *Chiliasto-mastix redivivus* (1657), 53.
[62] Bodleian Library (Oxford), MS. Clarendon 45, fo. 380[V]; *A Door of Hope*, 5; Sanders, *An Iron Rod* (both works).

> And women weak, with little toil,
> Went laughing some,
> Well laden home.[63]

With millenarianism, as with other popular ideologies, it is difficult to go beyond the words of the leaders to see how the rank and file perceived the message and what most attracted them. Gerrard Winstanley's subtle and non-violent doctrines, for example, contrast sharply with the crude threats against local farmers attributed (by enemies) to his followers. At a popular level, the millennium seems to have meant a future world freed from the insecurity of the seventeenth century. Wars would cease. Crops would be gathered without the age-old fear of harvest failure and famine. The worker alone, liberated from taxes, tithes, and rent, would benefit from his labour. Family life would be transformed by the assurance of perfect health and long life. Fears that a large family meant inevitable poverty disappeared with the guarantee of plenty in a land of milk and honey. In a period of recession, fighting, and confusion, such promises had an obvious appeal. Ministers and scholars stressed the importance of the Apocalypse and the approach of Judgement, so that popular millenarianism seemed to involve only a small step from orthodoxy. It was more comprehensible than the traditional picture of heaven itself and far more attractive. The 'saints shall be filled with joy', Mary Cary promised simply, 'joy without any mixture of sorrow at all'.[64]

---

[63] Fenwick, *Zions Joy*, 93.
[64] Cary, *Little Horns Doom*, 279.

8 Irreligion in the 'Puritan' Revolution

Christopher Hill

For the past thirty years or so I have been interested in making comparisons between the English, French, and Russian Revolutions. There are clearly general structural similarities. All three began with a 'revolt of the nobles'; in all three monarchy was overthrown and replaced by a period of parliamentary constitutionalism. In all three the original revolutionary leaders had to appeal for popular support outside the circle of those hitherto influential in politics; and these new circles produced new political demands, leading on to regicide and republic. But then the unity of the revolutionaries disintegrated, the republic was replaced by the dictatorship of Cromwell, Napoleon, or Stalin. In all three a wide extension of the franchise was demanded, and the land for the peasantry (stable copyholds in the English Revolution). Communist theories appeared in all three, though they triumphed only in the Russian Revolution. New ideas of the relation of the sexes, of marriage and divorce, were put forward in all three. Ideas for a decimal coinage were mooted in the English Revolution, put into effect in the French Revolution.[1] All three revolutions had international repercussions. Descending to minute particulars, there are extraordinary parallels between the three monarchs who lost their lives in consequence of their revolutions. Each was a well intentioned man with the obstinacy of the weak; each was dominated by a hated foreign wife. Charles I and Louis XVI were both second sons, who came to the throne only in consequence of the death of an elder brother. And so one could go on with examination questions beginning 'Compare the English, French, and Russian Revolutions in respect of . . . '.

[1] C. Webster, 'Decimalization under Cromwell', *Nature*, ccxxix (1971), 463.

But what about religion? Surely this is a 'contrast' question? 'Contrast the Puritan Revolution with the active dechristianization of the French Revolution, with the militant atheism which won out in the Russian Revolution'? I want to suggest that there were perhaps more analogies than the phrase 'the Puritan Revolution' would seem to allow. Some of the analogies are obvious. In all three revolutions the state church, as a bulwark of the old regime, came under attack, and religious discontent played a large part in forming the opposition — in the English and French Revolutions including opposition among the lower clergy. Tithes were denounced in the English Revolution, abolished in the French. In all three the universities were purged. The Quaker refusal of 'hat honour' and use of 'thou' to social superiors — these reappeared in the French Revolution. In England there was no dechristianization, or philosophical atheism. But, allowing for the different circumstances, perhaps we can find some anticipations even here.

Historians recently have started to undertake the difficult task of trying to rediscover the beliefs of ordinary people. Mr K.V. Thomas's magnificent *Religion and the Decline of Magic*, Professor Dickens's work, *Lollards and Protestants*, Mr A.L. Morton's *The World of the Ranters*, have knocked the bottom out of the idea that the common people of sixteenth- and seventeenth-century England accepted the religious orthodoxies of their betters. We are becoming more aware of popular heresies, dating back at least to fifteenth-century Lollards, and extending through sixteenth-century Anabaptists and Familists to seventeenth-century sectaries.[2]

[2] Among many other sources I would cite A. Hudson, 'The Examination of Lollards', *BIHR* xlvi (1973); *Selections from English Wycliffite Writings*, ed. A. Hudson (Cambridge, 1978); C. Cross, '"Great Reasoners in Scripture": the activities of Women Lollards 1380-1530', in D. Baker (ed.), *Medieval Women* (Oxford, 1978); I.B. Horst, *The Radical Brethren* (Nieuwkoop, 1972); J.W. Martin, 'English Protestant Separatism at its Beginnings', *Sixteenth Century Journal*, vii (1976); idem, 'Christopher Vitel: an Elizabethan Mechanick Preacher', ibid. x (1979); idem, 'Elizabethan Familists and English Separatism', *Journal of British Studies*, xx (1980); J.D. Moss, 'Additional Light on the Family of Love', *BIHR* xlvii (1974); idem, 'The Family of Love and English Critics', *Sixteenth Century Journal*, vi (1975); idem, 'Variations on a Theme: the Family of Love in Renaissance England', *Renaissance Quarterly*, xxxi (1978); F. Heal, 'The Family of Love and the Diocese of Ely', *Studies in Church History*, ix (1972); L.F.

Puritan preachers in the fifty years before 1640 offer much evidence of the unorthodoxy of the common people, particularly of their rejection of the wholesome doctrine of original sin: what Professor Collinson has called 'rustic Pelagianism'.[3] The nominal obligation on all English men and women to attend their parish church every Sunday was certainly not honoured by large numbers of the poorer classes, especially in towns. Indeed, in many London parishes the church could not have held them if they had all chosen to attend. Large numbers of rogues and vagabonds, itinerants, and squatters also absented themselves, and since they had no money it was not worth fining them for non-attendance. In 1644 the Presbyterian Parliament voted that JPs should compel them to come in, but this was soon cancelled by the Act of 1650 which abolished compulsory church attendance. This act lapsed in 1657, but the position was never recovered. In 1669 some Hertfordshire churchwardens thought it worth reporting that 'several of the inhabitants come constantly to church'. Eleven years later it was 'the general complaint of all the parishes' in Kent that 'the meaner sort absent themselves'.[4] This is what we may call 'passive irreligion', as opposed to more active and principled opposition to the church. Yet it is not always easy to differentiate. A Norfolk man was excommunicated in Edward VI's reign for crying 'We live like dogs and it is better not to come to church.'[5] A century later the Digger Gerrard Winstanley, who made a frontal attack on the established religion as the opium of the

Martin, 'The Family of Love in England', *Sixteenth Century Journal,* iii (1972); A. Hamilton, *The Family of Love* (Cambridge, 1981); B.W. Ball, *A Great Expectation: Eschatological Thought in English Protestantism to 1660* (Leiden, 1975); B. Manning, *The English People and the English Revolution* (1976); M. Spufford, *Small Books and Pleasant Histories. Popular fiction and its readership in seventeenth-century England* (1981); and my 'From Lollards to Levellers', in M. Cornforth (ed.), *Rebels and their Causes* (1978).

[3] P. Collinson, *The Elizabethan Puritan Movement* (1967), 37. For examples, see W. Perkins, *Works* (1609-13), i. 295-6, 537, 631; ii. 109, 290, 300; iii. 493-500, 583, 595.

[4] B.S. Capp, *The Fifth Monarchy Men* (1972), 195; C.W. Chalkin, *Seventeenth Century Kent* (1965), 224.

[5] I owe this to R.A. Houlbrooke, 'Church Courts and People in the Diocese of Norwich, 1519-1570' (Univ. of Oxford D.Phil. thesis, 1970), 85.

people, said 'We will neither come to church nor serve their God.'[6]

My subject is this more active irreligion. It is not always easy to detect, since before 1640 it was dangerous to draw attention to it, and we hear of it only through the reports of enemies. (Those who talk about the faith of our fathers forget that our seventeenth-century fathers lived under strict censorship.) But it is clear that, long before the Revolution, there was a good deal of materialist scepticism among the lower classes, sometimes crudely expressed, but often quite seriously thought out. I have no space to document this now, but take the following not untypical examples from the sixteenth century. The commons, a northerner said during the Pilgrimage of Grace, 'would never be well till they had stricken off all the priests' heads'.[7] The sentiment was repeated by a Norfolk man in 1570[8] and by many in the New Model Army and among the Levellers in the 1640s.[9] Londoners in Mary's reign used to refer to the consecrated bread in the sacrament as 'Jack-in-the-box'.[10] In 1600 in the diocese of Exeter and London it was 'a matter very common to dispute whether there be a God or not'.[11]

There was also a rather different upper-class scepticism, notably in Sir Walter Ralegh's circle: the diocese of Exeter which I have just mentioned included Sir Walter's areas of Devon and Dorset. Thomas Harriot, Ralegh's mathematician, could not accept the creation story in Genesis, and believed there were men before Adam. He denied the immortality of the soul, the resurrection, and the existence of Hell. Speaking of the doctrine of rewards and penalties in the after-life, Harriot said 'this opinion worketh so much in many of the common and simple sort of people that it maketh them have great respect to their governors, and also great care what they

---

[6] Winstanley, *Works,* 471.
[7] A.G. Dickens, *Lollards and Protestants in the Diocese of York, 1509–1558* (Oxford, 1959), 12.
[8] Houlbrooke, 'Church Courts and People', 344.
[9] *WTUD* (1975 edn.) 102; cf. R. Culmer, *The Ministers Hue and Cry* (1657), quoted by D.M. Wolfe in his introduction to *Complete Prose Works of John Milton,* ed. Wolfe (New Haven, 1953, continuing), iv. 94.
[10] H.F.M. Prescott, *Mary Tudor* (1952), 108.
[11] *RDM* (1971 edn.) 169, and see ch. 6 *passim.*

do'.[12] Recognition of the social role of religion was common to many in and around this group. Thus George Chapman's Bussy D'Ambois said that 'the witch policy' exaggerated the horrors of sin, making it 'a monster/Kept only to show men for servile money'. Robert Greene suggested that God and the after-life were 'mere fictions', 'only bugbears'; religion was 'a fable' invented 'to keep the baser sort in fear', and so to protect property and the social order.[13] Marlowe likewise thought that 'the first beginning of religion was only to keep men in awe'. He added that 'Moses was but a juggler', Christ was a bastard and/or a homosexual, and that he deserved his fate.[14]

The scepticism of this group was not politically radical. But it could link up with more popular irreligious traditions, as it did in 1593 when a shoemaker of Sherborne (Ralegh's area) reported a group who said 'that hell is no other but poverty and penury in this world; and heaven is no other but to be rich and enjoy pleasures; and that we die like beasts and when we are gone there is no more remembrance of us'.[15] Two generations later the sentiments were repeated verbatim by the antinomian libertines whom we loosely lump together as Ranters.

(Lest we should think the Ralegh circle unduly cynical about the social function of religion, here is the godly John Owen, Independent divine, writing in 1655: the majority of men must be 'overpowered by the terror of the Lord' and 'threats of the wrath to come' if mankind is to be preserved from 'the outrageousness and unmeasurableness of iniquity and wickedness, which would utterly ruin all human society'.[16] Many, many more examples could be cited.)

There were, then, long-standing traditions of irreligion. It

[12] *Thomas Harriot,* ed. J.W. Shirley (Oxford, 1974), 13, 24, 27, 108, 113; *WTUD* 144, 174-5; cf. T. Nashe, *The Unfortunate Traveller and Other Works* (1972 edn.), 68, 479; J. Dove, *A Confutation of Atheism* (1605), quoted by A.L. Rowse, *The Elizabethan Renaissance: The Cultural Achievement* (1972), 329.
[13] G. Chapman, *Comedies and Tragedies* (1873), ii. 39; R. Greene, *Selimus,* quoted in *WTUD* 163.
[14] *The Works of Thomas Kyd,* ed. F.S. Boas (Oxford, 1901), cxiv-cxvi; P.H. Kocher, *Christopher Marlowe* (Chapel Hill, 1946), chs. 2-3.
[15] P. Lefranc, *Sir Walter Raleigh, Écrivain* (Paris, 1968), 381.
[16] J. Owen, *Works* (1850-3), xii. 587.

would be difficult to find a seventeenth-century Englishman
who advocated atheism in intellectual terms. But the critique
of the established church made by many sectaries was so
radically anticlerical as to be virtually secularist in content.
They would have understood Voltaire's 'Écrasez l'infâme!'
Oliver Cromwell, William Dell, and many others expressed
anticlericalism by saying that the distinction between clergy
and laity was 'antichristian'.[17] Radicals like Milton, Saltmarsh, Dell, Levellers, Diggers, almost all the sects (Baptists,
Quakers, Muggletonians, many Congregationalists) rejected
the whole concept of a state church, together with the tithes
which paid for its ministers and the patronage system which
ensured that its clergy were appointed by the ruling class.
They insisted that ministers should be elected by the congregation and paid by the voluntary contributions of its
members; many rejected university education for the clergy
because it created a separate clerical caste. They would have
had a gifted layman preach on Sundays whilst labouring with
his hands the other six days of the week: some allowed women
to preach. They advocated toleration for all Protestant sects,
rejecting ecclesiastical censorship and all forms of ecclesiastical
jurisdiction in favour of a congregational discipline with no
coercive sanction behind it. They attached little importance
to many of the traditional sacraments of the church. Though
the motives of the sectaries were religious, the objective content of their demands was secularist. If a programme of this
sort had been adopted it would have destroyed the national
church, leaving each congregation responsible for its own
affairs with only the loosest contact between congregations:
the church would no longer have been able to mould opinion
in a single pattern, to punish 'sin' or proscribe 'heresy'. There
would have been no control over the thinking of the middle
and lower classes. 'If men be left to themselves', wrote the
Laudian, John Cosin, they may discuss 'whatsoever opinion
in religion, whatsoever debate between neighbours, whatsoever public matter in church or kingdom a man pleases to
make his interest.'[18] Cosin was talking of the necessity of set

[17] *Writings and Speeches of Oliver Cromwell,* ed. W.C. Abbott (Cambridge,
Mass., 1937–47), ii. 197; W. Dell, *Several Sermons and Discourses* (1709), 264–5;
cf. *Complete Prose Works of John Milton,* ii. 838; vi. 558.
[18] J. Cosin, *Works* (Oxford, 1843–55), v. 403.

forms of prayer to keep authorized ministers in check; how much greater the necessity of preventing preaching by unauthorized laymen!

Episcopal government in England, said a royalist divine in 1648, was 'the King's spiritual militia, and the most powerful, as commanding the consciences of subjects'.[19] Hence the strong feelings of popular hostility towards the clergy of which there is ample evidence in the 1640s when such feelings could be freely expressed. I quote Bishop Warner. 'The general opinion and carriage of the people (especially near London) . . . was such towards bishops that it was not easy to pass by them without reproach, yea (often) not without danger of their persons.'[20] 'So generally peevish and fanaticised were the people', said another account, that 'any particular discontent or personal quarrel' with a clergyman was generalized against 'these bishops, these parsons!'[21] In Cambridge clerical fellows of colleges 'became so hated by the weaker sort of the deceived people that a scholar could have small security from being stoned or affronted as he walked the streets'.[22] Finally, a real tear-jerker from London:

If any of the clergy, worn out with old age and former calamities, made use of a staff to support his aged weak limbs as he walked along the streets, he was pointed at as one that through drunkenness was not able to govern his steps. If he looked earnestly round about him with his dim eyes to find out any place he was to go in the City, some insolent scoffer would thus reflect upon him: 'that parson has devoured five fat livings, and see with what prying eyes he is seeking after a sixth.'[23]

Such anecdotes tell us rather more than their authors intended. There are many stories of clergy rabbled by their parishioners in the 1640s.[24] It was in 1642 that Thomas Fuller recalled that the famous Elizabethan Puritan, Richard Greenham, had said that atheism was a greater danger in England than popery.[25]

[19] [W. Chestlin], *Persecutio Undecima* (1681), 4 (first published 1648).
[20] E.L. Warner, *The Life of John Warner, Bishop of Rochester* (1901), 33.
[21] Chestlin, *Persecutio Undecima*, 7.
[22] *Querela Cantabrigiensis* (1646), 13.
[23] P. Barwick, *Life of Dr. John Barwick*, abridged and edited by G.F. Barwick (1903), 177.
[24] e.g. A.T. Hart, *The Man in the Pew* (1966), 149-50; cf. *WTUD* 30-1.
[25] T. Fuller, *The Holy State* (Oxford, 1841), 358.

The breakdown after 1640 of the old church, its courts, and its censorship, the establishment of religious toleration — which Thomas Edwards described as the greatest of evils — set men free to say in public and even in print what had hitherto only been muttered in secret. And what did they not say! 'We did look for great matters from one crucified at Jerusalem 1600 years ago', declared Thomas Webbe; 'but that does us no good.' It was more lawful, he added, 'to sit drinking in an ale-house' than to force men away out of the alehouse to go to church against their consciences. 'The Scriptures, that golden calf, was going down apace.' 'There's no heaven but women, nor no hell save marriage.' This didn't stop him getting a parish living — and a wife. 'I would have the liberty of my conscience', said a rebellious servant in similar vein, '*not* to be catechised in the principles of religion.' The Trinity was decried as 'a popish tradition'. William Erbery was alleged to have said he was as much God as ever Christ Jesus was.[26] John Hart claimed to have been made by the Earl of Essex and saved by Sir William Waller. The church is a spiritual whore-house, declared Roger Crab; priests are pimps and panders.[27] In 1653 an alehouse keeper was charged with having said (in a private letter from the East Indies) that he would rather be in bed with his girl-friend than in Heaven with Jesus Christ. He compounded his offence, when interrogated, by saying 'A pox on Jesus Christ.'[28] A journey-man shoemaker believed 'money, good clothes, good meat and drink, tobacco and merry company, to be gods; but he was little beholden to any of these; for his God allowed him but 8d. or 10d. a day, and *that* he made him work for'. 'The devil', he added, 'was but the backside of God . . . but a scarecrow.'[29]

Some of these remarks, of course, are pretty light-hearted: we should not make too much of them. But underlying this plebeian irreligion there is perhaps more theory, more theology if you like, than has been supposed. Protestant

[26] *Gangraena,* i. 21, 54, 106–7; ii. 21.
[27] *The Whole Works of John Lightfoot,* ed. J.R. Pitman (1823–4), xiii. 317; R. Crab, *Dagon's Downfall* (1657), 4–5.
[28] G.E. Aylmer, *The State's Servants* (1973), 307.
[29] A.L. Morton, *The World of the Ranters* (1970), 76–7.

Bible criticism, aimed at removing popish superstitions and corruptions, led on to so great an emphasis on the contradictions and inconsistencies of Scripture that some men ceased to believe it could be the word of God. The Leveller William Walwyn and the mortalist Clement Writer, the Ranter Laurence Clarkson and the Quaker Samuel Fisher, all followed up this line of thought. Milton and Bunyan were worried by it. The vulgar rather enjoyed it. 'Every . . . vagrant and itinerant huckster', a preacher told the House of Commons in 1647, denied the Trinity, the authority of the Bible, the historicity of Jesus Christ. 'If the Scriptures were a-making again', said a Wiltshire Ranter in 1656, 'Tom Lampire of Melksham would make as good Scriptures as the Bible.'[30] Gerrard Winstanley and the Ranters allegorized the Bible to such an extent that its literal meaning ceased to matter. 'Whether there were such outward things or no, it matters not much', said Winstanley of the biblical stories. There will never be peace, some Ranters urged, until all Bibles are burned — a saying which some of them put into literal practice.[31]

Secondly, materialism. It was traditional in Protestant polemic for anti-sacramentalism to take crude materialistic forms. From a Lollard lady in 1428 to Milton, speculations about the conversion of bread and wine into body and blood circled round the ultimate physical destination of the digested elements.[32] Opposition to magic, to sacramentalism, led to materialism. In the 1640s and 1650s it achieved the dignity of a theory, in the writings of Overton, Winstanley, Ranters, Muggletonians — and Hobbes and Milton.

Another road towards rejection of traditional Christianity was antinomianism. This was a caricature extension of the basic Protestant principle of the priesthood of all believers — the doctrine that God speaks direct to the individual conscience, dispensing with all mediators, whether the Virgin and the saints, or the hierarchy of the priesthood. Luther and Calvin had seen the elect as liberated from the law by the imputed righteousness of Christ. Milton too thought that

[30] *WTUD* 45, 228.   [31] *WTUD* 144, 262.
[32] J. Foxe, *Acts and Monuments,* ed. J. Pratt (1877), iii. 594; *Complete Prose Works of John Milton,* vi. 554.

believers could deviate from the ten commandments and even from the letter of the Gospel precepts in the higher interests of charity. 'The greatest burden in the world is superstition . . . of imaginery and scarecrow sins', which 'enslave the dignity of man.'[33] The Ranter Clarkson and the Digger Winstanley agreed.

So long as Protestantism was the creed of the bourgeoisie of Geneva, Amsterdam, La Rochelle, London, all was well: they looked into their own hearts, and found there respect for the Protestant ethic, an emphasis on hard work, thrift, monogamy. But as the lower classes were drawn into politics and religion, they found very different moral imperatives imprinted on their hearts. Yet who was to convince them that they were not also listening to God's voice in their consciences? Many radicals taught that God or Christ were in all the saints, and that perfection was possible in this life. We are as free from sin and therefore from the law, as Adam was before the Fall. Lieutenant Jackson believed in 1650 that he was 'as perfect now as ever he shall be'. He thought that 'there is no God but what is in himself and whole creation, and that he is alike in beasts as in men'.[34] Grindletonians, Winstanley, Dell, Erbery, Crab, Ranters, Quakers, all thought that sin had been invented by the ruling class to keep the poor in order. Murder, adultery, and theft were not sins, thought a London lady whom Edwards reported in 1646. All the Hell there was, was the darkness of the night.[35] The Leveller Walwyn accepted the label antinomian. The respectable Independent John Cook, more cautiously, was prepared to accept antinomian theory if not the practice of all antinomians.[36] The Ranters Abiezer Coppe and Laurence Clarkson defended from the pulpit the view that adultery, drunkenness, swearing, theft, could be as holy and virtuous as prayer. Sin existed only in the imagination. This was to extend the refined scepticism of the Ralegh group to the lower classes, who did not share their assumption that private property, inequality, and social subordination must at all costs

---

[33] *Complete Prose Works of John Milton*, vi. 639–40, 711; iv. 601; ii. 228.
[34] C.H. Firth, *Cromwell's Army* (1902), 408.   [35] *Gangraena*, ii. 8.
[36] Haller and Davies, 361; J. Cook, *What the Independent Would Have* (1647), 8.

be preserved. Winstanley stood traditional orthodoxy on its head: it was not the Fall of man and human sinfulness which explained private property, class distinctions, and the state which protected both; on the contrary, the establishment of private property explained covetousness and all other sins, together with the upper-class invention of Heaven and Hell.

Another approach reached similar conclusions — through the heresy of mortalism. The doctrine that after death the soul does not at once proceed to Heaven or Hell but sleeps until the final resurrection was a long-standing Christian heresy. Some Lollards,[37] Luther, and Tyndale shared it. The heresy assumes that soul and body are one, that the soul cannot exist without the body — materialism again. We must distinguish between those who believed in the sleep of the soul and those (like Richard Overton the Leveller and Milton) who believed that the soul died with the body and remained dead until the resurrection. An extension of this position was the belief that the soul was annihilated at death. Soul-sleepers heavily emphasized the ultimate resurrection. Annihilationists carried their materialism to the point of denying any resurrection. Those in between, like Overton and Milton, in practice were pretty perfunctory about the resurrection: their interest was mainly in the events of this life.[38]

One or other form of mortalism was widely accepted among Familists, Socinians, and Baptists, and was preached in England by the Leveller leader, Overton, the Bible critic Clement Writer, and by many General Baptists, Seekers, Ranters, and Muggletonians. Bunyan called the Quakers mortalists. Enemies of mortalists accused them indiscriminately of denying any after-life. If there is no Heaven and no Hell except on earth, libertinism would seem to the orthodox the natural conclusion to draw for action.

Familists had long taught that 'the whole man dies', and that at death the body returns to the elements from which it was composed. To a man like Lodowick Muggleton, who had dreaded the prospect of eternal damnation, mortalism brought

[37] J.A.F. Thomson, *The Later Lollards 1414-1520* (Oxford, 1965), 36, 41, 69, 82, 142, 160-1, 185-6, 248, 250.
[38] See my *Milton and the English Revolution* (1977), ch. 25; N.T. Burns, *Christian Mortalism from Tyndale to Milton* (Cambridge, Mass., 1972).

'much peace of mind'.[39] Bunyan, who shared the same fears, found the idea tempting.[40] Eloquent expression was given to this traditional view by the Leveller Richard Overton, the Digger Gerrard Winstanley, the Ranters Clarkson and Bauthumley. 'To reach God beyond the Creation', wrote Winstanley, 'or to know what he will be to a man after he is dead, if any otherwise than to scatter him into his essences of fire, water, earth and air of which he is compounded, is a knowledge beyond the line or capacity of man to attain to while he lives in his compounded body.'[41] Bauthumley said: 'Everything below God perisheth and comes to nothing. . . . They all shall return to their first principle of dust, and God shall . . . live in himself.' There is no Devil, no after-life.[42] Clarkson thought that at death 'that which was life in man, went into that infinite bulk and bigness, so called God, as a drop into the ocean . . . and the body rotted in the grave, and for ever so to remain'. 'For ever after I should know nothing after this my being was dissolved.'[43]

Denial of a separate existence for the soul apart from the body was a useful Protestant argument against Purgatory. But it was also, as Sir Thomas Browne and Henry More noted, an argument against the existence of ghosts. 'Deny spirits and you deny God', declared Henry More:[44] Joseph Glanville and many other early Fellows of the Royal Society devoted much time and energy to proving the existence of both spirits and God. Mortalism emphasized the importance of this life. Seeing man as a part of nature, as an animal, the mortalists were more scientific and rational than many of the scientists. Mortalism may have contributed significantly to that decline of belief in the supernatural which John Aubrey attributed to the 'liberty of conscience and liberty of inquisition' of the revolutionary decades.[45]

Mortalism could be combined with an allegorical inter-

[39] L. Muggleton, *The Acts of the Witnesses of the Spirit* (1764), 25 (first published 1699).

[40] *WTUD* 174.   [41] Winstanley, *Works*, 565.

[42] J. Bauthumley, *The Light and Dark Sides of God* (1650), 4, 49-53.

[43] L. Clarkson, *The Lost Sheep Found* (1660), 33. 'As a drop into the ocean' picks up a long-standing radical metaphor (cf. p. 203 below).

[44] See my *Reformation to Industrial Revolution* (1969 edn.), 117.

[45] J. Aubrey, *Brief Lives,* ed. A. Clark (Oxford, 1898), ii. 318.

pretation of the Scriptures to deny the after-life altogether. Heaven and Hell were in this world — and nowhere else. The Second Coming, the end of the world, and the Judgement were all events which took place within the individual conscience. Mrs Attaway, who agreed with Milton in being a mortalist and an advocate of divorce for incompatibility, believed that Hell existed only in the consciences of men and women, and there were many like her.[46] This became a general Ranter view, shared by Winstanley and many other radicals. Winstanley believed that the resurrection of Christ did not refer to a single person — or, if it did, its true significance was symbolic. 'Mankind is the earth that contains him buried, and out of this earth he is to arise', within us. 'The rising up of Christ in sons and daughters . . . is his second coming.'[47] That was all the heaven Winstanley expected: it was in this world only, as it was for Clarkson, Bauthumley, and other Ranters. Whether there was any life after death was a matter on which it was useless to speculate. We need not go to Heaven to find God, said Winstanley. 'Glory *here*!' is the brief claim of the Diggers' song — not in Heaven, not after death, but here and now.[48]

The annihilationist form of mortalism sometimes went with a kind of materialist pantheism, as for the heretic reported by Edwards in 1646: 'every creature in the first estate of creation was God, and every creature is God, every creature that hath life and breath being an efflux from God, and shall return into God again, be swallowed up in him as a drop is in the ocean.' 'There are some whole troops in the Army that hold such desperate opinions', Edwards tells us, 'as denying the resurrection of the dead, and hell.'[49] Mortalists in Somerset believed that 'God doth subsist in the creatures, and hereafter the whole creation shall be annihilated and reduced into the divine essence again'. Winstanley and many Ranters took over this idea.[50]

The view that 'all comes by nature', that God is an

[46] *Gangraena*, i. 27, 35, 116-19, 218; ii. 8, 150-1.
[47] G. Winstanley, *The Saints Paradice* (1648), 82-4; idem, *Works*, 161-2, 229-35.
[48] *WTUD* 145, 150.   [49] *Gangraena*, i. 21; iii. 107.
[50] *Gangraena*, i. 219; Winstanley, *Works*, 451.

unnecessary hypothesis, appears intermittently in the sixteenth and early seventeenth centuries, and circulated among
the radicals in the 1640s and 1650s: among others it attracted
George Fox.[51] There is 'no God but only nature', Clarkson
decided: no Moses, no Christ, no resurrection. The world was
eternal, and there were men before Adam.[52] One of the
disciples of William Franklin, the self-styled Messiah, also
believed there was only nature: so did many of Lodowick
Muggleton's acquaintances.[53]

The popularization of science, and especially of the
Copernican astronomy, also led to doubts. Where are we to
place Heaven and Hell if not above the sky and in the centre
of the earth? When a preacher explained to his congregation
that Heaven was so high that a millstone would take centuries
to fall to earth, a member of the congregation sensibly en-
quired how long it would take a man to get up there.[54] If
the universe was infinite, were there other worlds inhabited
by human beings? What then became of the Christian scheme
of salvation? Was it re-enacted in these other worlds? Once
the earth ceased to be the centre of the universe, doubts of
this kind were inevitably raised. 'An infidel is the best pro-
ficient in the school of nature' declared the mortalist Agricola
Carpenter.[55] No wonder the scientists of the Royal Society
were so anxious to prove that science demonstrates the
existence of God, or that early supporters of Cartesianism
like Henry More later rejected it because of its materialism.

One thing which emerged from the religious discussions of
the 1640s and 1650s was a greater understanding of the
psychology of religious experience; and this too worked in
a rationalizing direction, against the claims of prophets and
portent-mongers. Hell, said Walwyn, was the bad consciences
of evil men in this life; extreme fasting and continuance in
prayer might lead to hallucinatory visions.[56] Winstanley
thought that poverty led to religious despair, and that religion

---

[51] *WTUD* 174-9, 184, 206; *RDM* 168-72; *CSPD, 1648-9,* 425.
[52] Clarkson, *Lost Sheep Found,* 32-3.   [53] *WTUD* 173; *RDM* 171.
[54] *RDM* 161.
[55] A. Carpenter, *Pseuchographia Anthropomagica: Or, A Magical Description of the Soul* (1652), 22.
[56] Haller and Davies, 259-60, 296-7; Haller, ii. 288-91.

'torments people always when they are weak, sickly and under any distemper'.[57] 'Whilst we live in the fear of hell we have it': the words are attributed to the Ranter Richard Coppin.[58] For a man to say God 'hath spoken to him in a dream', the cool Hobbes summed up in 1651, 'is no more than to say he dreamed that God spake to him'.[59] As early as 1646 the doctor of William Franklin bled him as a remedy for his feeling that God had deserted him: the treatment was too successful, for Franklin came to believe that he was the Messiah.[60]

Religious toleration and freedom of the press had other far-reaching effects. The Koran and the Socinian Catechism were both translated into English. The latter was suppressed, but the former worried Bunyan a great deal.[61] Discussions about the admission of the Jews into England in the 1650s must have contributed to acceptance of the existence of more than one religion; so did the longer-term spreading of knowledge of the ancient non-Christian religions of India and China. The soldier who claimed the right to 'worship the sun or the moon like the Persians', the Wiltshire Ranter who 'would sell all religions for a jug of beer',[62] seem to have been thinking about comparative religion no less than the more philosophical Wildman who said that it was hard for any man 'by the light of nature to conceive how there can be any sin committed'; so to talk of sins against the light of nature was dangerous.[63]

The Ranters made the loudest anti-religious noises. Coppe announced that 'sin, and transgression is finished', and referred to 'the holy Scripturean Whore' as well as to his own former 'plaguey holiness'. 'A pox of God take all your prayers.'[64] Clarkson sang:

> Behold the King of Glory now is come
> T'reduce God and the Devil to their doom,

[57] Winstanley, *Works*, 568.   [58] *RDM* 170.
[59] T. Hobbes, *Leviathan* (1968 edn.), 411.
[60] H. Ellis, *Pseudocristus* (1650), 6.   [61] *WTUD* 266.
[62] D. Masson, *Life of Milton* (1859-80), iii. 525; *WTUD* 228; cf. Thomson, *The Later Lollards*, 67.
[63] A.S.P. Woodhouse (ed.), *Puritanism and Liberty* (1938), 161.
[64] *WTUD* 151, 334, 315, 202.

> For both of them are servants unto me . . .
> Thy worship and thy God shall die truly.[65]

But Winstanley was the man who carried the attack on existing religion the furthest. Hell exists in men because of the evil organization of propertied society; the conception is then used to bolster up that society by priests and others who benefit from it. 'Heaven above . . . the skies . . . is a fancy which your false teachers put into your hands to please you with while they pick your purses.'[66] Like Karl Marx two centuries later, Winstanley thought that belief in the after-life distracts men from changing the society they live in. Traditional Christians worship the Devil, covetousness, the God of this world — that is why Winstanley preferred to speak of Reason rather than God, and why the Diggers said: 'We will neither come to church nor serve their God.' To the accusation that his teaching 'will destroy all government and all our ministry and religion', Winstanley's answer was 'it is very true'.[67]

I have established, I hope, that sectarian religion drove Winstanley, Clarkson, and many others, to the verge of denying Christianity altogether. It may be objected that Ranters and Diggers were a small minority, and this is true. But there is evidence that such views circulated fairly widely. We need not accept the alarmist accounts of professional heresy-hunters like Edwards, Baillie, Rutherford, Pagitt, Ross, and several more — though Edwards's *Gangraena* at least is well documented and seems to stand up quite well to examination: we need a critical edition. Nor need we rely on remarks like that of Walter Charleton in 1652, that present-day England produced more 'atheistical monsters' than any other age or nation, even though such remarks are confirmed by men so different as Robert Boyle, Thomas Fuller, Francis Osborne, Bishop Stillingfleet, and the author of *The Whole Duty of Man*.[68] Just as the best evidence for the unpopularity of Elizabethan and Stuart bishops comes from the bishops themselves, so the strongest evidence for the prevalence of

---

[65] L. Clarkson, *A Single Eye* (1650), sig. A1ᵛ.   [66] Winstanley, *Works,* 226.
[67] Ibid. 471.   [68] *WTUD* 179–80.

religious doubts in the 1640s and 1650s comes from those who at one time shared these doubts even though they later overcame them. John Rogers, later the Fifth Monarchist, doubted the existence of God; Richard Baxter and his wife doubted the truth of Scripture and the life to come. Thomas Traherne went through a period of general scepticism in which he doubted the Bible: so did Michael Wigglesworth in New England. George Fox at one time thought 'all things come by nature'. Bunyan had doubts about the existence of God and the Day of Judgement. Were the Scriptures not 'written by some politicians on purpose to make the poor ignorant people submit to some religion and government?'[69]

The author of *The Whole Duty of Man* made the point that the religion of the more radical sects moved towards what conservatives thought total irreligion. 'Atheism', he wrote, 'seems to be the gulf that finally swallows up all our sects.' 'Its bold monopolising of wit and reason', denial of the existence of God, of Judgement, of Hell: "tis only this liberty of discourse that hath propagated atheism.'[70]

A man like Richard Baxter had no doubts about the social types who rejected established religion. The profane multitude, the rabble, he argued in 1659, were hostile to ministers and all religion. 'If any would raise an army to extirpate knowledge and religion', he wrote later, 'the tinkers and sow-gelders and crate-carriers and beggars and bargemen and all the rabble that cannot read . . . will be the forwardest to come in to such a militia.'[71] So he supported the restoration of King, bishops, and church courts in 1660, and the suppression of popular heresy.

There is no room here to discuss the aftermath. Bishops came back, but church courts did not long retain their power over the laity. The great persecution of the restoration period was instigated by the gentry in Parliament, implemented by

[69] Ibid. 172-5.
[70] *The Works of the Author of the Whole Duty of Man* (1704), ii. 109-11; cf. 261-4.
[71] R. Baxter, *The Holy Commonwealth* (1659), 92-4, 226-9; *The Poor Husbandman's Advocate to Rich Racking Landlords* (1691), edited by F.J. Powicke and G. Unwin as *The Rev. Richard Baxter's Last Treatise* (Manchester, 1926), 20-4.

justices of the peace. Its object was to restore social control.
Those of the sects which survived the persecution did so by
abandoning political aims, concentrating on a kingdom which
was not of this world; by strict discipline over their members,
and by shedding those who were not strongly convinced that
theirs was the only way to salvation. There was no sect of
irreligionists, and the irreligious fringe of the sects did not
stand up to persecution. Why suffer gratuitously in this
world if you do not believe you will be rewarded in the next?
So membership of the sects was cut back to those who had
strong other-worldly convictions, and this stamped an in-
delible image on them. The Quakers, who stood up to persecution most bravely, threw off their radical, near-Ranter wing.

We do not know to what extent irreligious ideas survived
after the censorship closed down again in 1660. It is difficult
to believe that they disappeared. Hobbist atheism, of course,
was rather smart in court circles, and Pepys gives us plenty
of evidence for anticlericalism. In 1663 Robert Blackburne,
Secretary to the Admiralty, said to him that 'the present
clergy . . . are hated and laughed at by everybody . . . [they]
will never heartily go down with the generality of the
commons of England, they have been so used to liberty'. The
royalist, Samuel Butler, likewise spoke of the 'general ill-will
and hatred they [bishops and clergy] have contracted from
the people of all sorts'. Lord North thought that few Englishmen in his time believed in life after death, 'especially among
the vulgar'.[72] At the turn of the century a lay clerk and
master of boys at Norwich cathedral held the Ranter belief
that there was no Heaven but a quiet mind, no Hell but
the grave.[73]

Presbyterian Puritans had tried to impose a stricter discipline on England. They had tried to enforce church attendance even on vagabonds, and where the Presbyterian discipline
flourished it was fierce against the simple pleasures of the
poor. So when in the reaction against Army rule in 1659-60
the alternatives seemed to be bishops or Presbyterianism,

[72] S. Pepys, *Diary,* ed. H.B. Wheatley (1946), i. 314–15; S. Butler, *Characters
and Passages from Note-Books,* ed. A.R. Waller (Cambridge, 1908), 318; *RDM*
172.
[73] R.W. Ketton-Cremer, *Norfolk Assembly* (1957), 85.

there appears to have been a genuine *popular* preference for bishops as the lesser evil. There was thus a dual process: as the sects selectively shed their fellow-travellers until they were whittled down to small groups of highly committed believers, so the state church became the receptacle of the non-committed; it remained the church of all non-believers. Anyone who has been in the army will confirm this. When I was waiting to complete my forms on joining up in 1940, one question of which asked for 'religious denomination', I heard a corporal say about the man ahead of me: 'He says he is an atheist, sarge.' 'Put him down C. of E.', was the inevitable answer. Atheist was not a recognized sect.

Well then: I have established to my own satisfaction, and I hope to yours, that there was a good deal, if not of atheism, at least of positive irreligion in the English Revolution. I hope I have established that in this respect the analogy with the dechristianization of the French Revolution and the militant atheism of the Russian Revolution is not too far-fetched. Allowing for the fact that the English Revolution came first and that the two later revolutions drew on its ideas and practice, I think we can see tendencies among English radicals towards the greater irreligion of the next two revo-lutions — rather as Winstanley foreshadows the communism of Babeuf and Lenin. This consideration seems to me yet another reason for finally abandoning the phrase 'the Puritan Revolution', which I include in my title in the hope of drawing attention to its inadequacy. It was after all only invented in the nineteenth century: contemporaries, like modern historians, thought in more sociological terms. Neither the causes nor the outcome of the Revolution were primarily religious. It may well be, as Dr Manning suggests, that what started as a constitutional conflict had changed to a conflict which was also religious by 1643, thanks to the incursion of the lower classes into politics.[74] But this means that it had also become a social conflict; and in the long run the radicalization of politics had a secularizing effect. What matters, the Leveller Richard Overton said, is 'not how great

---

[74] B. Manning, 'Religion and Politics: The Godly People', in Manning (ed.), *Politics, Religion and the English Civil War* (1973), 120.

a sinner I am, but how faithful and real to the Commonwealth'.[75] Certainly the sort of people I have been discussing
do not fit into most normal definitions of the word 'Puritan'.
(Definition is the way to solve most seventeenth-century
problems. If you want to show that Puritans were hostile to
the theatre, you start by defining 'Puritan' as someone hostile
to the theatre: then the fact that most of the well-known
opponents of the theatre were pro-episcopalian Anglican
parsons doesn't matter. If you want to prove that Puritans
contributed nothing to the Royal Society, you start with a
definition of 'Puritan' which excludes anyone who accepted
the restoration. And so on.)

This perhaps leads on to more general reflections. If there
is the pattern in great revolutions which I have suggested, the
facts to which I have been drawing attention should tell us
something about popular attitudes towards religion in general.
When the lid is taken off, what bubbles out must have been
there all the time. Was active — as opposed to passive —
irreligion there all the time? English experience suggests that
this was indeed the case. The roots of the irreligious ideas of
the English revolutionaries can be traced back to the Lollards;
they may well have a continuous underground history from
their disappearance in 1660 to their revival by the Chartists.
This suggests perhaps that the formal Christianity of the
established churches never had so complete a monopoly
as appears.

In sixteenth- and seventeenth-century England Puritans
conducted an active campaign to make an England that
should be Christian in their sense: god-fearing, actively
religious, prepared for Christ's kingdom. Some, like Milton
in *Aeropagitica,* believed that liberty of discussion would
conduce to this end: but when it came they discovered how
wrong they had been. Free discussion opened the doors to
scepticism. As the Revolution pushed further to the left, the
godly pulled back in alarm. Most Puritans after 1660 abandoned the attempt to build Christ's kingdom, and were prepared to settle for what Philip Henry called 'a face of godli-

[75] Haller and Davies, 231.

ness',[76] outward acceptance, leaving the godless masses to formal membership of the Church of England. Under the great persecution of the restoration period there was no possibility of the sects evangelizing the lower classes; even the Quakers seem to have concentrated on survival. When at last greater religious liberty came with the Toleration Act of 1689, the old dissent had lost its missionary zeal. Apart from some chivvying by the societies for the reformation of manners — 'a face of godliness' — the lower classes, not perhaps altogether to their dissatisfaction, were pretty well left alone until Wesley and Whitfield interested themselves in their fate. Wesley's *Journal* reports many discussions with antinomians which read exactly like the dialogue between Quakers and Ranters a century earlier. But then came Tom Paine and the French Revolution, and with them the beginnings of an irreligion which no longer took 'religious' forms. And that, as they say, is not my period.

[76] Quoted, with other examples, in my *Society and Puritanism in Pre-Revolutionary England* (1969 edn.), 249.

Index